The Line Through the Heart

The Line Through the Heart

Natural Law as Fact, Theory,
and Sign of Contradiction

J. Budziszewski

Wilmington, Delaware

"The line dividing good and evil cuts through the heart of every human being."

—Aleksandr Solzhenitsyn

To my teachers

Budziszewski, J., 1952–

The line through the heart : natural law as fact, theory, and sign of contradiction / J. Budziszewski. —1st ed. —Wilmington, Del. : ISI Books, c2009.

p. ; cm.

ISBN: 978-1-935191-17-9
Includes bibliographical references and index.

1. Natural law. 2. Natural law—Religious aspects—Christianity. 3. Religion and law. 4. Law—Political aspects. I. Title.

K460 .B83 2009   2008939402
340/.112—dc22   0905

ISI Books
Intercollegiate Studies Institute
3901 Centerville Road
Wilmington, DE 19807-0431
www.isibooks.org

Manufactured in the United States of America

Contents

Preface

This book is about natural law—about the foundational principles of good and evil inscribed in created human nature. Although it reflects a single point of view, no one could fail to notice that it was put together from essays written at different times. For that reason, it may be helpful to say something about how the chapters fit together. To summarize them would be too much like giving away the ending of a novel. I do think that I ought to "motivate" them. Before even that, the design of the book should be explained, since I may seem to have given birth to Siamese twins—a short book about ethics, joined at the hip with another short book about politics. No, the two parts do make a single book.

One excuse for connecting them is that the study of politics is a *branch* of the study of ethics. This old claim strikes most people as impractical and unrealistic, not to say bizarre. On the contrary, it is utterly hard-headed. What could be more impractical and unrealistic than to imagine that a bad man can be a great statesman, or that a people can have a wholly different government than it deserves?[1] We may look at the matter from another side too. Ethics is the study of the good, and even a corrupt government rests on some corrupt idea of the good—for example, that the good is gaining power, amassing wealth, or protecting the position of the privileged. The politics of an age may rest on a crumbling foundation derived from a mistaken ethics, but it will have an ethical foundation.

The second excuse for the structure of the book is that it offers a connecting term between its two parts: the concept of law. The foundational principles of good and evil are the natural or moral law; of regime design, constitutional law; and of day-to-day legislative enactment, ordinary law. Some people will consider this emphasis a good and timely thing. After all, despite what Pope Benedict XVI has aptly called the dictatorship of relativism, the natural law tradition is enjoying a certain renewal and refreshment. Other people will consider it a bad and untimely thing. I cannot help that; with two short exceptions, which I take up shortly, the rest of my excuse must be the rest of the book. But this brings us back to the chapters.

Chapter 1, "Natural Law as Fact, Theory, and Sign of Contradiction," sets the tone. It begins, some would say, as offensively as possible, by quoting the pope himself. These days, much less than a quotation from the Holy Father is enough to give offense, and that fact is very much to the point. One day some years ago I was lecturing to a classroom of undergraduates about the strategies devised by the Framers of the U.S. Constitution for coping with political passion, self-interest, and virtue. Concerning passion, their goals were to avoid arousing it in the first place, and to slow down legislative deliberation in the event that it was aroused. Needing an example of passionate controversy, I mentioned the congressional debate about partial-birth abortion, which was going on at that time. Surprisingly, many of the students were altogether unfamiliar with the issue and asked me to explain. In my most dispassionate voice, I gave a one-sentence, purely clinical definition of the procedure; perhaps I should have realized what would happen. A woman of about thirty years of age, somewhat older than most of the class, began screaming at the top of her lungs. It took me a moment to realize that the shriek was articulate; she was claiming that the procedure was used "only when necessary to save the woman's life." Besides being false, this claim was beside the point, for I had not even raised issues like when it was used or whether it could ever be necessary. But saying so was no use (I tried). Relief came only when I remarked to the rest of the class, "Now you know why the Framers were concerned about strong passions"—at which point the young woman abruptly fell into silence. Apparently, people can be driven to hysteria by the mere act of *defining* the things which they say they approve. Doesn't this fact raise questions about the human heart, and therefore about natural law? I think so. The chapter explores these questions.

Chapters 2 and 3, "The Second Tablet Project" and "Nature Illuminated," take up the relation between the knowledge of good and the knowledge of God, along with the relation between what our minds require revelation to know and what they can know without it.[2] Some thinkers drive a wedge between the first tablet of the Decalogue (duties to God) and the second (duties to neighbor). In fact they drive two wedges. The first wedge is the idea that although we can find out basic morality by reasoning, reason tells us nothing about God. The second wedge, which is much more intriguing, is the idea that ignorance of God does no harm to the knowledge of morality anyway—that our grip on, say, "Thou shalt not steal" is just as firm even if we lose our grip on "Thou shalt put no other gods before Me." Together, these two ideas give rise to the ill-starred project of trying to get by with the second tablet alone, a project which I criticize in Chapter 2. The further question of what revelation *adds* to the conclusions of reason is touched upon in Chapter 2, and deepened in Chapter 3.

The theme of the fourth chapter, "The Natural, the Connatural, and the Unnatural," is the mystery of how things that seem to run against the grain of human nature can become "second nature"—how we can become habituated to seeking the good in ways that are destructive to our good—and what this does to our rationality. I confess that classroom experiences add poignancy to this topic, too. For example, there was the day when I was explaining to philosophy students the concept of natural teleology—that human powers and experiences have inbuilt purposes and indwelling meanings which we discover and do not invent. Two students in the back asked what view Saint Thomas Aquinas would have taken of certain fashionable uses of the sexual powers. I proposed that they reflect on the inbuilt purposes of these powers and work it out logically. The discussion proceeded very calmly and reasonably until, at the very point when it reached its conclusion, a young woman in the front began to weep, sobbing out a plaint about how hurtful and uncompassionate it is to "judge" and "condemn" people. Sensitive to the claims of bruised reeds and smoldering wicks, I explained as gently as I could that no one was being judged; the question of condemnation had not even come up. But surely, I said, true compassion requires caring for the true good of other persons. If so, then to exercise compassion toward them it is not enough to know what they wish; one must find out whether their wishes are truly good. As this drama unfolded, I was acutely aware that whether I could *explain* compassion to the young woman was incomparably less important than whether I could *show* it to her. Only God knows whether I succeeded, but this returns us to the point. Wouldn't one think that teaching would be merely the presentation of logical arguments? I have not found it to be such. The reasons for this deserve much more attention from natural lawyers than they receive. It isn't enough that one's philosophy is *about* human beings. It must be capable of being addressed *to* them in all of their humanity and brokenness. Yet this too reflects something about our nature, does it not?

The fifth chapter, "Accept No Imitations: Naturalism vs. Natural Law," takes up so-called evolutionary psychology, also called evolutionary ethics. At the bottom of the discussion is an idea widely current among scientists, general readers, and not a few philosophers that natural law is just biology in fancy dress. There is something to the notion; teleology is more at home in biology, which deals with organisms—interdependent structures of purposes—than in other branches of science, which deal merely with processes. Moreover, the meaning of human actions doesn't *push aside* the organic purposes of the powers they employ, rather it builds on them. We share in the biological purpose of sex because we are animals; we share in the human meaning which supervenes upon this purpose because we are not *merely* animals, but animals with rational souls. Rationality raises everything biological to a higher level. One might say that it makes the body not less significant, but more. But here we run into a problem. An atheist can certainly recognize natural purposes and meanings; nothing prevents him from agreeing that eyes are for seeing, legs for walking, or kisses for showing affection. But he has no answer to the "So what?" question. If nature has no Author, then these natural purposes and meanings have no authority. Why *shouldn't* he violate these purposes and meanings? If he saves all his kisses for mockery, so what? If he puts out his eyes to play Lear, so what? We might have evolved differently; our indwelling meanings are really meaningless; our inbuilt purposes are really purposeless. The genes are just another vile jelly. Out, out! I suggest that this outlook is dreadfully mistaken, and that the milder versions of naturalistic reductionism are mistaken, too.

Part II turns to politics—politics in the broadest sense, the organization of our common life. Aristotle recognized that one of the first questions of our common life is, "Who is a citizen?" But one must be a person to be a citizen, and so the more fundamental question is, "Who is a person?" This controversy, the topic of the sixth chapter, "Thou Shalt Not Kill . . . Whom?" has obsessed two generations. One of my own teachers, lo these many years ago, held that the state may intervene to protect a born child, but not to protect a fetus. His reasoning was simple: If a child is not properly cared for, then when he grows up he will be incompetent to function as a citizen. By contrast, aborted fetuses present us with no such problem, for the simple reason that they will never grow up. I never understood why my teacher cut his argument short. Why restrict it to fetuses? Since his sole stated object was to keep from having to deal with incompetent adults, he should have reasoned that although we should not mistreat people who are already grown up, it would be perfectly licit to kill infants, toddlers, and adolescents. Today, those who take his side of the question go even further. The fashion is to say that although we may not deliberately take the lives of innocent persons, *not all humans are persons*—not even all adults. The question for them is not who shares in the community of human nature, but simply which of those who share in it shall be suffered to go on living. Not many ordinary people realize that this is already the shape that the question has taken in law courts, hospital ethics boards, and other councils where certain people decide whether others are people at all.

I anticipate that some readers of the sixth chapter may be surprised by the seventh, "Capital Punishment: The Case for Justice." A fashion on my own side of the question of human personhood is to say that it is *always* wrong to take life—that abortion, capital punishment, just war, and presumably self-defense are each wrong, always wrong, and wrong for all the same reasons. Against this "seamless garment" view, I defend the older tradition that the evil of murder lies in taking *innocent* life. Abortion, therefore, is different than the others. In particular, capital punishment has a necessary though limited place—not despite the sacredness of life, but because of it. Some thinkers in my own communion mistakenly plead the authority of the Church against this view. On the contrary, the papal magisterium has lately emphasized not that capital punishment is always wrong, but that under rightly ordered institutions it should be *rare*. And surely this teaching is true. Its much-neglected corollary is the importance of seeing to it that our institutions are ordered rightly. Presently, the various parts of the system of justice work at cross-purposes.

The next two chapters turn from the most basic concerns addressed

by human law—human life and personhood—to human law itself. Someone who reads only the eighth chapter, "Constitution vs. Constitutionalism," might think that I want to do away with the Constitution; someone
who reads only the ninth, "Constitutional Metaphysics," might think that I
regard it as sacrosanct. Neither view would be correct. The Constitution is
worthy of high esteem, but we should also acknowledge its flaws. Whereas
the former chapter concerns the fact that we aren't sufficiently on our guard
about it, the latter concerns the fact that we don't sufficiently cherish what
is good about it either. A certain difficulty chafes those who try to discuss it
at all. As George Carey has explained,[3] serious efforts to teach and understand what the Constitution meant to those who wrote and enacted it will
inevitably seem partisan. In a sense they are. Those of us who speak of
these things have different commitments than the proponents of a "living
Constitution," which means a Constitution that means whatever they say
it means. We are no more "neutral" than they are; we are only more objective.[4] A fair examination of the founding documents does not support the
claim of such proponents to fulfill the original meaning of these texts, so
they must ultimately take refuge in hocus pocus like "non-interpretivism."
A fair presentation of their goals shows them at war with the natural law,
so they must ultimately speak jabberwocky about a "different" natural law
that authorizes everyone to invent his own interpretation of reality. For a
while people can be overawed by such incantations, but eventually they say,
"I don't get it—it seems like smoke and mirrors." At that point one can say,
"It is," and show them the mirrors, if only they are willing to look. It seems
a terrible waste of time that so much of our teaching must be unteaching,
that so much our effort must be expended just to prepare for Lesson One.
All things considered, however, we do well to reach Lesson One—if we do
reach it. Certainly the Federalists and Anti-Federalists reached no further.
Let us be humble and grateful.

The final chapter, "The Illiberal, Liberal Religion," returns to the
problem broached in this introduction, the relation between the City of
Man and the City of God. Here especially I risk the charge that I've "left
off philosophizing and gone to meddling." According to a certain interpretation of the history of recent centuries, credit for the achievement of
relatively peaceful relations among the religions in places like the United
States belongs largely to the practice of religious toleration. I don't dispute
this claim; indeed I hold that proper toleration and respect for the dignity
of conscience are duties of natural law. What I do challenge is a double

distortion of history which is usually bundled up with the claim. One side of this distortion concerns who discovered toleration; the other concerns what toleration really is. The idea that this virtue was discovered in modern times is an outstanding example of what happens when celebrities start believing their own press releases (in this case, celebrities in the history of ideas). What modernity did eventually develop was not the virtue of religious toleration as such, but a new, incoherent, and less than candid theory of it—along with certain new modes of religious oppression.

I have little doubt that this preface has already provoked certain objections. Allow me to anticipate two. One is an objection to the book's focus on natural law; the other is to the way the book discusses it.

Perhaps the most interesting reason for considering it untimely to discuss natural law goes back to a terse, fascinating, and widely misunderstood article written a half-century ago by the philosopher G. E. M. Anscombe.[5]

In brief, Anscombe argued that modern moral philosophers had backed themselves into a corner. On the one hand, they thought of morality as *law*. On the other hand, few of them believed in all the other things one must believe in order to speak of law coherently.[6] It makes no sense to propose a moral *law* unless there is a moral lawgiver, and not many philosophers of that time believed in God. Anscombe thought that such incoherencies were at the root of the various other difficulties that plagued the theories then current, such as utilitarianism and Kantianism. It was as though people were trying to theorize about sums without believing in addition, or about ribs without believing in bones.

What she proposed to these skeptics was not that they abandon moral philosophy, but that they carry on the enterprise in a different way. Henceforth they would admit that they had no business talking about morality as law; instead they would content themselves with describing the psychology of the moral virtues. They would allow themselves to say "This is what it means to have honesty" or "This is the sort of person we admire as being courageous," but they would not indulge in the conceits that "Be honest" and "Be courageous" are moral laws. This suggestion prompted a great revival of philosophical reflection about virtue.

I am all for thinking about virtue. But there are several difficulties with the philosophical agenda "all virtue, all the time." First, it isn't what Anscombe meant. She didn't oppose talking about moral law; she believed in it herself, and for her this was perfectly reasonable, because she believed in all the presuppositions of law, such as the lawgiver. Her suggestion to stop talking about moral law was only for those who *didn't*.

Second, there are two different ways for a thinker who believes in law without a lawgiver to escape incoherency. Anscombe mentions one: Abandon belief in the law. But as her own case shows, there is another: Believe in the lawgiver. In fact, the natural law tradition is not the only thing enjoying a renaissance. Since Anscombe's time, so is theism. To be sure, a certain kind of atheism is still the unofficially established religion of the opinion-forming strata of our society—the courts, the universities, the news media, the great advertising agencies, the whole pandering sector of the economy. The kind of atheism that these boosters favor is *practical* atheism. They don't really care whether people believe in a God; what disturbs them is belief in a God the existence of whom makes a difference to anything else. *Theoretical* atheism, by contrast, ran out of ideas quite a while ago. Notwithstanding certain recent highly promoted pop culture books peddling atheism of the crudest and most ill-considered sort,[7] all of the new and interesting arguments are being made by theists[8]—and the sort of God whose existence they defend makes a difference to everything there is.

Third, talking about law and talking about virtues aren't mutually exclusive. *Every* complete theory of moral law requires a theory of virtue. In fact, I suspect that every complete theory of virtue requires a theory of moral law. Even Aristotle, who is supposed to be the paradigm case of a moral philosopher who talked only about virtue and not about law, talked about law. He holds that the man of practical wisdom acts according to a rational principle; this principle functions as law. He holds that virtue lies in a mean, but that there is no mean of things like adultery; this implies that there are exceptionless precepts, which also function as law. He holds that besides the enactments of governments and the customs of peoples there is an unwritten norm to which governments and peoples defer; this norm too is a law. Consciousness of law creeps in through the back door even when it is pushed out the front, and Aristotle wasn't even pushing.

But another objection can be offered to this book. Granted that one must drag ethics into politics, granted that one must drag natural law into ethics, granted even that one must drag God into the discussion of natural law—still, why it is necessary to drag in *theology* concerning God? Why not just nice, clean philosophy? In the most ancient meaning of the term, theology *was* a branch of philosophy, "first philosophy," systematic reasoning about God, the supreme cause and principle of all things. And it is quite true that a certain thin sort of natural law theory can get by with first philosophy alone. Today, though, the term "theology" is used for systematic reasoning about *revelation* concerning God. Must the cat be allowed to drag *that* old thing through the door?

We may as well admit that the cat has already had his way. Philosophy is full of questions and notions that it borrowed from theology and then forgot that it had borrowed. Consider but a single example, the concept of "personhood," on which I have touched already. It turns out that the very idea of a "person"—of a rational *who* with moral attributes, the ultimate possessor of his acts and even his nature—originates in Christian theology. If we purged philosophy of its theological acquisitions, it would look as though moths had eaten it. Is that what we really want?

Ultimately, a discussion among Protestants, Catholics, Jews, Muslims, and atheists, each of whom is invited to discuss his theological premises, will be more rich and interesting than a conversation among Protestants, Catholics, Jews, and Muslims, each of whom is expected to impersonate an atheist. Such a conversation may even be more courteous—just because, for a change, no one is insisting that the others shut their mouths.

1

Natural Law as Fact, as Theory, and as Sign of Contradiction

The Christian faith holds that the creation has been damaged. Human existence is no longer what was produced at the hands of the Creator. It is burdened with another element that produces, besides the innate tendency toward God, the opposite tendency away from God. . . . This paradox points to a certain inner disturbance in man, so that he can no longer simply be the person he wants to be. . . . There is a collective consciousness that sharpens the contradiction. . . . [T]he stronger the demand made by the law, the stronger becomes the inclination to fight it.[1]

—Joseph Cardinal Ratzinger

I

Before his consecration as Pope Benedict XVI, Joseph Cardinal Ratzinger wrote to several Catholic universities requesting that they sponsor and encourage public talks about natural moral law and contemporary society. His reasons deserve thought. "The Catholic Church," he wrote, "has become increasingly concerned by the contemporary difficulty in finding a common denominator among the moral principles held by all people, which are based on the constitution of the human person and which function as the fundamental criteria for laws affecting the rights and duties of all." For centuries unquestioned, he says, these truths of the natural law "constituted a valid starting point for the Church's dialogue with the world, with cultures and non-Christian religions." The urgency of "renewing an understanding of the natural moral law" arises, he says, from the fact that its truths are now "obscured," not only in secular dogma, but even sometimes in "the teaching which takes place in Catholic universities." He clearly believes that renewing the understanding of natural law is not a task for philosophy alone, but for philosophy in partnership with revelation, because, as he explains, it requires "a deeper understanding of the theology of creation, as this flows from the unity of God's salvific plan in Christ." To guard against misunderstanding of this important point, he quotes John Paul II to the effect that "it is not a case of imposing on non-believers a vision based on faith, but of interpreting and defending the values rooted in the very nature of the person," "principles upon which depend the destiny of human beings and the future of civilization."

Strong words. The cardinal, now pontiff, makes sharp observations not only about the moral confusion of the times, but also about Catholic teaching, which ought to help to clear up the confusion, but sometimes merely joins in the muddle.

Ratzinger seems to view the natural law under three distinct aspects. In the first place, he views it as a fact. Natural law is a feature of the world, having to do with the constitution of the human person, and behind that, with the constitution of created reality as a whole. The cardinal's expression "the constitution of the person" calls several things to our attention. One is that the human being is a person, not just a mess of chemicals and electrical impulses. Personhood is not a mystification but a reality, and persons are meant by God to know reality, including the reality of themselves, as He knows them. But the expression also emphasizes that the human person is constituted in a certain way. If we lost sight of this fact, true personalism would collapse into a personalistic relativism in which we could no longer tell what counted as using a person wrongly, as a means to an end. After all, anyone can plead the second version of Kant's categorical imperative, "Never treat another as a mere means to an end." A woman denied an abortion might protest that she should not be reduced to a "means" to her baby's survival; a man denied assistance in killing himself might complain that he should not be reduced to a "means" to the peace of his doctor's conscience.

To say that natural law is a fact does not mean that theorizing about it is unnecessary. Calling attention to a fact is always an act of theory. Even so, we are apt to forget that before the theory must come the thing that the theory is about; natural law theorizing is about something that is already and unquestionably there. I use the word "unquestionably" with a qualification. Of course the "thereness" of natural law is questionable in a certain sense; everything is questionable in a certain sense. One might maintain that it is *not* there. But insofar as we are serious about being Christian philosophers, committed to an adequate view of the human person, a view which makes use of all of the resources of faith and reason as they co-illuminate each other, we should already know the answer to that logically possible question. At this stage of the game it would be frivolous—a squandering of what has been given to us—to waste breath on the question of whether the human person has a constitution, just as it would be frivolous for a mineralogist to ask whether there are minerals, or an oceanographer to ask whether there is ocean. The mineralogist and oceanographer have better questions to ask. So do we.

Only in second place, then, does the cardinal view natural law as a theory. We are to be realists. The theorist must humble himself before the fact, which in this case means the reality of human personhood. This is where those "better questions" that I mentioned come in: What do we actually know about the constitution of the human person? How are its principles "natural," and how are they "law"? How can we explain them in a way that makes them intelligible even to the people of our time? I suggest that if theory does come in second place, not in first, then it will be a different sort of theory than the kind we have become accustomed to during the last several centuries. It will not be the belly-button-searching kind that demands exhaustive investigation of whether we can know anything at all before asking what, if anything, we know. Instead it will realize that we must already know something, and know that we know it, even in order to ask how we do come to know it. A truly adequate theory of the natural law will not always be turning into metatheory of the natural law, a theory about theories. It will resist that tendency. It will keep its eyes focused on the data, contemplating the constitution of the human person itself, rather than turning its eyes skull-inward in a futile attempt to catch itself at the act of contemplation that it was engaged in a moment before. The study of how we know is important, even indispensable, but it is only the maidservant of the study of the things that are known, not the master.

We have not reached the end of the story, for in third place, the cardinal seems to view natural law as a scandal, as a sign of contradiction.[2]

I take his remark that its truths have been "obscured" as a gentle way of saying that they have been widely repudiated. Whether or not he intended to make that point in his letter of invitation, it is certainly an aspect of his broader teaching; it is the point of the quotation I have set at the head of this chapter. And it is certainly true—a point which theologians acknowledge, but, curiously, is not often discussed by philosophers. The fact is that natural law exasperates. It offends. It enrages.

By the way, this gives us a reason—a serious reason—to consider the questions that I called frivolous a few moments ago. It may be frivolous for the oceanographer to ask *on his own behalf* whether there is ocean, but it would not be frivolous if he lived among people who denied water even though living on a raft. In the same way, it may be frivolous for us to ask *on our own behalf* whether the human person has a constitution, but it is not frivolous if we live among humans who deny the personal structure of their being. There is even a sense in which it is not frivolous to ask the question even on our own behalf, for faith in God—even faith in the God-given constitution of our personal being—is inevitably a choice against the ever-present possibility of doubt. Commenting on a scene in a play by Claudel, the cardinal writes,

> Fastened to the cross—with the cross fastened to nothing, drifting over the abyss. The situation of the contemporary believer could hardly be more accurately and impressively described. Only a loose plank bobbing over the void seems to hold him up, and it looks as if he must eventually sink. Only a loose plank connects him to God, though certainly it connects him inescapably and in the last analysis he knows that this wood is stronger than the void which seethes beneath him and which remains nevertheless the really threatening force in his day-to-day life.[3]

The scandal of natural law is both chronic and acute. It is acute because of the suicidal proclivity of our time to deny the obvious, a proclivity, by the way, which itself cries out for explanation. We have reached that day that Chesterton foresaw when he wrote, "Everything will be denied. Everything will become a creed. . . . Fires will be kindled to testify that two and two make four. Swords will be drawn to prove that leaves are green in summer. . . . We shall be of those who have seen and yet have believed."[4] The circumstance of living during an acute phase of the scandal makes it especially important that we not let our own eyes be darkened. Even today there is a common ground, because humans still bear a common nature; whether people are commonly willing to stand on that ground is another matter altogether. It is a slippery common ground, wet with the moisture of our evasions. Therefore we must not suppose that the definition of "common ground" is "what everyone concedes" or "what no one denies." There is nothing that everyone concedes; there is nothing that no one denies. We must be willing to be bold.

I have commented on the acuteness of the scandal in our time. But the scandal is also chronic. Natural law is a sign of contradiction, not merely incidentally because of the times, but essentially because of all times. One reason is the Fall. Our condition contradicts our constitution; our state is out of joint with our nature. The natural law scandalizes us because our actual inclinations are at war with our natural inclinations, because our hearts are riddled with desires that oppose their deepest longings, because we demand to have happiness on terms that make happiness impossible. To understand the scandal at an even deeper level, natural law is a sign of contradiction because Christ the Redeemer is a sign of contradiction. The cardinal is quite clear about this. Consider again his remark, quoted earlier, that an adequate understanding of natural law implicates "the theology of creation, *as this flows from the unity of God's salvific plan in Christ.*"[5] Some people would say that in making such a claim, the cardinal is no longer proposing philosophical ethics, but demanding the abdication of philosophy to theology. On the contrary, he is rejecting a false view of philosophy, a view which supposes a relationship of faith and reason which is ultimately insupportable. Yes, we can and must find ways to make ourselves comprehensible to those who do not share the insights of revelation, but this does not mean that we can do so without relying on these insights. Nature presupposes supernature, and the present disorders of nature merely stun the mind when contemplated apart from the graces of creation and redemption. For this reason, a truly adequate understanding of nature's malaise requires some hint, some glimpse, some trace of its supernatural remedy.

How awful such reflections are for those of us who crave the approval of our secular colleagues. The timid flesh crawls at the thought of their skeptical glances. Yet in the long run, there is no other way to make headway. How could we expect natural law to be plausible to those whose nature experiences only its humiliation, and not its rising again? These remarks risk scandal of yet another kind too. I mean methodological scandal, and this is unavoidable. The philosophical method of our day is minimalist. It assumes that people can consider propositions about reality only in small doses, one dry pill at a time. I suggest that at least sometimes, the very opposite is true. The reason the pill goes down so hard is that it is *only* a pill, for the mind, like the stomach, desires a meal. Just as some foods are digestible only in combination with other foods, so also some ideas are plausible only in combination with other ideas. In order to stand firm they must have context, as the single stone requires the arch. So let us not worry about scandal, but go ahead and do the unminimalist and unsecularist thing.

II

The rest of this chapter merely elaborates the three aspects under which we must view the natural law: natural law as fact, as theory, and as sign of contradiction. First, then, as fact. As I conceded earlier, to call attention to a fact is always an act of theory. Even so, it is not the *same* act of theory as what we do about the fact afterward, so let us consider the pretheoretical realities that provoke natural law philosophy and with which it has to deal. For convenience I will distinguish four categories of such experiences. First come those facts, those pretheoretical realities, that provoke us to philosophize about practical reason as such; second come those that provoke us to do so in terms of natural law rather than in other terms. The former category can be subdivided into facts that provoke us to philosophize about practical reason *as practical,* and facts that provoke us to philosophize about it *as reason.* In turn, the latter category can be subdivided into facts that provoke us to philosophize about natural law *as law,* and facts that provoke us to philosophize about it *as natural.*

To begin at the beginning, the pretheoretical reality that provokes us to philosophize about practical reason as practical is that we are, so to speak, magnetized toward other things, other persons, and other states of affairs.[6] We are not just knowers, but seekers, who spontaneously incline toward certain realities other than ourselves. When I say that this inclination is spontaneous, I do not mean that it is arbitrary, because that is not the way that we experience it. One way of saying this is that we do not merely experience ourselves as drawn to things; we experience the things themselves as being such as to draw us. Our word for their being so—and there is such a word in every language—is "good"; goodness is the quality of being such as to draw us. So another way to express what I am saying is that we experience certain things as good, and experience ourselves as drawn to them because of their goodness; we are designed to be so drawn. With an air of demystification, subjectivists like Thomas Hobbes tell us that it is the other way around. They deny that we are inclined toward things because they are good. Instead, they say, we call them good because we happen to be inclined toward them (as we may happen to be inclined to different things tomorrow). Goodness is merely a name, and inclination does not point outside itself after all; it just is.[7] But this is not just bad theory, it is a bad description of the experience. If you ask a man "Why do you love that woman?" he does not normally reply by telling you about himself—"I just do"—but by telling you about her—"Because she is wonderful."

It might be objected that some people do reply "I just do"—for example, in Country and Western songs. Quite so, but Country and Western songs are more or less explicitly about disordered loves, not ordered ones, and the perception of the disorder is internal to the experience itself: "I'm crazy for crying, crazy for trying, crazy for loving you." Even then the lover does not say that the beloved is not lovable. What he suggests is that her good is mixed with bad in such a way that by inclining toward the former, he ends up suffering the latter. "I knew you'd love me as long as you wanted / And then some day you'd leave me for somebody new."[8]

So much for the pretheoretical reality that provokes us to philosophize about practical reason as practical; what then is the one that provokes us to philosophize about it *as reason*? Here I must apologize for my earlier metaphor of magnetism, for our inclination toward the good is only a little bit like actual magnetism. For animals, perhaps the resemblance is closer. The tom enters the field of influence of the estrous queen and is drawn in to mate, the wolf enters the field of influence of the unprotected fawn and is drawn in to devour. If an animal is inclined toward two objects at once, it pursues the most attractive. Everything is simple. For us it is not like that. We *deliberate* about which good to follow; the goods that attract us are not *causes* of action, but *reasons* for action. Deliberation is a strange and mysterious thing, not at all like what an animal does.

It might be objected that this is untrue. The animal is drawn to the highest good as estimated by sense; we too are drawn to the highest good, but as estimated with the further help of discursive imagination. On this account, deliberation merely extends our senses by allowing us to compare in our minds goods that are sensibly present with goods that are not. The animal glances back and forth between one thing and another with the eye of the body; we do the same, but with pictures in the mind. But this poorly describes what we actually do when we deliberate. In the first place, deliberation cannot be merely an extension of sense, for we are capable of being attracted by non-sensible objects like knowledge and justice. Still stranger is that we invest even sensible goods with non-sensible meanings; a meal, for example, becomes a reminder of my love for my family. Strangest of all—because perverse—is that although we agree that it is prudent to pursue the highest good, we often fail to do so. We seem capable of pursuing things that *even in our own considered estimate* are not worthy of pursuit. Nothing like that is even possible among the animals. In view of the fact that the only way to be attracted to something at all is to see it as somehow good, it is hard to see how it is possible even for us.[9] But let us pull back from the frontier of these mysteries and go on to the next thing to be examined.

The most important aspects of pretheoretical reality that provoke us to philosophize about practical reason in terms of *natural law*—and specifically about natural law *as law*—are certain experiences that we later, as theorists, attribute to conscience. Not every culture has a word for conscience, arousing a suspicion among some people that these experiences are rooted not in the constitution of the human person *per se* but only in the constitution of the Western person, in fact the *late* Western person, his superego shaped by the Judeo-Christian tradition of a divine lawgiver. On the contrary, the distinction of the late Western person is not that he has these experiences, but that he has more ample resources for understanding them. The universality of the experiences themselves is most famously illustrated by Sophocles, who, without any help from the traditions of his culture, nevertheless makes his heroine Antigone proclaim that the ordinances of the tyrant Creon are invalidated by the laws of the gods—laws unwritten and unchanging, that are not only for today or yesterday, but for always. Indeed the wisdom traditions of peoples and nations across the globe acknowledge some such law.

The plot thickens, for we are really speaking of at least three different experiences of graduated intensity. Those who fail to heed conscience in the first mode meet it again in the second; those who refuse to acknowledge it even in the second mode meet it yet more darkly in the third. Antigone testified to its first, cautionary mode: She experienced the performance of her duties toward her dead brother not only as good but as obligatory. This may seem unsurprising, but there is something remarkable about it. Theorists of practical reason often overlook the fact that the inclination to a thing as an object of duty is more than the inclination to it as good per se. The second mode of conscience is accusatory: It indicts us for wrong we have already done. Ordinary slips of prudence lead merely to disappointment; had I only done P or had I only not done Q, I could have enjoyed a certain good or avoided a certain bad. In hindsight, I wish that I had done differently; how stupid, how unfortunate, what a waste. Bad conscience is not that kind of disappointment. True, its occasion would seem to be the same; by doing something or failing to do something, I have unnecessarily brought about a result contrary to my desire. But the experience itself is not the same, for it is more than the awareness of a foolish mistake, or even of a lack of self-control. I am conscious rather of trespass, of breach, of transgression. There is another difference, too, for the emotional and behavioral corollaries of imprudence and bad conscience are not at all the same. In the one case I suffer mere regret, but in the other I suffer remorse. In the one case I may be angry with myself, but in the other I have the sense that I am under wrath. In the one case I probably hope to keep my foolishness a secret, but in the other I suffer an urge to confess. In the one case I probably hope to escape paying the price of my foolishness, but in the other I find myself impelled to seek atonement. I have the sense of having violated a boundary, which I did not make, but which my deepest self agrees with utterly. The good that I betrayed was not merely *commended* by inclination, but *commanded* by authority. I am not only dismayed, I am accused.

What about the third mode of conscience? Even when remorse is absent, as it sometimes is, guilty knowledge generates objective needs for confession, atonement, reconciliation, and justification. These other Furies are the greater sisters of remorse: inflexible, inexorable, and relentless, demanding satisfaction even when mere feelings are suppressed, fade away, or never come. And so it is that conscience operates not only to caution, not only to accuse, but also to avenge, punishing the soul who does wrong but who refuses to read the indictment. I say more about the revenge of conscience in the final part of this chapter. For now suffice it to remark only how exact is the correspondence between the supernatural experience of the sacrament of confession, and the natural experience of bad conscience. They exhibit the same "moments," the same stages, the same phases; it is really true that nature is a preparation for grace.

But I am getting ahead of myself, for I have not yet discussed the experiences that provoke us to philosophize about natural law *as natural*. Although we are speaking of more than one reality, we may briefly consider them together. One of these realities is that a propensity for the experiences that we have already been thinking about is built into our design and woven into the fabric of the normal adult mind. Of course, to speak this way is to suppose that we do have a design, that our minds do have a fabric, that the way we are is not arbitrary or meaningless. Theoretically one may deny that this is so, but at the moment, we are enumerating facts, and it is a fact that human beings of all times and places perceive their lives as having such meaning. Natural law theory holds that they are right.

By the way, the experience of our lives as having meaning cannot be accounted for on grounds of so-called natural selection (which ought to be called "accidental selection," because "nature" is precisely what it is not about). A subjective perception of meaning, reflective of nothing in reality, has adaptive value for an organism only if there is a preexisting subjective *need* for meaning—and what would be the adaptive value of *needing* meaning? Within the context of accidental selection, the answer seems to be "none." Another provocation for philosophizing about natural law *as natural* is the spontaneous intuition of almost all people that moral experience is rooted in what really is. According to this intuition, a rule like the prohibition of murder reflects not a mere illusion or projection, but genuine knowledge. It expresses the actual moral character of a certain kind of act. If this is so, then in a certain sense the law is built not only into human nature but into the rest of nature too. Nature must be *a kind of thing that can sustain* the meanings that we find in the acts that we perform in it. And as though that were not enough, there is yet one more sense in which the law strikes us as built-in. We all find in experience that when we cross the grain of the universe, the universe kicks back. To this interesting fact I will return.

III

Enough with the pretheoretical realities; let us turn to our attempts to account for them, to the theory. The central claim of natural law theory can be expressed in just a few sentences. Law may be defined as an ordinance of reason, for the common good, made by him who has care of the community, and promulgated.[10] Nature may be conceived as an ensemble of things with particular natures, and a thing's nature may be thought of as the design imparted to it by the Creator—in traditional language, as a purpose implanted in it by the divine art, that it be moved to a determinate end.[11] The claim of the theory is that in exactly these senses, natural law is both (1) true law, and (2) truly expressive of nature.

Let us consider these matters step by step, starting with the definition of law. Legal positivists define law merely as the will of the sovereign. This definition simply misconstrues what is asked for. The legal positivist is answering the question, "What qualifies an enactment as belonging to our system of enactments?" His answer, by the way, is circular; he consults the sovereign to recognize the law, but then consults the law to recognize the sovereign.[12] The natural lawyer is trying to answer the entirely different question, "What qualifies an enactment as a rule and measure of human action?" Truly human action is personal and rational rather than merely impulsive, so its norm must be personal and rational too. This norm must serve the common good, because it is a rule and measure for all, not just for some. It must be enacted by public authority, for otherwise it will not bind conscience; it will give rise not to a moral duty, but only to an inconvenient circumstance, a sanction, that cautious people will keep in mind. Finally, the norm must be promulgated, because it cannot be followed if it cannot be known. Does natural law really satisfy this definition? Evidently so; all four conditions are satisfied. Consider the natural law forbidding murder. It is not an arbitrary whim, but a rule which the mind can grasp as right. It serves not some special interest, but the universal good. Its author has care of the universe, for He created it.[13] And it is not a secret rule, for He has so arranged His creation that every rational being knows about it. So it is that when we speak of natural "law," we are not merely dropping into metaphors. It is law. It is not merely a standard for human law, although it serves as a standard too. Nor is it merely a consideration that becomes law when humans enact it, as in the *Leviathan* of Thomas Hobbes. Rather, it is already law, original law. Apart from it, the decrees of the powerful are not truly law, but only enacted frauds.

One might object that although a so-called natural law might either be really natural or really law, it could not be both *at once*. The argument would be that nature cannot contain ordinances of reason because it is mindless; that it cannot promote the common good because it has no ends; that it cannot be regarded as an enactment of authority because it "just is"; and that it cannot be regarded as promulgating anything because it isn't a text. What gives this objection its apparent force is that it slips in a "ringer." In place of the classical understanding of nature as meaningful and designed, it substitutes its own understanding of nature as blind fatality. It is talking about a different thing. Benedict XVI has called attention to this ancient and dangerous mistake. In informal remarks following an address in Saint Peter's Square, he quoted Saint Basil the Great, who said that some, "deceived by the atheism they bear within them, imagined the universe deprived of a guide and order, at the mercy of chance." Benedict remarked, "I believe the words of this fourth-century Father are of amazing timeliness. How many are these 'some' today?"[14] His question, of course, was rhetorical; we know the answer all too well. Their number is legion. But why should we accept their view of nature? What arguments have they? Or what objections do they offer to our own?

One objection to the classical understanding of nature is that it is rubbish to talk about natural purposes, because we merely imagine them. According to this way of thinking, the purposes of things aren't natural; they are merely in the eye of the beholder. But is this true? Take the power of breathing. When we say that its purpose—viewed from another angle, its meaning—is to oxygenate the blood, are we making it up? Plainly not. This purpose isn't in the eye of the beholder; it is an inference from the design of the lungs. To say that the purpose of P is to bring about Q, two conditions must be satisfied. First, P must actually bring about Q. This condition is satisfied because breathing does oxygenate the blood. Second, it must be the case that the fact that P brings about Q is necessary for explaining why there is P in the first place. This condition is also satisfied, because apart from the oxygenation of blood there is no way to explain why the power to breath should have developed.[15] We can ascertain the purposes of the other features of our design in the same way that we ascertain the purpose of breathing.

A second objection to the classical understanding of nature is that it doesn't make any difference even if we can ascertain the purposes of natural things, because an "is" does not imply an "ought." This dogma, too, is false. If the purpose of eyes is that they see, then eyes that see well are good eyes, and eyes that see poorly are poor ones. Given their purpose, this is what it means for eyes to be "good."[16] Moreover, good is to be pursued; the appropriateness of pursuing it is what it means for *anything* to be good. Therefore, the appropriate thing to do with poor eyes is try to turn them into good ones. If it really were impossible to derive an ought from the is of the human design, then the practice of medicine would make no sense. Natural law theory has contemptuously been called "metaphysical biology"; so be it, for biology needs metaphysics. But we are speaking of more than biology. In exactly the same way that we infer that the purpose of the eyes is to see and the purpose of breathing is to oxygenate the blood, we can infer the purpose of the capacity for anger, the purpose of the power of reasoning, and so on. Natural function and personal meaning are not alien to each other, they are connected. In a rightly ordered way of thinking, they turn out to be different angles of vision of the same thing.

The third objection to the classical understanding of nature is the most radical. This time the objector holds that even if nature does generate a sort of *ought*, that makes no difference, because any such *ought* is arbitrary. Man, says the objector, is the product of a meaningless process that did not have him in mind.[17] Had the process gone a bit differently—had our ancestors been carnivores instead of omnivores, had they laid eggs instead of borne live young, had they started watching television earlier than they did—then we would have had a different nature with differnt norms. Call such norms "natural laws" if it pleases you, the objectors say, but don't imagine that they mean anything. I think this third objection is the strongest, for nature is undoubtedly a contingent being, and one cannot ground transcendent meaning in a contingency. But on closer consideration, the objection answers itself, for contingent beings never "just are"; they too must have causes. If their causes are contingent, then they must have causes. To avoid endless regress, the chain of causes must at least end in a necessary being, and since the effects that this being produces are personal, He must be personal as well. But if this is true, then natural law theory is not trying to ground meaning in a contingency after all. Nature takes meaning from supernature; creation from its Creator; the created structures of personal goodness from the uncreated personal Good Who is their source.

I remarked earlier that the natural law truly satisfies the promulgation condition—that it is not a secret rule, for the Creator has so arranged His creation that every rational being knows about it. This needs to be more fully spelled out. The claim here is not that everyone knows the theory of natural law. That is plainly false; not everyone has even heard the *expression* "natural law." However, everyone is acquainted with the thing itself. To speak in the words of Thomas Aquinas, the foundational principles of morality are "the same for all, both as to rectitude and as to knowledge."[18] To say that they are the same for all "as to rectitude" means that they are right for everyone; in other words, deliberately taking innocent human life, sleeping with my neighbor's wife, and mocking God are as wrong for me as they are for you, no matter what either of us believes. To say that they are the same for all "as to knowledge" means that at some level, everyone knows them; even the murderer knows the wrong of murder, the adulterer the wrong of adultery, the mocker the wrong of mockery. He may say that he doesn't, but he does. There are no real moral skeptics; supposed skeptics are playing make-believe, and doing it badly.

To be sure, the game is played very hard, and not only by skeptics. I must not take innocent human life—but only my tribe is human. I must not sleep with my neighbor's wife—but I can make my neighbor's mine. I must not mock deity—but I can ascribe deity to a created thing instead of the Creator. These are the lies that we tell ourselves. In our time we are finding out just how hard the game can be played, and this development puts natural law in a new theoretical situation. It might once have been thought sufficient to say that some moral knowledge is universal. As it turns out, however, the determination to play tricks on moral knowledge is universal too. A law is written on the heart of man, but it is everywhere entangled with the evasions and subterfuges of men.

But that is a problem for the final part of this chapter, on natural law as a sign of contradiction. For now, let us return to how natural law is known. There are, I think, four ways. I have sometimes called them the four "witnesses," as a memorial of Saint Paul's remark to the pagans of Lystra that although in times past God allowed the Gentile nations to walk in their own ways, even then "He did not leave Himself without witness."[19] The context shows that he is not speaking of human witnesses, but of impersonal testimonies built into the very pattern of God's providence. To be sure, these witnesses are wordless. The same thing might be said of them that the psalmist says of the heavens: "There is no speech, nor are there words; their voice is not heard; yet their voice goes out through all the earth, and their words to the end of the world."[20]

The first witness may be called conscience, but in a different sense than that word bears in everyday speech. We think of conscience as one thing. The classical natural law tradition distinguished two things—I think rightly. One is *synderesis*—some prefer to call it *anamnesis*, remembrance—which might be called "deep conscience." Deep conscience is the interior witness to the most general norms of practical reason, including, by the way, not only principles like "good is to be done and evil avoided," but also its proximate corollaries, well-summarized by the Decalogue. The other thing is *conscientia*, which might be called "surface conscience." Surface conscience is the application of the knowledge that deep conscience provides. Like memory, this knowledge is not always in the mind "actually" but is always there latently; we are in the "habit" of knowing it, even though we may not be thinking of it, even though we may not be aware of knowing it, and even though we may even suppress it. The habit is natural, not acquired; it is a feature of the design of the created practical intellect.[21]

I have just spoken of design, and must now speak of it again, for the second witness is the evident designedness of things in general. We perceive immediately that nature requires an explanation beyond itself; that the things in nature are indeed designed; and that design requires personal agency. Working out the logic of these perceptions is one of the tasks of philosophy, but the perceptions themselves are prephilosophical. Saint Paul alludes to them when he says that the reality of God and of some of His qualities have been known "since the creation of the world," having been "clearly perceived in the things that have been made."[22] It might be thought that although the perception of the designedness of things is theologically interesting, it is not *morally* interesting. On the contrary, it does at least three things for moral knowledge. In the first place, it vindicates the previous witness, deep conscience, for if deep conscience is designed as a witness to moral truth by a God who knows what He is doing, then its witness to this truth is reliable.[23] It also confirms that we have duties not only to neighbor but to God Himself, to whom we owe the very possibility of the experience of anything good. Finally, it informs us that just as deep conscience is designed, so the rest of us is designed; we are a canvas for His purposes, a parchment of His meanings.

That leads us to the third witness, the particulars of our own design. Design is obvious not just in our bodies but across the whole range of human powers, capacities, and actions. The function of fear is to warn; of minds, to deliberate and know; of anger, to prepare for the protection of endangered goods. Everything in us has a purpose; everything is for something. A power is well used when it is used for that purpose and according to that design. Nor is this just about the *functions* of things; as I have already suggested and as natural lawyers are coming to realize more deeply, it is also about the meanings of things. Our very bodies have a language of their own; they say things by what we do with them. Bone speaks to bone, organ to organ, skin to skin. A smile means something friendly; one cannot give that meaning to a slap in the face. One can use a kiss to betray, but only because the kiss, in itself, means something else. Conjugal sex means self-giving, making one flesh out of two. And so on.

Some of the most interesting features of our design show up not at the level of the individual but at the level of the species. A particularly striking example is the complementarity of the sexes: Short of a divine provision for people called to celibacy, there is something missing in the man which must be provided by the woman, and something missing in the woman which must be provided by the man. Indeed, complementarity is not *bypassed* by the celibate but provided with a higher fulfillment. When we speak of such things as being "married to the Church," we are dealing not with euphemisms but with profound realities. Design features like complementarity establish conditions for human flourishing that would not have been deducible just from the fact that, in some thin sense, we are rational. They require us to recognize the *personal* character of rational being.[24]

The fourth witness to natural law is the natural consequences of its violation. Those who cut themselves bleed. Those who betray their friends are betrayed by their friends. Those who abandon their children have no one to comfort them when they are old. Those who travel from bed to bed lose the capacity for intimacy and trust. Especially interesting are the *noetic* penalties for violation, for those who suppress their moral knowledge become even stupider than they had intended. We see that the ancient principle that God is not mocked, that whatever a man sows he also reaps,[25] is sewn into the fabric of experience. A clarification is necessary, for in calling natural consequences one of the witnesses, I should not wish to be misunderstood. Natural law theory is not "consequentialist"; the penalty for violation is not what *makes* the wrong act wrong. It functions rather as an announcement and a form of discipline. In fact, the most intriguing thing about the natural consequences of things is that they point to the natural purposes and meanings of things. For example, the natural link between sex and pregnancy is not just a brute fact to be circumvented by latex; it declares that sex serves the *meaning* of self-giving and the *purpose* of procreation, of having and raising children in the love and fear of God.

I have enumerated four witnesses. An endless confusion of cross-purposes has been caused by the fact that the various theories of natural law do not all focus on the same witness. In hostile challenge to the Scholastic thinkers, Thomas Hobbes zeroed in on the witness of natural consequences—indeed on just one such consequence, violent death. In ways that are often overlooked, and despite the thinness of his teleology, John Locke relied on the two witnesses of design.[26] In provocative though incomplete ways, the "new" natural law theory of Germain G. Grisez, John Finnis, and Joseph M. Boyle gives central place to the design of deep conscience, the deep structure of practical reason, while attempting to avoid *direct* reliance on the other aspects of our design.[27] The classical tradition, epitomized by Thomas Aquinas, attempted to provide an integrated account of all four witnesses. Unfortunately his good example is rarely followed.

IV

At last we return to the sheer scandal of natural law. By its scandal, I mean more than just that some things about it are very puzzling. But since that fact causes difficulty, allow me to begin there.

There are a number of different things one can study about natural law. Some natural lawyers focus on its foundations in the common moral sense of the plain person. These are "dialectical" foundations, because the plain person knows all sorts of things that he doesn't know he knows. A scholar, by contrast, may know very few things, but he is perhaps more likely to know, or think he knows, how he knows them. If natural law theory is to be made plausible to its critics, then the whole problem of latent knowledge, of how we can know something at one level, even though not knowing that we know it, needs to be more thoroughly investigated.

Other natural law thinkers focus on casuistry, on the solution of difficult moral problems. This enterprise is precariously balanced between two extremes. At one extreme is the oversimplified notion that if there really is a law written on the heart, there *could not be* any difficult moral problems. At the other is the overcomplexified notion that *every* moral problem is difficult. For young people, the most dangerous and tempting extreme is the former. They confuse what feels right at the moment with natural law, and if their feelings are confused, they become disillusioned and conclude that there is no natural law. For natural lawyers themselves, however, the most dangerous and tempting extreme is the latter. They sometimes make such circuitous paths to such obvious destinations that the destinations themselves come into doubt.

Still other natural law thinkers focus on metaphysics, on the study of what the world must be like for there to be a natural law in the first place. This project is indispensable, but it is prone to confuse the theory with the fact. We see this especially in our teaching. Which is the better way to explain the idea of natural law—to ask, "Have you noticed that there are some things about right and wrong that we all really know and can't help knowing?" or to say, "It's all about the convertibility of being and goodness?" Obviously, the former—even though the latter is also true.

These scandals are avoidable. However, not all scandals are avoidable. Ultimately, the natural law is a sign of contradiction for much deeper reasons. Even in the prelapsarian state, their noetic powers intact, our first parents were tempted to "be like God, knowing good and evil"—to imagine that they could be First Causes of their own moral knowledge and their own constitution as persons. How much more are we postlapsarians liable to this temptation, our noetic powers damaged by the Fall, our wills no longer innocent but depraved.[28] Our problem then is not ugliness, but sullied beauty, and our tragedy is twofold, for not only are we unable by our own powers to restore our loveliness, but we are wroth with the very offer of restorative grace. Such is sin.

For natural law theory, the consequence of the Fall is that we *don't want to hear* of natural law. We cannot fully ignore it, because its first letters are written on our hearts. But we resist the inscription, and the letters burn. Here begins the terrible game that I mentioned earlier. The crisis of natural law in our time owes partly to the deepening intensity of the game, but partly to the fact that we ignore it. We persist in taking pretended moral ignorance at face value, in philosophizing as though the problem of moral failure were merely cognitive. We suppose that when the opinionators of our time repudiate God, celebrate the destruction of life, and rejoice in sexual debasement, they simply do not know any better. We imagine that if only we present them with airtight arguments, they will change their minds. That is not how it will happen, for there is such a thing as motivated error. Indeed the problem is graver still. Our opinionators have not destroyed deep conscience, but suppressed it. That may sound better, and in a way it is, but in another way it is worse. Like a man who is buried alive, conscience kicks against the walls of its tomb. The defiant intellect—which is that tomb—therefore fortifies the walls.

A single example will suffice. We *can't not know* the wrong of deliberately taking innocent human life. The appalling thing is that we make use of this knowledge even in order to defy it. The arguments for abortion amount to claiming either that the act is not deliberate, or that it is not a taking, or that the unborn child is not innocent, not human, or not alive.

A moment, please: not innocent? Even that, for there is no limit to what can be denied. Legal scholar Eileen L. McDonagh calls the unborn child a "private party" who uses "violence" to "coerce" the woman "to be pregnant against her will"; it is "objectively at fault for causing pregnancy." The woman has a "right to consent to a relationship with this intruder," and is entitled to "the use of deadly force to stop it," even if this intruder "acquires the highly charged label of 'baby.'" "Some might suggest," McDonagh says, "that the solution to coercive pregnancy is simply for the woman to wait until the fetus is born, at which point its coercive imposition of pregnancy will cease." But "this type of reasoning is akin to suggesting that a woman being raped should wait until the rape is over rather than stopping the rapist."[29]

What is one to make of such an argument? It is hard to know whether it is more horrible or more absurd. The difficulty is not that it cannot be answered, for it can. Rather the difficulty is that in order to find it plausible in the first place, a person must already be beyond or very nearly beyond argument. The level of self-deception required is stupendous. Nor is this rare, for there are many such arguments-beyond-argument. Physician Warren M. Hern, has written a learned article explaining that pregnancy is "an illness requiring medical supervision," which "may be treated by evacuation of the uterine contents," but "has an excellent prognosis for complete, spontaneous recovery if managed under careful medical supervision." If you can believe it, the article was published in a journal called *Family Planning Perspectives*.[30]

I remarked earlier that guilty knowledge sometimes generates remorse, and always generates objective needs for confession, atonement, reconciliation, and justification. Arguments like those of Hern and McDonagh illustrate the perversion of the need for justification. However, the perversions of the other four impulses are equally deadly to truth-seeking discourse. The normal outlet of remorse is to flee from wrong; of the need for confession, to admit what one has done; of the need for atonement, to pay the debt; of the need for reconciliation, to restore the bonds one has broken; and of the need for justification, to get back in the right. But if these Furies are denied their payment in wonted coin, they exact it in whatever coin comes nearest. We flee not from wrong, but from thinking about it. We compulsively confess every detail of our transgression, except that it was wrong. We punish ourselves again and again, offering every sacrifice except the one sacrifice demanded, a contrite and broken heart. We simulate the restoration of broken intimacy by recruiting companions as guilty as ourselves. And we seek not to become just, but to justify ourselves—to concoct excuses.

Each one of these perversions makes its own contribution to the distortion of scholarship and public discourse. I have spoken of justification; how about the other four? The confessional character of some of our intellectual enterprises is unmistakable; confession actually becomes a kind of advocacy. Or consider the way that recruitment becomes seduction to intellectual evil. One might suppose that I am tendentiously labeling the practice of persuasion as enlightenment when practiced by my side, but as seduction when practiced by the other. On the contrary, the seducers themselves are often guiltily aware of their dark motives. Everyone knows scholars like an atheist of my acquaintance who boasts of the "fun" he had "ruining all the Catholic kids" at the liberal arts college where he taught. The verb "ruining" was precisely accurate even by his lights, for the fun lay not in liberating these innocent and impressionable young minds from what he considered error, but in deflowering and desecrating them. Perhaps the strangest impulse to incoherency in our intellectual discourse is the perversion of the need to atone. The dishonest intellect, at some level aware of having committed the sin against the truth, attempts to make up for its transgression by mortifying itself; ultimately it denies that there is such a thing as the truth, or at least that truth can be known. "Here you shall pass among the fallen people," Virgil said to Dante, "souls who have lost the good of intellect."[31] It is not only in hell that we meet them.

Abortion is not the only issue that generates such levels of denial, nor are they found only among the professional advocates of evil. Denial is the normal response of the intellect that is tortured by its conscience but refuses to repent—"normal" in the sense that fever is the normal response to infection, or that unconsciousness is the normal response to a severe blow to the head. It is part of the system of natural consequences to which I alluded earlier—a noetic and personal, rather than a physical and biological, penalty for the violation of natural law. And it comes near to being the normal condition of our era.

An even grimmer consideration is that the inherent tendency of denial is to become deeper and deeper over time, and to express itself in graver and graver transgressions. Consider the argument that human person-hood is not a category of being but a mere cluster of functional attributes, such as the ability to communicate and plan, so that those who lack these abilities are not persons. The original motive for adopting such a view may be to rationalize only one kind of killing, but inevitably it justifies others. Notice that functionalism also generates a caste system, for if personhood depends on attributes that vary in degree, then personhood itself must vary in degree. Good communicators and planners will be held to possess the highest degree of personhood, second-rate ones will be held to possess the next degree, and third-rate ones will hardly be held to be persons at all. Surely the interests of those who are more fully persons must trump the interests of those who are less, one reasons, so the range of mandated outrages grows ever broader. A functionalist might be dismayed by this implication of his premises. His dilemma is that he cannot give them up without admitting that the one cherished outrage which drove him to embark on this process of rationalization was wrong all along. If he continues to set his face against repentance, then by the very logic of the case he is compelled to be obstinate about more and more.

One might object that even if all this is true, my complaint is out of place. The objection would run like this: I seem to think that the noetic consequences of the violation of natural law pose a problem for natural law philosophers, but if I am right about those consequences, then we are speaking of people who resist argument—and if they do resist argument, then philosophy has nothing left to do. But this does not follow. In the first place, we can philosophize *about* denial even if we cannot philoso-phize with those who are *in* denial. In the second place, there are many ways of talking with people, and philosophy is only one of them. The vari-ous modes of public discourse have always been recognized as legitimate topics for philosophy. If the noetic consequences of transgression pose obstacles to sane public discourse, then why not philosophize about the obstacles too? Why not philosophize about *less* than sane public discourse, and how it might be brought back to sanity?

Historically, one reason the natural law tradition has advanced is that new crises raised new questions. For our age, the crisis is an old one made newly acute, and the questions it raises are twofold: why natural law is a sign of contradiction, and what can be done about the scandal. I am con-vinced that if we fail to grapple seriously with these questions, we will be derelict not only in intellect but in love. To Bernard of Clairvaux is attributed the epigram "Some seek knowledge for the sake of knowledge: that is curiosity. Others seek knowledge that they may themselves be known: that is vanity. But there are still others who seek knowledge in order to serve and edify others, and that is charity." The times are dark, and darkening. If ever there was a time for Christian philosophers to exercise such charity, it is now.

2

The Second Tablet Project

I

According to the mainstream of the natural law tradition, the reality of God and the reality of our indebtedness to Him are among the things everyone really knows. They are part of "general" revelation; we have natural knowledge not only of the Second Tablet of the Decalogue, but of the first. Needless to say, some people find this claim scandalous. They deny the natural knowledge of God, deny the natural knowledge of the First Tablet of the Decalogue, and deny the natural knowledge of the first precept of the summary of the Law, to love God with all that is in you.[1] Apart from direct or "special" revelation, they think ethics should acknowledge neighbor only. Passions run high among such thinkers. A book reviewer angrily declares "God does not belong" in discussions of how to live. A scholar of my acquaintance devotes the last phase of his intellectual career to what he calls "pushing God out of the natural law"—or at least, he says, "into the wings." This goal is widely shared. Insofar as it wishes to get by on the Second Tablet without the first, we might call it the Second Tablet Project.

The Second Tablet Project is probably more popular among lukewarm religious believers who wish to make the moral law palatable to nonbelievers than it is among nonbelievers themselves. Nonbelievers who want to get rid of the first tablet usually have doubts about the second too—and for the same reasons. God, they think, is a dubious proposition, but why should morality be less dubious than He? Aren't these two matters both pretty dim? As to the notion of "things we can't not know," they don't believe that there are such things—we have only a motley of incompatible opinions about God and how to live, all of them equally controversial because none of them can be known to be true. Under the circumstances, they think, the only sensible thing to do is to eject the whole lot of these opinions from the public square. This is the mentality that finds it scandalous to post the Ten Commandments on a schoolroom or courtroom wall. The argument seems to be, "Because we don't agree with each other, you must do as I say"—for if anyone should protest, "But your opinion that these norms are *not* common knowledge is far more controversial than the norms themselves," they respond, "See what I mean?" Or perhaps, like John Rawls, they respond that *their* opinion should have special privileges because it is "political, not metaphysical."[2] Here the argument seems to be, "The ultimate truth of things is unknowable, and *that's* why you must do as I say." Of course, any view of what is knowable or unknowable presupposes something about what is, so that is another sleight of hand.

For those who do believe in natural law or general revelation, the fact that the Second Tablet Project so often turns into a No Tablet Project raises an important question. What difference does it make to the knowledge of the moral law that we do have some knowledge about God? If we didn't have that knowledge, that could we retain knowledge of morality? If we could retain it, would it be different? Would it be complete?

The inquiry requires two parts, because there are two ways to know about God: the vague, partial, natural knowledge of God which is available to every human being, and the additional knowledge of God which is offered (for those who accept it) in the biblical tradition of direct revelation. Though my emphasis is on the first way, I will also comment on the second. To be sure, Holy Scripture is not included in the things one can't not know. But every perspective for discussing what we can't not know is *some* perspective for discussing what we can't not know, and my perspective is biblical.

By the first way to know about God I mean the *sensus divinitatis,* the spontaneous awareness of the reality of the Creator. I do not exclude the clarity that philosophy can add to this awareness; I only wish to point out that the philosophical arguments for the existence of God do not start from nowhere. However complex they may be, they merely elaborate pre-philosophical intuitions, such as the everyday idea that anything which does not *have to be* requires a cause. "Why is there something, and not rather nothing?" is a question that anyone can ask.

As to the second way of knowing about God—the biblical tradition of direct revelation—I use the qualifier "biblical" advisedly. Other religions have traditions, too, but traditions of direct revelation are quite rare. Every major religion which claims to record God's direct revelations to human beings in actual historical time accepts at least part of the Bible; this includes Judaism, Christianity, and Islam. No major religion outside of the biblical sphere of influence claims to record God's direct revelations to human beings in actual historical time.

II

Apart from any consideration of an alleged direct revelation, what difference does it make to the natural law that we *naturally* have knowledge of God? It seems to make not one difference, but at least four.

The first difference has to do with what C. S. Lewis called the "abolition of man." If God has designed and endowed us with our nature—this is not a question of how He did it or how long it took, but only of who is responsible—then we can be confident that we have the nature that we ought to have in accord with His good purposes. This premise in no way slights the Fall; even a crushed foot remains a foot. The proposition that we are in conflict with our nature in no way implies that it is not, in fact, our nature.

Let us imagine someone who denies divine design. He admits that human beings have a nature, just in the sense that certain ways of living go against the grain; he only refuses to allow that we were endowed with this nature by God. Put another way, the direction of the grain is meaningless. With a different evolutionary history, we would have had a different nature. Given the nature that we do have, certain things go against the grain, hence a certain natural law; given some other nature, different things would have gone against the grain, hence a different natural law. What strikes our nature as evil might for that nature be good. The entire basis of morality, on this account, is the particular nature that we have at the moment. There would be nothing wrong with having a different nature and thus a different natural law. We just don't.

But what if we could? What if we could *change* our nature? According to those who hold this view, we already have. Our ancestors were as different from us, they say, as a prosimian is different from a man. Generation by generation, the ur-men of the long gone past adapted to a changing environment. Our great-grand-primates were the products of adaptation to a life in the branches of trees. Our grand-primates were the products of adaptation to a life on the savanna. Our parents were the products of adaptation to the practice of agriculture. And our descendants will be the products of adaptation to the most enduring features of our own environment, whatever those turn out to be. Perhaps television.

Notice that on this theory, some of the circumstances to which our ancestors adapted were the results of their own prior actions. It was they who came down from the trees, and had therefore to adapt to the savanna. It was they who invented agriculture, and had therefore to adapt to a different diet. In a sense, then, we have been influencing our own evolution all along. We have already changed our nature. We just didn't know that we were doing it. If there is nothing wrong with having a different nature—and if we have already changed our nature without knowing—then why shouldn't we take the process in hand? Why shouldn't we deliberately change ourselves as we wish to be changed? Why shouldn't we *determine* the nature of our descendants?

Such proposals are no longer idle talk. In October 2000, news leaked that an American company named Biotransplant and an Australian company named Stem Cell Sciences had successfully crossed a human being with a pig by inserting the nuclei of cells from a human fetus into the pig's eggs. Although the embryos were destroyed when they reached the 32-cell point, they would have continued to grow had they been implanted in the womb of a woman—or a sow. Since then, other companies in other countries have continued this line of research.

According to J. Bottum in the *Weekly Standard,* "There has been some suggestion from the creators that their purpose in designing this human pig is to build a new race of subhuman creatures for scientific and medical use. . . . [T]hen, too, there has been some suggestion that the creators' purpose is not so much to corrupt humanity as to elevate it." His comments are worth quoting at some length:

> It used to be that even the imagination of this sort of thing existed only
> to underscore a moral in a story. . . . But we live at a moment in which
> British newspapers can report on [nineteen] families who have cre-
> ated test-tube babies solely for the purpose of serving as tissue donors
> for their relatives—some brought to birth, some merely harvested as

embryos and fetuses. A moment in which *Harper's Bazaar* can advise women to keep their faces unwrinkled by having themselves injected with fat culled from human cadavers. . . . In the midst of all this, the creation of a human-pig arrives like a thing expected. We have reached the logical end, at last. We have become the people that, once upon a time, our ancestors used fairy tales to warn their children against— and we will reap exactly the consequences those tales foretold. Like the coming true of an old story—the discovery of the philosopher's stone, the rubbing of a magic lantern—biotechnology is delivering the most astonishing medical advances anyone has ever imagined. But our sons and daughters will mate with the pig-men, if the pig-men will have them. And our swine-snouted grandchildren—the fruit not of our loins, but of our arrogance and our bright test tubes—will use the story of our generation to teach a moral to their frightened litters.[3]

Plainly, Bottum is not pleased with what the researchers have done. As he writes, it makes no difference whether they plan to create subhumans or superhumans, for "either they want to make a race of slaves, or they want to make a race of masters. And either way, it means the end of our humanity." The evil is not that the experiment might turn out badly. It is that our nature would be abolished.

But our atheist will ask: What exactly is the objection to abolishing our nature? Why *not* abolish it? We won't be around to mind. Our descendants won't mind either, because we can build into their natures that they are satisfied with the natures they get. If we like, we can make an entire graded set of natures, along the lines of Huxley's *Brave New World*. "I'm glad I'm a Beta," say his Betas. So why *should* we reap the consequences that the tales of old foretold? Why should the pig-men use the story of our generation to teach a moral to their frightened litters? Why should these litters be frightened by what, to them, would be the story of Genesis?

Genesis, I think, is the crux of it: Not the text of Genesis, but its idea of creation. To abolish and remake human nature is to play God. The chief objection to playing God is that someone else is God already. If He created human nature, if He intended it, if it is not the result of a blind fortuity that did not have us in mind—then we have no business exchanging it for another. It would be good to remember that Genesis contains not only the story of creation but the story of Babel, of the presumption of men who thought they could build a tower "to heaven."

Here then is the first difference that the knowledge of God makes to the natural law. A godless natural law would revere the laws of human nature only insofar as we continued to be human. Denying that our humanity is a creation, it would have no reason to preserve this humanity, and no objection to its abolition.

III

The second difference it makes to have natural knowledge of God concerns what we might call "oughtness." A moment ago we spoke of a godless natural law. But in what sense can a godless mind revere the laws of human nature at all? The early modern Dutch legal philosopher Hugo Grotius famously remarked that even if there were no God (as he conceded that it would be impious to believe), yet the natural law would have a kind of force. What seems to impress most people who read this remark is that Grotius thinks it *would* have a kind of force. More interesting is his qualifier: It would have a *kind* of force. The suggestion is that it would not have the kind that it would have if God were real.

Taken with that emphasis, the remark of Grotius might be true. Although a godless natural law would lose the force of "oughtness," it would retain the lower force of prudence. But perhaps it would lose that force too. Let us look into this further.

The argument for saying that the natural law would lose the force of oughtness but retain the force of prudence runs like this: If there is no God, then the universe is not a creation. One immediate consequence is that I owe nothing to anyone for the fact that I am in it. If there is a reason to keep the moral laws, it cannot lie in honoring the one who made us. Another consequence is that the universe has no meaning beyond itself. The patterns in it *just are;* they do not reflect the goodness or the intentions of a Designer.

And this makes a difference. A theist who attributes the order of nature to God can say things like this: "I see that the sexual powers cause conception, and that the fact that they do so is part of the explanation of why human nature has been endowed with such powers in the first place. This tells me that conception is a *purpose* of the sexual powers, a part of what they are *for*. When I employ them, I ought to respect this fact; I ought not to use them in ways that are incompatible with their purpose." Adding inference to inference in this fashion, he gradually works out a comprehensive account of the right use of the sexual powers and the respect which is owed to the natural institutions which direct and contain them, and he can reason similarly about the other natural powers and institutions.

But an atheist might reply like this: "I use the word *purpose* too, and I am even willing to concede that you use it correctly. If one thing causes another, and if that fact is part of the explanation of why the first thing occurs, then the second thing is a purpose of the first;[4] even a Darwinist like me can concede that much. So what? How do you get from 'One of the purposes of the sexual powers is procreation' to 'I should not use the sexual powers in ways that are incompatible with procreation'? So far as I can see, the only thing that follows from the connection between procreation and sex is that when I do have intercourse, it would be prudent to watch out." Stretching a point a bit—taking into account the entire set of things there are to "watch out" for (not only conception, but jealousy, emotional emptiness, disease, loss of trust, and so forth)—perhaps a purely prudential justification of marriage and family and so forth could be developed. Perhaps a purely prudential justification for each of the other natural laws and institutions could be developed in the same way. And perhaps that is the sort of thing that Grotius had in mind.

Unfortunately, a truly "oughtless" prudence would have nothing to say to free riders, for anyone who thought he saw a way to obtain the benefits of these laws and institutions without their costs would do so. Nor would it have anything to say to what might be called "crazy riders," for anyone who was willing to accept the costs of transgressing them would do so. In an oughtless world, why not? To speak again of marriage, some men prefer seducing married women. Others say they can do very well without trust. Still others say that although they fear exposure, they would rather risk it than forgo their pleasures. Some even enjoy the risk; for them, it isn't a cost.

To be sure, the oughtless sort of prudence is rather thin. The thicker prudence of the natural law tradition would point out that free riders sacrifice greater goods for lesser ones; they *ought* to desire better for themselves than they do. But they have no *ought*—remember? In their sort of prudence, the good is nothing but the desirable, and the desirable is nothing but what they actually desire. From their point of view, the good for which they feel the greatest desire is the greatest good—just because they desire it most.

IV

Some people would say that the thinness of the oughtless sort of prudence is a problem only for the naïve sort of atheist. With a little more sophistication, the atheist can reply that in the same way things *just do* have causal and functional properties, so they *just do* have moral properties. The argument saves oughtness by sheer fiat—or so it seems. But does it really save anything at all? In one way, it makes the atheist's moral case even weaker, because it concedes the arbitrariness of the universe in which he thinks he is living. So we come to the third difference it makes that we have natural knowledge of God: It determines whether we can expect the universe to make any sense at all, morally or otherwise.

In the colloquy between theist and atheist presented several paragraphs ago, both parties assumed that the universe is causally and rationally patterned: this causes that, that explains this other thing, such-and-such is a reasonable explanation of so-and-so. But what right has the atheist to this assumption? Why should there be any patterns whatsoever? If the universe *just is,* then why shouldn't the things in it *just happen?* There is no reason to expect them to yield to reasoning, no explanation of why they should even have an explanation. Moreover, we are not out of the woods even if we do find patterns in the universe, for if these patterns too *just are,* then there is no warrant for assuming that they are more than local, accidental, superficial, inconsistent, and ephemeral. The sun may not rise tomorrow morning. Fire may not burn this afternoon. Two plus two may equal now four, now six, now one. For me, conception may *not* be caused by sexual intercourse (that is how teenagers think). Even if today I am myself, next week I may be someone else (that is how postmodernists think). So why should the natural law have even the force of prudence, much less oughtness? Why should there even be logic? Why should I "watch out" for anything? How could I?

But perhaps the only problem with our sophisticated atheist is that he is not sophisticated *enough.* If without God he has no right to assume Pattern, very well: Let him be a sort of Platonist, and posit that Pattern itself is God. Of course Pattern would not be what the theist means by God, but it would be God in the impersonal sense: deepest reality, the underlying principle of everything, that on which all else depends.

But if he is to be a sort of Platonist, then what does he make of Plato's problem? There are a great many patterns, not just one. This raises the question of what organizes them, what binds them all together in a unity, a Design. We know of only one thing which is capable of Design, and that is mind—intelligent agency. It is not enough for the universe to resemble a mind in *having* design; let us have no tricks, like calling the patterns "ideas" when we have not earned the right to do so. Behind the universe there must be a *real* mind which is capable of the things that real minds do, like designing. Nor let us overlook the significance of the fact that the things this mind designs include persons, for a cause cannot be exceeded by its effect. All this brings us back to God—God as the theist means God: God with a mind, God in the personal sense.

If our atheist accepts this implication, then he is back in the fold; he is no longer an atheist. But if he denies it, then it will not help him even if Pattern really is the deepest reality, because in that case "Pattern" is merely a fancy name for "patterns," and plurality of patterns without design is merely chaos; "mere anarchy is loosed upon the world." After all, Plato merely gave names to the ways things hang together; he never explained why they had to hang together, where there was any necessity to it. For example, he said that all good things participate in a sort of superpattern, or transcendental, called Goodness, and in token of the fact he assumed an underlying unity among the virtues—courage, wisdom, justice, moderation, and all the rest. But with nothing to *bring* these good virtues into unity, there is no reason why they should *be* in unity. Perhaps cowardice is the fount of justice, wisdom comes only to the wanton, and courage makes fools of us all. Perhaps righteousness and peace have not kissed each other, as the psalmist claims, but tear each other daily into pieces. Don't many people think in exactly this way?

Another of Plato's convictions was that goodness is but *one* of the transcendentals. He supposed there were two more, truth and beauty. Supposing this to be true, one might think that it helps matters, but it only makes them worse. For why should the *three* transcendentals hang together? Why shouldn't goodness be ugly, beauty lie, and truth be inimical to good—not because they *have* come apart, as they seem to in this fallen world, but because they *must* come apart, because that is just how they are?

Natural selection gives no reason to expect them to cohere; a clash between, say, truth and goodness would not keep an organism from passing on its genes. In fact there *is* no reason—unless there is something else at work, *someone* else at work, Whom Plato may have known but did not name. In the end we find that the sophisticated sort of atheist is no better

off than the naïve sort. His universe is just as mad, and perhaps more ter-
rifying still. It may contain just as much oughtness as he likes: But what
ought to be, what charms us, and what *is* are all at war, and the house of
Ought is divided against itself.

V

Our question for the last few sections of this chapter has been what difference it makes to the natural law that we naturally have knowledge of God.
So far I have been treating this question as though it meant, "What difference would it make to the natural law if we *didn't* have such knowledge?"
But there is another way to take it: "What difference would it make to the
natural law if we do have such knowledge but *tell* ourselves we don't?"
In other words, we may ask about the consequences of lying to ourselves
about Him. One of these consequences is a kind of metastasis—as in the
growth of tumors. This is the fourth way it matters to have natural knowledge of God.

Do we not lie to ourselves about ordinary right and wrong? The desire
to know truth is ardent, but it is not the only desire at work in us. The
desire not to know competes with it desperately, for knowledge is a fearsome thing. That is why we so often groan about how difficult it is to
know what is right, even though we know perfectly well what is right.
Every honest person can confirm this from his own experience. Just how
much lying goes on was recently confirmed during the high-level political
scandals of the last fifteen years, beginning during the Clinton admin-
istration, when everyone from television interviewer Geraldo Rivera to
comedian Jerry Seinfeld seemed to agree that "everybody lies about sex."
As Seinfeld put it in an interview with Michael Blowen, "Truth and sex
don't go together." Presumably he had in mind not only our lying to other
people but our lying to ourselves, because one just can't do that much
lying without rationalizing it to himself somehow.

But the problem of lying to ourselves goes far beyond sex. Along with
the mainstream of the natural law tradition, I have suggested that one of
the things about reality and goodness that we know perfectly well is the
reality and goodness of God. Biblical tradition agrees. When psalm four-
teen remarks, "The fool says in his heart 'There is no God,'" it doesn't call
him a fool for thinking it, but for saying it even though yet deeper in his
heart he knows it isn't true. From this point of view, the reason it is so dif-

ficult to argue with an atheist is that he is not being honest with himself. He knows that there is a God; he only tells himself that he doesn't.

One need not take this from a theist like me. Consider the remarks of the Harvard population biologist Richard Lewontin—an atheist who thinks matter is all there is—in the January 9, 1997, edition of the *New York Review of Books*: "Our willingness to accept scientific claims that are against common sense is the key to an understanding of the real struggle between science and the supernatural. We take the side of science *in spite of* the patent absurdity of some of its constructs, *in spite of* its failure to fulfill many of its extravagant promises of health and life, *in spite of* the tolerance of the scientific community for unsubstantiated just-so stories, because we have a prior commitment, a commitment to materialism." He continues, "It is not that the methods and institutions of science somehow compel us to accept a material explanation of the phenomenal world but, on the contrary, that we are forced by our *a priori* adherence to material causes to create an apparatus of investigation and a set of concepts that produce material explanations, no matter how counterintuitive, no matter how mystifying to the uninitiated. Moreover that materialism is absolute for we cannot allow a divine foot in the door."

What Lewontin is admitting here is that he and those who think like he does are only selective skeptics. They are hostile to belief in God because of a prior commitment to a dogmatism which excludes God—a dogmatism about which they are not skeptical at all, which they accept not because of the evidence but in spite of it, and to which they will cling even when it forces them into absurdities.

For another example, consider the remarks of the philosopher Thomas Nagel in his book *The Last Word*. The purpose of the book is to defend philosophical rationalism against subjectivism. At a certain point Nagel acknowledges that rationalism has theistic implications. For the moment, the important thing is not whether that is true, but that Nagel thinks that it is. Note well what he says next. After suggesting that contemporary subjectivism may be due to "fear of religion," he writes, "I speak from experience, being strongly subject to this fear myself: I want atheism to be true and am made uneasy by the fact that some of the most intelligent and well-informed people I know are religious believers. It isn't just that I don't believe in God and, naturally, hope that I'm right in my belief. It's that I hope there is no God! I don't want there to be a God; I don't want the universe to be like that." Nagel adds, "My guess is that this cosmic authority problem is not a rare condition and that it is responsible for much of the scientism and reductionism of our time. . . . Darwin enabled modern secular culture to heave a great collective sigh of relief, by apparently providing a way to eliminate purpose, meaning, and design as fundamental features of the world." If Nagel is right, then those who say that theism is a crutch have got it backwards. For our contemporary intellectual culture, it is atheism that serves as a crutch. It couldn't have been easy to admit that.

So it seems that these men come close to agreeing with me. To be sure, they don't agree that God is real. But they agree that there is something not quite honest in their rejection of Him—something driven either dogmatically, as in Lewontin's case, or emotionally, as in Nagel's—rather than forced upon them by the evidence. The preposterous view that the atheist is not being honest with himself—that He knows that there is a God, but only tells himself he doesn't know—is looking better and better. If this is true—as I think it is—then it changes everything. For then the important question is not, "Is there a God?" but, "Can I concede one part of my moral knowledge while holding down another?" or to put a point on it, "Can I admit to myself that I know about, say, the goodness of love and the evil of murder, while *not* admitting to myself that I know about the goodness of God and the evil of refusing Him?"

One certainly can do that—lots of people do—but one can never do it well. The gambit slips from one's control because, at bottom, it is a lie, and lies metastasize; the universe is so tightly constructed that, in order to cover up one lie we must usually tell another. This applies with just as much force to the lies we tell ourselves as to the lies we tell other people. One could imagine a universe so loosely jointed that lies did not require the support of more lies, but the one we live in is not like that. In this one, deception begets deception, and self-deception begets more self-deception; the greater the lie, the greater its metastatic tendency. This tendency is strongest precisely in the case of the greatest self-deception, pretending not to know that God is real, because there are so many things one *must not think of* in order to not think of the reality of God.

One cannot predict in advance *what* stories one will tell himself to make believe that he does not know the reality of God and his obligation to Him; every agnostic and atheist devises a different set of plausibility gambits, a different pattern of omissions, forgettings, and avertings of gaze. But it is extraordinarily difficult—I think impossible—for such self-deceptions not to slop over at some point into what he admits about the moral law. Our minds won't go like that.

VI

We have been asking how it matters that we have *natural* knowledge of God, and we have found that it makes four differences: to whether man may be abolished, to whether morality has oughtness or only prudence, to whether we have reason to expect the universe to make any moral sense at all, and to whether, having lied to ourselves about God, we can be honest about the rest of our natural knowledge.

The next part of the inquiry is how Scripture *illuminates* our understanding—how it matters that there is a biblical revelation *over and above* the natural knowledge of God. This direct revelation makes at least three differences, and the first difference has to do with forgiveness.

Clear vision of the moral law is crushing, because the first thing that an honest man sees with this vision is how far he falls short of it. He cannot escape the awareness of a debt which exceeds anything he can pay. Apart from an assurance that the debt can somehow be forgiven, such honesty is too much for us; it kills. The difficulty is that without a direct revelation from the Author of the law, it is impossible to know whether the possibility of forgiveness is real. Therefore we look away; unable to accept the truth about ourselves, we might keep the law in the corner of our eye, but we cannot gaze upon it steadily. Apart from an assurance that the debt can be forgiven—an assurance which transcends what human reason can find out on its own—no human being dares to face the law straight on.

Yet we can't quite wipe the law from our intellects. It is woven into the deep structure of our minds, as linguists say the threads of language are. Unable to make it go away, we use every means we can devise to pretend that we are really being good. Evasions and rationalizations spread through our intellects like the mycelium of a fungus in its host. That is why the ancient world was brutal, as we of all people should understand. Not even the greatest of the pagans could admit what was wrong with infanticide, although they knew that the child was of our kind. Neither can we admit what is wrong with abortion and a host of other evils.

It is hard enough to face the moral law even *with* the possibility of forgiveness. It offends our pride to be forgiven, terrifies it to surrender control. Without the possibility of forgiveness it would be harder still: How could we ever face how wrong we had been about anything? How could we bear to change our minds? The history of ethics would be a history of digging in against plain truths. Consider how many centuries it took natural law thinkers even in the Christian tradition to work out the implications of the brotherhood of master and slave. At least they did eventually. Outside of the biblical orbit, no one ever did—not spontaneously.

It may seem that the possibility of forgiveness matters only on the assumption that there is, in fact, a God—that without the lawgiver, there would be no law, and therefore nothing to be forgiven. The actual state of affairs is more dreadful, for the Furies of conscience do not wait upon our theological assumptions. One who acknowledges the Furies but denies the God who appointed them—who supposes that there *can* be a law without a Lawgiver—must suppose that forgiveness is both necessary and impossible. That which is not personal cannot forgive; morality "by itself" has a heart of rock. And so although grace would be unthinkable, the ache for it would keen on, like a cry in a deserted street.

VII

The second difference it makes to acknowledge biblical revelation has to do with providence. Self-interest is not the only thing that tempts us to commit injustice. One of the strongest motives to do wrong is to try to make everything go right, for sometimes justice requires allowing some bad things to happen to other people. If we forbid hanging innocent men, the mob may break out in a riot. If we forbid bombing noncombatants, the war may be prolonged. If we forbid giving perjured testimony, the murderer may go unpunished. Surely it isn't right, we reason, that there are riots, longer wars, and murderers free in the streets. Let us do evil for the sake of good. It doesn't seem *just* to do justice.

Christian faith undercuts the urge to fix everything on our own through conviction of the final helplessness of man, and confidence in the final providence of God—through certainty that only God can set everything to rights, and faith that in the end He will. Man can merely ameliorate, not cure; but there will be a Judgment, and there will be a hand that wipes every tear from the eyes of those who mourn.

The final helplessness of man to fix himself may seem fatuously obvious after a century that killed hundreds of millions of people, all with the idea of improving human life. If it is a fatuity, however, it is unbearable fatuity, one that we persistently refuse to accept. I commented earlier on the idea that one *may* play God if no one is God already. What we have in view here is the conviction that one *must* play God if the Creator is not Judge and Healer. Immanuel Kant thought that morality would be undermined without a belief in divine judgment, but Kant did not know the half of it. The wrongs of the world would not merely dismay the desire to do right. They would taunt, torture, and drive men to a despair which could be relieved only by committing yet greater wrongs, on the principle that if God does not save us then we must save ourselves.

There may be some few who could resist this terrible conclusion. I have not met them. It is no accident that not even the Stoics, who invented the very term "natural law," ever rose to the idea of principles which hold without exception, principles which may not be violated even to prevent violations. The problem was not that they failed to find these principles written upon their hearts, but that they could not bring themselves to attend closely to the inscription. It would have been too awful to believe that the goodness of the ends did not justify the wickedness of the means, because how else could the ends be achieved? The same people who said *Fiat justitia ruat caelum* ("Let justice be done, though the heavens fall") also said, *Salus populi suprema lex* ("The safety of the people is the supreme law")—and as they understood these two mottoes, the second unraveled the first. Have the Germans begun another uprising? Then raze their villages, rape their virgins, and show them what the Pax Romana means. All for justice, all for order, all for peace.

Without confidence in providence, our vision of every commandment goes askew. "Thou shalt not murder" seems to change before our eyes to "Thou shalt keep alive the greatest number possible—at the expense of others, if that is what it takes." In the novel *Sophie's Choice*, a Nazi guard at Auschwitz commands a young mother to choose which of her children will be sent to the ovens. If she cooperates in the crime, the one she selects will be burned; if she refuses, then both children will be taken to their deaths. After a long, hanging moment, the mother pushes away her little girl, and cries out that he take her—not her favorite, not the boy! Her choice is plainly evil; for the sake of a better result, she has united herself with the sin of the murderer. And in the end her favorite child dies too. But without faith in a God who hears the cries of the poor, how could she choose otherwise? One day I was surprised to hear one of my seminar students argue that it would have been "selfish" for Sophie to refuse to mark one of her children for death. How so? His reply was that she should have been willing to "sacrifice herself"—by which he meant *sacrifice her conscience.* It took me some time to realize that although my agnostic student considered "I must promote life" to be a real moral duty, he viewed "I must not have complicity in murder" to be a merely personal scruple on the order of "I am not the sort of person who skips bathing." He didn't deny that conscience speaks differently, but he thought that for the sake of a "better" result, Sophie should have been willing to suffer the agonies of its accusations.

And if there is no God, why not? The motto "do the right thing and let God take care of the consequences" makes sense only on the assurance that He will take care of the consequences. Without that assurance, doing the right thing *means* taking care of the consequences—or trying to. And so it is that unless there is providence, the urge to do good irresistibly consorts with evil; unless God is just, our judgments become unhinged.

VIII

The third difference biblical revelation makes to moral understanding concerns our ability to recognize our neighbors for what they are. To be a person is to be a proper subject of absolute regard—a "neighbor" in the sense of the Ten Commandments—a being of the sort whom the Commandments are about. It is *persons* whom I am not to kill, *persons* whom I am to love as I love myself. But what is a person? If we accept the biblical revelation that man is the *imago Dei,* the image of God, then every human being is a person—a person by nature, a kind of thing different from any other kind, a being whose very existence is a kind of sacrament, a sign of God's grace. Trying to understand the nature of man without recognizing him as the *imago Dei* is like trying to understand a bas-relief without recognizing it as a carving of a lion.

The problem with rejecting this biblical revelation is not that one loses the dim, inbuilt sense of awe that clings to human life; we intuit the image of God even if we do not know what it is. The problem is that this inbuilt sense is not enough. We need an explanation of what it is that we are intuiting—of what we experience when we experience the sense of awe. Without this explanation, I may try to hold onto my knowledge of the evil of murdering my neighbor, but I will find it difficult to recognize my neighbor when I see him. It is not impossible; as I show in a later chapter, more or less adequate explanations *can* be constructed from materials accessible to natural reason. But that is the long way around, and most people weary long before they reach the end of it. By and large, the ones who do stay on the trail are the same ones who acknowledge the biblical revelation of the *imago Dei*.

Denial of the *imago Dei* is something new and much more dangerous than a simple return to paganism. As Frances Schaeffer once remarked, the worst that could be said of the pagans was that they had not yet heard that man is made in the image of God. Although they naturally recognized the dignity of man and the justice that is due to him, their understanding of this intuition was deficient. By contrast, our thinkers have heard that man is made in the image of God, *but deny it.* This puts such a strain on the inbuilt structures of moral knowledge that justice flips upside down. Refusing to learn, they finally distort even what they already know.

IX

What shall we say about the Second Tablet Project? Just that it cannot succeed. The Second Tablet depends on the first; whoever denies his duty to God will find, if he is logical, that he can no longer make sense of his duty to his neighbor. Conscience will certainly persist, reminding him of both, but it will seem to him an absurdity in a sea of absurdities. Though he may admit that he has a nature, he will be unable to say why he should keep it. Though he may admit that this nature is governed by certain laws, he will find that their oughtness creeps out the door and that even their prudence slips away. All this will be needless, for he does have the knowledge of God; he merely denies it. But denial only makes his crisis deeper, for lies metastasize, and the greatest lie metastasizes to the greatest degree.

Then should we say that the two tablets are enough if only we take them as a pair? More's the pity, no: not even the pair of them is enough by the light of nature alone. Though natural knowledge is sufficient to illuminate our duty, duty by itself is despair. It cannot assure us of the possibility of forgiveness when we fall short; it cannot assure us of the certainty of providence in the face of evil; and it cannot explain to us the fallen dignity we bear as images of God. In want of the first assurance, we seek refuge from guilt by denying our sins. In want of the second assurance, we seek to make everything go right by doing wrong. In want of the explanation, we find it all too easy to pretend that we do not recognize our neighbors for what they are.

In these senses, moral knowledge is protected and illuminated by the knowledge of God, and the natural knowledge of God is protected and illuminated by the knowledge of His word. Faith and reason contain and depend on each other. May we be spared the illusion of an ethics that stands wholly by itself.

3

Nature Illuminated

I

According to a famous statement of the Second Vatican Council, "It is only in the mystery of the Word made flesh that the mystery of man truly becomes clear."[1] What does this say about natural law, which is commonly supposed to be an affair of human reason?

One might suppose that it says nothing about it: The "mystery" of man which we need revelation to understand has nothing to do with his nature but only to do with his destiny. Or perhaps the "mystery" becomes *fully* clear in Christ only in the sense that only Christ was *perfect* man. In either case, isn't reason alone still sufficient to investigate man's nature? Surely we need not resort to supernatural realities to say what a human being is.

As the late John Paul II recognized, this compartmentalizing interpretation just will not work. "With these words," he wrote,

> the Second Vatican Council expresses the anthropology that lies at the heart of the entire Conciliar Magisterium. . . . Christ alone, through his humanity, reveals the totality of the mystery of man. Indeed, it is only possible to explore the deeper meaning of this mystery if we take as our starting point man's creation in the image and likeness of God. Man cannot understand himself completely with reference to other visible creatures. The key to his self-understanding lies in contemplating the divine Prototype, the Word made flesh, the eternal Son of the Father. *The primary and definitive source for studying the intimate nature of the human being is, therefore, the Most Holy Trinity.*[2]

Then is man's very *nature*—not just his destiny—so intimately tied up with supernature that it cannot be grasped fully by reason alone? If so, then it might seem that the whole idea of a philosophy of natural law is destroyed. Nothing is left—it might seem—but theology.

Suppose this really were the result. One might ask, "So what? What difference does it make whether we get our insight into man from theology rather than from philosophy? There is more than one way to skin a cat." Ah, but that is just the problem: In this scenario theology would be the *only* way to skin the cat. The only way to have a meaningful conversation with an unconverted person about our shared human nature would be to convert him first.

That is certainly what many people think, but it is not what the Council teaches. "All this holds true not only for Christians," it says, "but for all men of good will in whose hearts grace works in an unseen way."[3]

Well, then what does *that* mean for the philosophy of natural law? Is it destroyed, or isn't it?

II

Something is destroyed by the conciliar teaching, but not philosophy. What is actually abolished is a too simple idea of how revelation and so-called unaided reason are related. In fact, revelation and reason are in intimate converse, each one entangled with the other. In the first place, revealed truth about man's nature presupposes the natural law. In the second place, it underwrites reflection upon it. More to the present point, supernature illuminates the *natural* realities with which human reason is concerned. This is true in an immediate and direct way for those who acknowledge that this revelation is true. What I hope to show is that in an indirect way it is even true for those "men of goodwill" who do not.

Now there are two ways in which one might inquire about these matters, two ways to investigate how the mystery of man is illuminated by the mystery of the Word. One way is to focus solely on the Word Incarnate, Jesus Christ. Now this Man was God. Because we are not God, it might seem that this fact tells us nothing about ourselves, but the sheer fact that the human and divine could commune in a single person brings out with shocking clarity the depth of the older teaching that the one is the image of the other. The sharpest, clearest definition of human nature is simply *imago Dei*. In surrender to God, then, we lose nothing; only in Him can we discover ourselves.

Or consider the hope of redemption, grounded in Christ's death and resurrection. The fact that this directly concerns our destiny rather than our nature does not make it irrelevant to our nature. What it tells us is that it was no mockery for the Creator to set eternity in the hearts of men,[4] that the thirst for Himself with which He endowed us can be satisfied after all, that we can drink from Him forever. Perhaps there is no logical contradiction in the idea of an image of God who is destined to futility, but there is certainly a performative incoherency in it. As Benedict XVI points out, hope that life will not end in emptiness is a requirement of our nature: "Only when the future is certain as a positive reality does it become possible to live the present as well."[5]

The approach that I have just described—considering only what Christ shows us about ourselves—may seem to be the high road. But although the mystery of the Word made flesh is the highest arch of the structure of revelation, the Word was not imparted to us only in the flesh. All expressions of the Word are connected; we do not throw away scripture, sacrament, and apostolic teaching because we have Christ. In reality, everything in revelation illuminates the mystery of man. This more general matter is what I wish to explore.

I mentioned three ways in which revelation is related to natural law. It *presupposes* natural law in that it makes no sense without it. Time after time God commends His commandments to our admiration. "What great nation is there," He asks the children of Israel, "that has statutes and ordinances so righteous as all this law which I set before you this day?"[6] Plainly the question expects the Israelites to compare the relative righteousness of the verbally revealed ordinances of God and the humanly enacted ordinances of other nations. But how can they compare, unless they have the power of comparison? How can they have such a power, unless they already know something about righteousness? And how can they already know something about it, unless God has already revealed that something by other means? We find the same pattern throughout the word of God: Even when His disclosures exceed what natural reason could have figured out for itself, we can distinguish them from nonsense. They depend on natural reason for their intelligibility.

Revelation *underwrites rational reflection* on the natural law by acknowledging the ways in which created reality itself is a kind of revelation; nature itself bears a kind of testimony to the truths of its Creator. A law is written on the heart, even in the person who "has not the Law."[7] We bear a certain order and design, which gives the way we are put together a significance it could not have if it were merely the unintended result of an accidental sequence of events. The principles of this design can be recognized—for example, the complementarity of the sexes. Finally, our actions have natural consequences; the law of the harvest, that we reap as we sow, is not a mere product of the myth-maddened mind. This four-fold testimony teaches us, in a manner not unlike the way in which the properties of soil and seeds instruct the farmer. Experience assists human wisdom because Eternal Wisdom has seen to it that it shall; the universe has been designed to make this possible.

More to the point of this essay, supernature *illuminates* the natural realities that are the business of natural law philosophy by inviting the intellect to reason more fully and adequately about matters that it may in principle be capable of finding out on its own, but rarely does. Philosophy has rightly been called a preamble to theology; but theology is also a preamble to better philosophy. An everyday parallel may make this clear. Persons of my own sex often fail to notice things that ought to be per-fectly obvious, and are in fact obvious to most women. "Have you seen my glasses?" "Yes, you're holding them." "Are we out of milk?" "Turn around; it's on the table." "Why did Sheila speak so unkindly to that young man?" "Because she likes him." Philosophy is like that too. The facts of created reality may be right under our noses without our noticing. We may be nearly blind to them until their Creator says, "Look here," as the pagan thinkers were nearly blind to the sacrificial quality of love.[8] Does this "look here" allow natural law thinkers to dispense with arguments acces-sible to nonbelievers? Obviously not, but it allows them to peer into the phenomena of our common life with greater confidence and penetration than they otherwise could. It provides hints and insights about all sorts of matters which natural reason can later confirm by its own proper meth-ods. So reason grasps the things within its ken more quickly, deeply, and surely when revelation calls attention to them.

Astonishingly, it also grasps these natural realities more readily when supernatural realities *not* within its ken are revealed to it—as we will see. But to see this we need more equipment—say, a prism.

Through the prism of revelation, at least five different colors of light shine on the natural realities. We may call these *preceptive, affirmative, narrative, promissory,* and *sacramental.* Although these lights clarify every facet of our nature, for simplicity I deal mostly with the facet of conjugal sexuality.[9] One cannot talk about everything, and the Word made flesh did after all perform His first supernatural miracle at a wedding. I make no claim to break new ground concerning sexuality per se. The purpose is merely to show how the natural and supernatural realities are related.

III

The first supernatural light upon nature is the light of precept: God commands or forbids something that the mind itself can recognize as right or wrong. Telling us what we already know or could have known may seem superfluous. Yet, as equatorial sunlight prickles the skin, so revelation prickles the mind and wakes it up, and it does this in several different ways.

Precept *confronts* us because certain matters of right and wrong are so obvious that at some level everyone already knows them. According to Thomas Aquinas, these include all of the things covered by the Decalogue, such as the wrong of adultery and the wrong of theft. If we already know them, then why is confrontation necessary? Because the matter is more subtle than it appears. In one sense, it is impossible to be mistaken about the moral fundamentals; they are right before the eye of the mind. Thus Saint Thomas declares in one place that "the natural reason of every man, of its own accord and at once, judges [these things] to be done or not to be done."[10] In another sense, however, it is quite possible to be mistaken about the moral fundamentals, for the eye can be averted. Thus he remarks a few pages later, "and yet they need to be promulgated, because human judgment, in a few instances, happens to be led astray concerning them."[11]

Attention to this subtlety clears up one of his examples. As Saint Thomas famously remarks in another passage, "[T]heft, although it is expressly contrary to the natural law, was not considered wrong among the Germans."[12] Many readers think he meant that human reason can be totally ignorant even of precepts so basic as "Thou shalt not steal." On the contrary, not only was theft a punishable offense among the Germans, but, considering the source that Saint Thomas cites (the sixth book of Julius Caesar's commentaries on the Gallic War), he would have been well aware of the fact. Caesar does not mention the routine Germanic penalties for theft, such as compensation. On the other hand, he says that the Germans considered such offenses so detestable that to propitiate their gods they sought out thieves and robbers to be burned alive.[13] Has Saint Thomas overlooked the passage? There is no need to think so. When he says that theft "was not considered wrong among the Germans," what he doubtless has in mind is a later passage where Caesar explains that the Germans approved stealing from tribes *other than their own*.[14]

The manner in which the judgment of these barbarians was "led astray," then, is not that they were ignorant of the wrong of taking what properly belongs to one's neighbor, but that they refused to recognize the members of the other tribes as neighbors. They didn't justify theft as such—just some theft. They told themselves that they weren't really thieves. This is very much like the way a philandering man invents excuses for his affairs. Perhaps he tells himself that he isn't really unfaithful to his wife, because he'll lie to make sure she isn't hurt. Or perhaps (especially if he has studied ethics) he tells himself that the "question" of faithfulness is "complicated," because the other woman is more truly his "wife" than his actual wife is. This is why confrontation is so important; the divine reminder of what we already know has a tendency to cleanse the mind. Such cleansing can operate not only at the level of an individual but at the level of an entire culture; with our favorite evasions burned away, we think more clearly. About what? Geometry? No, but certainly about things like theft and adultery.

Precept also *corrects* us. Here I am not speaking of the foundational matters, of the principles of right and wrong that we "can't not know," but of their more or less remote implications. A great many points of morality that lie within the mind's capacity of discovery, and that, after reflection, wise people consider obligatory, nevertheless have to be explained to persons who lack wisdom. In fact, even the knowledgeable may make mistakes. "In order, therefore, that man may know without any doubt what he ought to do and what he ought to avoid," Saint Thomas remarks, "it was necessary for man to be directed in his proper acts by a law given by God, for it is certain that such a law cannot err."[15] Consider adultery again. As we saw above, though we may need confrontation about it, strictly speaking we don't need correction about it; the good of marriage is just too obvious for us to pretend that we don't get it about adultery. Granted, it is not so obvious to the adulterer; habitual duplicity dims the powers of judgment. The good of chastity in all of its dimensions, on the other hand, is not so obvious even in the first place. To most people it seems rather a stretch. They may consider it admirable—a remote, ideal beauty—but it is unlikely to strike them as obligatory. Consequently, concerning lines of conduct like divorce, fornication, perversion, "polyamory," and even prostitution, they do need correction.

The difference between these two spheres of moral knowledge should not be overstated. Are people *completely* ignorant of the moral character of unchastity? Probably not. Even today, most people involved in sexual sin recognize its impurity more clearly than they let on. But do they see the *depth* of the problem? That is most unlikely. We need only listen to the way that they speak: "I'm not a tramp. I only sleep with men I like." Even so, an element of honest ignorance mingles with the element of denial, and so we are right to say that revealed precept does more than admonish us, "You know better." Concerning the remote implications of the natural law it actually corrects the error, stays the wandering judgment, and imparts certainty where confusion reigned before.

Correction about one vice has consequences for other vices, and ultimately for our grasp of natural law. We have been speaking about the good of chastity, but in order to be deceived about that good, a man must also be deceived about a whole range of other goods. The truest friendship is partnership in a good life; in that respect his friendship is impaired. Justice requires acute perception of what is really due to the other person; in that sense his justice is impaired. Courage requires not mere fearlessness but a right estimate of what things are worth fighting for; in that sense his courage is impaired. Unfaithfulness requires constant deception; in that sense his frankness is impaired. Deceived in so many ways, his wisdom is askew. Insofar as wisdom regulates all of the moral virtues, the pattern of his life is askew. Lacking the stability and discipline necessary for clear and honest thought, constantly tempted to rationalize, his thinking about natural law is askew. If sexual purity were a recognized prerequisite for those who pursue such studies, matters would be different, but as it is, philosophers need corrective precepts about purity just as much as everyone else.

Finally, revealed precepts illuminate the natural realities by *invitation*. Pondering the structures of creation, we can discern reasons why the revealed precepts are so fitting; this is part of what the Scriptures call Wisdom, who speaks personified in Proverbs:

> The LORD created me at the beginning of his work, the first of his acts of old. Ages ago I was set up, at the first, before the beginning

of the earth. . . . [T]hen I was beside him, like a master workman; and I was daily his delight, rejoicing before him always, rejoicing in his inhabited world and delighting in the sons of men. And now, my sons, listen to me: happy are those who keep my ways. Hear instruction and be wise, and do not neglect it. . . . For he who finds me finds life and obtains favor from the LORD; but he who misses me injures himself; all who hate me love death.[16]

Reflection on the reasons for God's commandments was one of the great projects of rabbinical Judaism. Rabbi Saadia Gaon declares that if all relied on theft instead of work for livelihood, "even stealing would become impossible, because, with the disappearance of all property, there would be absolutely nothing in existence that might be stolen."[17] In similar fashion, Maimonides says that the eating of flesh torn from living animals—a violation of the Noahide commandments—"would make one acquire the habit of cruelty,"[18] and Rabbi Hanina explains about the commandment to administer justice that "were it not for the fear of it a man would swallow his neighbor alive."[19] Such arguments might seem to presuppose what they are trying to prove, but the circle is not vicious, because the longer we reflect, the deeper we are able to go. Consider, for example, Rabbi Saadia Gaon's remark. Why *would* the disappearance of property leave nothing that might be stolen? Merely in the formal sense that stealing is taking what another person owns? No, in another sense too. No one takes care of what might be gone tomorrow; without *personal* care and responsibility the *common* good suffers. If property is rightly conceived as a form of stewardship—for "every beast of the forest is [God's], the cattle on a thousand hills"[20]—then property is far better training even in charity than those alternative institutional arrangements in which no one owns anything, in which "everyone" owns everything, or in which each one owns something but tells the others to go to hell.

The same is true of the precepts of chastity that we were considering before. Without revelation, just through reflection on the created realities, we may or may not have arrived at them. But once they are revealed and the revelation is accepted, they are known, and once they are known, the mind goes on to ask what makes them true. In other words, we ask *what it is* about our constitution that makes sexual purity so crucial and impurity so catastrophic. Why ask at all? Does God require consent in order to command us? No, but He made us in His image and delights to see it reflected back to Him. He might have ruled us as He rules the animals, but instead He makes us finite participants in His wisdom. Not only does He provide for us, but He has endowed us with the ability to understand in some measure the principles of His providence, and to care for each other in imitation of His loving care for us.[21]

By the way, it is for this reason alone that human enacted law is possible. God could have arranged matters so that we never had to deliberate about what is to be done, never had to labor in order to grasp how the general principles of the natural law should be applied to the particular circumstances of our earthly communities. Such is not His way with us. We may ask, "Why didn't you make it easier?" That is really like asking, "What is man that Thou art mindful of him, and the son of man that Thou dost care for him?"—but in the mode of a complaint. The psalmist replies that He has made us little lower than the angels, and has crowned us with glory and honor.[22]

IV

The next supernatural light upon nature is the light of affirmation. Affirmation is not a command to do or not do something, but a declaration that something is or is not the case. Whereas a command *presupposes* that something is so, provoking the mind to discover what it is, affirmation *declares* that something is so, provoking the mind to see it for itself and work out the implications. The faculty of reason responds to preceptive illumination like this: "I see now that I am to live in such and such a way; can I find out by my own proper methods what it is in the design of creation that makes this right?" But it responds to affirmative illumination like this: "I see now that such and such is true; can I find out by my own proper methods what might follow from this fact?"

Conjugal sexuality is richly illuminated by the light of affirmation, as in the following passage from the prophet Malachi:

> Has not the one God made and sustained for us the spirit of life? And what does he desire? Godly offspring. So take heed to yourselves, and let none be faithless to the wife of his youth. For I hate divorce, says the LORD the God of Israel, and covering one's garment with violence, says the LORD of hosts. So take heed to yourselves and do not be faithless.[23]

If the intellect concedes Malachi's claim that the sexual powers have a procreative purpose, then the logic of the rest of his argument is not hard to work out. After all, marriage is the only form of association in which the family-building aim of the sexual powers can be adequately realized. If a couple should say, "But we never meant to have children," we should not think that they have a different, dissoluble kind of marriage, but that they do not have a marriage. What they have is an affective liaison characterized by sexual intercourse outside of the conditions which allow the purpose of such intercourse to be fulfilled. These conditions are stringent, because procreation is more than making children. It also means raising them. We can make them outside marriage, but raising them that way is like trying to churn butter in a furnace. For at least two reasons, the bond must also be permanent. One is that the knowledge that it will endure into the future radically affects its quality in the present. The other is that the children of the union will go on to have their own children. Not only will they need parental help to establish their new families, but the grandchildren will have need of their grandparents.

I began the previous paragraph with an "if." *Should* reason concede that sex has a procreative purpose? Moderns object that the purposes of things aren't natural, that they are merely in the eye of the beholder. Supposing that nature is purposeful is derided as "metaphysical biology." But do we say this about the other natural powers? On the contrary, sex is the only natural power about which we do say it. The purpose of respiration is to oxygenate the blood; apart from it there would be no reason to have lungs. The purpose of circulation is to deliver nutrients and other substances to the places they are needed; apart from it there would be no reason to have a heart and vascular system. If we are consistent, we will reason this way about sex. We will say that its purpose is to generate posterity; apart from this purpose there would be no reason for sexual organs. Instead of saying this, we interrupt the argument to say that the purpose of sex is pleasure.

On its face, the interruption is absurd. Of course sex is pleasurable, but in various kinds and degrees, pleasure accompanies the exercise of *every* voluntary power: eating, breathing, even stretching the muscles of the leg. The problem is that eating is pleasurable even if I am eating too much, breathing is pleasurable even if I am sniffing glue, stretching the muscles of the leg is pleasurable even if I am kicking the dog. For a criterion of when it is good to enjoy each pleasure, one must look beyond the fact that it is pleasurable.[24]

We have been considering the unitive implications of the procreative realities, but the unitive realities can also be considered in themselves. Here, the prime example of affirmative illumination is the declaration, "So God created man in His own image, in the image of God he created him; male and female he created them."[25] A great deal is happening in this brief passage. What it has to do with natural law might at first seem obscure, because God is not part of nature; He is not something created, but the Creator. Although unaided intellect can draw inferences about Him from the evidence of what He has made, it can neither see Him as He is nor take the measure of His relation with us. Here is the astonishing thing: Although the fact *that* we are His image exceeds unaided reason's power of discovery, the things that are true about us *because* we are His image do not exceed it. To mention but two of these things: If God is personal, and we are His image, then it pertains to our essence that we are personal too. And if two kinds of personal reality are required to image Him, male and female, then male and female must complement each other not just in gross anatomy but in the very root of their personhood.

The antecedent parts of these statements, the *ifs*, go beyond what unaided reason could confirm. We need revelation to know that God is personal, that we are made in His image, and that it takes two kinds of personal reality to image Him. But the consequent parts of the statements, the *thens*, lie entirely within reason's range. Revelation interrogates reason. It asks, "Now that I point it out to you, can't you see for yourself that your fundamental reality is personal?" "Yes," replies reason, "I do." This stirs us to penetrate still more deeply into personhood, and through even longer reflection, we finally come to see that an individual person is a complete individual reality, existing in itself, different from all other somethings, made for rationality, the ultimate possessor under God of all it is and does. A person is not just a piece or part of something, it is not just an instance or process of something, it is not just a clump of different somethings. Nor is it merely a thing to be owned, a thing to be used, or a *thing* of any sort at all. It is not just a *what*, but a *who*.[26] This insight has transformed the Western world.

But there is more. Revelation goes on to ask, "And can you not see for yourself that your two kinds of personal reality, male and female, depend on and co-illuminate each other—that neither can be understood in isolation?" It would be impossible to understate the depth of this affirmation, or the abyss of the error from which it saves us. How does it do this? In the language of philosophers, personhood is incommunicable. I cannot transfer the mystery of who I am to another person. Unfortunately, it is all too easy to leap from this true statement to a mistaken conclusion. I may falsely imagine that because I am complete in a certain sense, therefore I am complete in every sense; that because I cannot transfer myself, therefore I cannot give myself; that the *incommunicability* of persons precludes the *communion* of persons. That would be bad enough, but in a fallen world, the difference of sex deepens the error and gives it sharper teeth. To the mutual alienation of man and man is added the further disaffection of men and women. They come to seem adverse to one another, natural enemies like fox and bird, perhaps drawn together by their senses, but sundered by difference in kind. As the truth of personhood transformed the Western world, so the distortion of personhood bids fair to destroy it.

Revelation stays the error, showing that reality is the other way around. If it takes both kinds of us to image our Creator, then our two kinds of personhood presuppose each other, and everything about us is made for communion. Notice that just as before, the antecedent part of the statement, the *if*, goes beyond what unaided reason could confirm. Just as we need revelation to see that we image God, so we need revelation to know in what mode we image Him. But just as before, the consequent part of the statement, the *then*, lies entirely within reason's powers. Once it is called to the intellect's attention, the intellect can say, "Yes, thank you—now I see it for myself." I am complete in the sense that I am a whole person, not part of a person, yet when provoked to think more deeply, I perceive that I am *not* complete in the further sense that I could know myself if estranged from the opposite sex. Wonderful to relate, the gap between the sexes turns out to be the very condition of the crossing of it. To speak even more generally, the incommunicability of personhood does not preclude the communion of persons. On the contrary, it is exactly what makes it possible. Because I exist in myself, therefore I can give myself; if I were not a person, I would be incapable of such a gift.

V

Yet another wavelength in which supernature illuminates the natural realities is narrative: We learn more about natural law by thinking about the story.

God differs from human authors in that, by His infinite power and wisdom, He arranges and orchestrates not just words, but real things. Consequently, although the literal sense of the revealed narrative is deeply important, it falls infinitely short of exhausting its meaning. Certain correspondences occur between earlier and later stages in salvation history; for example, Israel foreshadows the Church. Others occur between lower and higher things; for example, the earthly sanctuary signifies the heavenly. Still others occur between events outside us and events within us; for example, the wanderings of the Israelites describe the wanderings of the soul.

What does that have to do with natural law? The answer is that if God is not only the Author of History but the Lord of Creation, then he can also orchestrate correspondences between events in the biblical story and truths about human nature. Narrative illumination is this sort of correspondence.

More than one wavelength of light can shine out from the same passage. Consider again the great passage in Genesis 1:27 that we have already discussed: "So God created man in His own image, in the image of God he created him; male and female he created them." Reading it in the light of affirmation, it says, "We are made like this." But reading it in the light of its place in the origins narrative, it says, *"And then we were* made like this." In other words, instead of viewing it as a statement about what is the case, we can view it as the *report of an event that implies* something about what is the case. Does this chronological addition make a difference? Certainly. By viewing it as an event, we relate it to other events, such as the Fall: Yes, we were created in such and such a fashion, *but then we fell.* The Fall does not deprive us of our nature—a broken foot still has the nature of a foot—but our nature is not in its intended condition.[27] For natural law, this is no insignificant consideration. If we had never seen healthy feet, it might have taken us a long time to discover that broken feet were broken—to reason backwards from their characteristics even in their present broken condition, to the principles of their purpose and design, to the fact that their condition deviates from that design. In the meantime we might have taken their broken condition as normative. Even if we grasped that something was wrong with our feet, we might have misunderstood what it was. We might have thought that feet are bad by nature, or that they are good but corrupted by shoes. Apart from revelation we make the same mistakes about human nature.

But not all passages radiate in more than one wavelength; some illuminate the natural law *only* when read in their narrative context. "God created man in His own image"—we don't need to know what happened next in order to understand at least part of what this passage tells us about man. By contrast take the next line: "And the man and his wife were both naked, and were not ashamed." Presumably this, too, tells us something about ourselves, but what? To know what the narrative implies, we have to take it seriously as narrative.

In our times, the most spectacular attempt to discern what the narrative *as narrative* tells us about human nature is the series of general audiences of Pope John Paul II published as *Theology of the Body*. This remarkable work is both exegesis of Scripture and philosophy of natural law, but it respects the fact that these are different things—neither dividing the reality that they are talking about nor confounding their ways of knowing it. John Paul takes his departure from Christ's reply to the question of why Moses permitted divorce: "For your hardness of heart Moses allowed you to divorce your wives, but *from the beginning* it was not so."[28] Christ's answer forcefully redirects attention to the account of our origins in Genesis. Taking the cue, John Paul draws insights into our nature from three crucial aspects of the narrative: original unity, original solitude, and original nakedness.

Consider only what he says about original nakedness. These days carnality is underrated. Our obsession with sex doesn't show that we take embodiment seriously; actually, it shows that we don't. Like gnostics, we regard our bodies as separate from our true selves. We *use* them merely to get pleasure, attention, and other things for self—and nothing taken seriously is merely used. But the gnostics were wrong. As John Paul emphasizes, body is not separate from self; it is the emblem and vesture of self. The body is the visible sign by which the invisible self is actually made present, the medium of the language that it speaks. We *mean* things to each other by what our bodies do, and when the speech of the mouth contradicts the speech of the body, the latter abolishes the former. To crush your windpipe with my thumbs is to say to you, "Now die," even if I tell you with my mouth, "Be alive." To join in one flesh is to say, "I give myself," even if my mouth shapes the words, "This doesn't mean a thing."

In some ways bodily speech is just as complex as vocal speech. In particular, just as we can say inconsistent things with the spoken word, so we can say inconsistent things with the embodied word. The important thing to remember is that even so, certain meanings are creationally embedded in the language of the body. When you kiss to betray, you are certainly contradicting the primordial meaning of affectionate greeting, but you have not thereby abolished it. You have only parasitized it; you are *using* the meaning to betray. When you employ what is called a "barrier" during sexual intercourse, you are certainly fuddling the meaning of sex, but you have not erased it. You have only overlaid it; overtop the engraved inscription, "I join without reservation," you have scribbled, "but I hold back." Self-giving, moreover, is decisive. When I give a thing external to myself, I can set a term for it, after which I will take it back. When I give my very person, I give away the power of taking back; there is no authority left by which the gift can be revoked. Totality and indissolubility turn out to be inherent in the meaning of the mutual act by which marriage is physically consummated.

We now have (among other things) two complementary demonstrations of the indissolubility of marriage. One develops the unitive implications of the procreative realities, the other delves into the unitive realities *per se*. Both kinds of demonstration lie within the reach of natural reason. Yet even though both of them build on facts experienced at some level to every mature human being, it took centuries to work them both out. Not until Thomas Aquinas, perhaps, did we have an adequate presentation of the former argument; not until John Paul, perhaps, did we have an adequate development of the latter. Even now we quibble. As to the procreative realities, I may claim that nannies, daycare workers, or bureaucrats can care for children better than parents can, or that it is better to have no parents than quarreling ones, or that a mom can be a mom, dad, grandma, and grandpa all rolled up into one. As to the unitive realities, I may claim that only "free love" is real love, or that the language of the body is merely conventional, or that there is no such thing as a gift of self. The argument is never really over.

Why isn't it? It isn't as though claims like the ones I have mentioned are hard to refute. The problem is that our ability to grasp the refutations—even more, our willingness—is all too easily undermined by the demons of greed, weakness of will, evil habit, vicious custom, and depraved ideology. And so we see once again that even though the natural realities of marriage are fully *knowable* by unaided reason, they may not be fully known by it. There seems no reason in the world why Aristotle, who knew a thing or two about marriage, could not have penetrated the procreative and unitive realities as deeply as two celibates, Saint Thomas Aquinas and John Paul II. Nevertheless, he didn't—and this was no accident. Through revelation, they had a leg up on the natural facts. He did not.

VI

The next beam from supernature onto nature is the light of divine promise. Two revealed promises are especially important. The first is the promise of forgiveness—divine assurance that God restores repentant sinners who accept the means of grace. From this we learn not to despair of our sins against others. The second is the promise of providence—divine assurance that in the end, God will set everything to rights. From this we learn not despair of the sins of others against us. Only because of these two promises can conscience serve not as a rock to crush us, but as a dog to hound us home.

Here I can be brief, because these matters have been broached in the previous chapter. Suffice it to say that without the former promise, the face of natural law would be only a face of accusation. Few could bear to look at it at all; none could bear to look at it steadily. Without the latter promise, the same accusing face would be turned outward. Contemplation of the wrongs of the world would drive us to yet greater wrongs, on the principle "let us do evil that good may result." Whether by its own guilt or by rage at the guilt of all others, intellect would be undermined, and the counsels of natural law would be pulled in perverse directions.

Since every promise affirms something, the promissory sort of light might seem just a variation on the affirmative sort that we have considered already. Such a conclusion would miss the point, because promises affirm a different class of truths, illuminating the intellect in a distinctive manner. How so? Ordinary affirmations—man is made in God's image, spouses join as one flesh, divorce betrays posterity—draw the attention of natural reason to creational realities right under its nose, which it might otherwise have slighted or overlooked. Promises do something different, because they inform natural reason of something it never could have known: the place of natural law in the economy of salvation.

Although both kinds of light act upon the thinker's mind, they do so in different ways. One merely adds to his data, the other one purges his will. Assured of God's mercy, the thinker no longer needs the false comfort of thinking himself better than he is. Assured of God's providence, he is also freed from the equally false need to play God with others. Cleansed of both kinds of despair, he can think about the natural law more honestly because he is no longer desperate or afraid. Hope turns out to be not only a spiritual virtue but an intellectual virtue as well.

VII

Finally we come to the supernatural light shed on nature by the sacraments. It may seem impossible that sacrament could illuminate the natural law. Doesn't the grace of the sacraments exceed the resources our nature contains? Doesn't the truth about this grace exceed what reason could have discovered by itself? Strange though it may seem, revelation about things that are above reason provides reason with clues about things that are not above reason.

Consider Saint Paul's explosive remarks about marriage in the fifth chapter of his letter to the Ephesians. From the outset, the language is daring. Wives are to submit to their husbands as to the Lord; husbands are also to submit, but in another and asymmetrical sense, loving their wives as Christ loved the Church and gave himself up for her.[29] A turning point comes with Paul's astonishing declaration that this is a "mystery" and it is somehow "about" Christ and the Church.[30] Suddenly we see that his figures are more than analogies. He is saying that a certain natural reality and a certain supernatural reality not only happen to correspond, but were made for this correspondence; that in the depth of providence, the marriage of the spouses invokes the Marriage of the Lamb, and in some measure makes it present. Paul calls this wonder a *mysterion*, something hidden and now revealed, but the Greek term is much more potent than its English cognate. It is the same word that the Greek Fathers used from the fourth century onward for the sacraments; the Douay-Rheims Bible even translates it "sacrament." It would be extravagant to read all the later developments of sacramental theology back into the text, but it is not extravagant to say that the grace Paul has in mind is the same kind we now call sacramental. For he is claiming nothing less than this: that because of Christ and among His people, the natural event of marriage is not just a sign of a spiritual event, but a participation in it—an event of such potency that a man and a woman are really and permanently made one,[31] receiving the grace to be bound with the love that binds Christ with the Church. Transmundane meaning and power are supernaturally transfused into vessels of flesh.

Not only does the possibility of such grace tell us something about supernatural reality, it also tells us something about natural reality. Why? Because though grace exceeds nature, it never violates it; nature could receive nothing from grace had it not been fashioned ahead of time to receive it. This is certainly true of matrimony, for sacramental marriage builds upon the covenantal and "donational" properties of natural marriage. Apart from the form of the covenant, the sacrament would be unintelligible; apart from the grace of the sacrament, the donation might seem almost impossible. Among the laws of the intellect, one of the foremost is this: What we barely fulfill, we can hardly discern. The sacrament remedies this defect, so we can see the covenant better if we know the sacrament.[32]

The same possibility of insight into natural reality accompanies each of the sacraments. Consider a dock. Even if we have never taken the trouble to look at the dock, we can infer something about it from the shape of the ship meant to berth there. Afterward, we can examine it to see if our inferences are borne out. Nature is the dock of grace, the place where the Glory chooses to come into berth. And so, in just the same way as the ship and the dock, if we know something about the sacrament, then we can infer something about the natural institution that the sacrament ennobles. By knowing something about the sacramental grace, we can more easily perceive the shape of the presacramental reality that is ordained to receive this grace.[33] Afterward, natural reason can inquire to see if these inferences are true. And so in an odd and indirect way, it turns out that the sacraments are proper subjects not only for theology, but even for natural law.

In the case of marriage, sacramental illumination clears up many things that would otherwise be obscure. There is a taste of Godward longing even in natural marriage; somehow it participates in the *sensus divinitatis*. In almost all times and nations people have dimly perceived something of transcendent importance about it,[34] and the temptation to make idols of the potencies behind it is very strong. Alas, whatever we treat as God that is not God betrays us, and from repeated betrayal arises an opposite temptation: to *suppress* the obscure longing for transcendence and treat marriage as *less* than it is. Outside of the influence of the sacrament, no society has found the balance. None has been able to give the sacred quality of conjugal union its due without idolizing it; none has been able to avoid idolizing it without debasing it; and all too often these tendencies have worked together. No wonder! For nowhere outside of the truth of the sacrament can the supernatural end of natural marriage be understood. Nature is ordained the receptacle of grace: neither divine, nor simply profane, but a natural chalice for supernatural good.

VIII

It might be held that all this talk of light from revelation is bad news for natural law. Getting people to take natural law seriously is hard enough as it is. If it gets out that the tradition has been cheating for all these years— that most of the so-called conclusions of natural reason are cribbed from divine oracles—then the game is up. According to the objector, only one cure is possible. When God comes around with His cheat sheets, honest natural lawyers should say, "No, thank you, I'll do my own thinking." Only then can they expect to be taken seriously in a pluralistic world.

There are two problems with this supposed cure. First, it is based on a false diagnosis. When a schoolboy struggling with arithmetic sneaks the answer key, that's cheating; when he allows the teacher to show him how to work the problem, that isn't cheating, but honest learning. The kind of boost that natural reason receives from revelation is not the former kind but the latter.

The second problem with the supposed cure is that it has been tried. That was the Enlightenment's project. Little by little, natural law thinkers scrubbed from their little cups of theory whatever grime of influence might have remained from the centuries of faith, whatever benefit they might have gained from the teacher's help. First went the idea of nature; then the idea of law; finally, in our day, the idea of thinking the truth. In the end they found that they had scoured away the ground that they were standing on.

Where does this leave us? In wading through the mire of an era whose inmates have tired of supposed Enlightenment and loiter at the gates of the Dark, we should not be too glad-handed with the pearls of faith—"The Bible says!" persuades only those who are already substantially convinced. But the philosopher should not be *afraid* of revelation either. Although much of it concerns supernatural realities that the natural force of reason is too weak to confirm on its own, yet the light that it sheds on the creational realities is shed to the end that the intellect may see them for itself. Seeing, it may show them to others. What finally justifies our hope is that they really are there to be seen.

4

The Natural, the Connatural, and the Unnatural

I

Can the unnatural become natural to us?

I am not asking whether human nature can change; if it could, it wouldn't be our nature. Nor am I asking whether we can create a new morality to suit ourselves. Morality is something that obligates us whether we like it or not. If we can change it to suit ourselves, then it is not morality.

Yet from time to time we do hear someone say that something unnatural as such is "natural for me." What could this be about?

One of the strangest and most intriguing things about human nature is its openness to what Plato and subsequent philosophers have called "second nature."[1] We are designed in such a way that things which are not part of our design can become so habitual, so ingrained, that they seem as though they are. Another old-fashioned term for this phenomenon is "connaturality." Consider the grace of a classically trained ballerina. Human beings do not spontaneously move like that; she must learn that exquisite poise, that heartrending beauty in movement. To that end, she retrains every nerve, muscle, and reflex until clumsiness would take effort, artlessness would take art, and her very walking looks like dancing. It isn't that grace becomes effortless for her even then, although she makes it look as though it is. But her limbs have internalized the aesthetic of the dance; beautiful movement, or at least beautiful movement of that kind, has become connatural. It is second nature to her.

Can something that goes *against* the grain also become ingrained? Can something in conflict with nature also become second nature?

In one sense, apparently, yes. Consider coffee. We naturally avoid bitter flavors, and I have never heard of anyone liking coffee at first taste. Yet it is possible to learn to enjoy that particular bitter flavor, even to savor it. For me, this happened on a cold day in Chicago in my eighteenth year, when black coffee was the only hot thing around. In fact, in this sense, every acquired discipline, including moral discipline, goes against our natural inclinations. Consider the ballerina again. The young dancer persists in unpleasant practice for the sake of an end which is so fascinating, delightful, and vitalizing that the boredom, pain, and exhaustion of the means are worth enduring. That is just how it is with the virtues. Initially, it is difficult to be good, to be brave, to be true—difficult and most unpleasant. Yet if, with the help of grace, one persists in this unpleasant discipline, then one can see a day coming from afar when it will be more difficult and unpleasant *not* to be good, honest, and true than to be that way. On that day, the actions that virtue requires will be second nature.

Anyone who knows the tradition of natural law will recognize something wrong with the claim that I have just made. I seem to have been saying that virtue is against nature—or, to turn it around, that something contrary to nature can still be good. Not really, but it is true that I have been playing a trick. There is an ambiguity in the way we use expressions like "nature" and "natural inclination," and I have been playing on this double meaning. Each such expression has two meanings, not one, and the two meanings are nearly opposite.

According to what might be called the lower meaning, the natural is the spontaneous, the haphazard, the unimproved: Think of our first parents in the jungle, or for that matter, think of the jungle itself. From this point of view, a human being is at his most natural when he is driven by raw desires, "doing what comes naturally," as we say. But according to what might be called the higher meaning, the natural is what perfects us, what unfolds the inbuilt purposes of our design, what unlocks our directed potentialities. This time think of our first parents not in the jungle but in the Garden, or for that matter, think of the Garden itself. From this point of view, a human being is most genuinely "doing what comes naturally" when he is at his best and bravest and truest—when he fulfills his creational design, when he "comes into his own." The lower way of speaking makes nature and second nature enemies. The higher makes them friends, at least potentially.

Natural law thinkers use terms like "nature" and "natural inclination" in both senses, but they distinguish them. If you want to say that virtue conflicts with human nature in the lower sense but completes and perfects human nature in the higher sense, the natural lawyer cheers you; you have stated the matter correctly. He only asks you to remember that when he urges you to follow the natural law, he is talking about nature in the higher sense, not the lower. He is not encouraging you to let it all hang out. He is urging you to live up to your humanity, to come into your inheritance, to acquire that second nature which makes you *actually* what you already are potentially, though hindered by the Fall. By the way, the ambiguity of the term "nature" is not the only obstacle to clarity. Another such obstacle is that the expression "second nature" is a kind of oxymoron. Second nature isn't *really* nature, just because it *is* second; it has to be acquired. Yet in another way, second nature does pertain to nature—first because our design is open to such acquisitions, and second because it requires them for its fulfillment.

We are now in a position to restate our original question. I asked whether the unnatural can become connatural, whether something that goes against the grain can become ingrained. Something that goes against the grain of lower nature can surely become ingrained, otherwise no one would drink coffee, become brave, or learn to dance. But can something that goes against the grain of higher nature become ingrained? To put the query another way, can the *radically* unnatural become connatural—is our design open, vulnerable, susceptible to what frustrates the purposes of our design?

Let us call this The Problem of Unnatural Connaturality.

II

Saint Thomas Aquinas speaks of connaturality in a variety of related meanings. Things or beings can be connatural *to each other* in the sense that they have the same nature. For example, Saint Thomas speaks of the connaturality and coeternity of the Divine Persons,[2] and remarks that because all men are of one species, they have one connatural mode of understanding.[3]

Relationships of connaturality can be asymmetrical as well. For example, one being can be the connatural *principle of being* of the other, as parents are to children. This means that the nature of the children stems from the nature of the parents. One thing can also be the connatural *principle of government* of others, as a country is to its citizens. This means that the population receive the nature of citizens through being constituted as a country under government.[4]

A being is said to be connatural *with a thing* in the sense that the thing is naturally suitable to the being, so that the being is by nature drawn to the thing. Thus Saint Thomas speaks of the appetitive subject's connaturality with the object of its appetite, and of a heavy body's connaturality for the center.[5]

Turning the idea around, a thing can also be called *connatural to a being* in several senses. One sense is that the thing is contained within the being's nature, as the intelligible species by which angelic intellects know things are contained within the angelic nature—they are neither acquired from the things themselves, nor adventitiously infused by God.[6]

Something can also be said to be connatural to a being in the sense that it is in accordance with the principles of that being's nature. This is the sense Saint Thomas has in mind when he says that it is connatural to the human intellect to know things by receiving knowledge from the senses—a mode of knowing very different than that of the angelic intellect.[7] In the same sense he says that comparison of one thing with another "is the proper and connatural act of the reason," that "it is connatural to us to proceed from the sensible to the intelligible," and that the "connatural" way to acquire knowledge is discovery and instruction.[8]

Yet again, something can be said to be connatural to a being in the sense that it is the sort of object to which the natural principles of the being are adapted. This is the sense in which Saint Thomas is speaking when he says that the connatural object of the intellectual faculties of the human soul falls short of the excellence of separate substances.[9] In the same sense, he says that the reason why activities that raise the soul above sensible things cause weariness is that "sensible goods are connatural to man."[10]

In a closely related sense Saint Thomas speaks of a thing's *connatural end* (or connatural good). The connatural end or good is the end or good to which the thing tends in accordance with its nature—with which, in this sense, it is said to have "a certain conformity."[11] The connatural end of human beings, for example, is that happiness to which we are adapted by our own natural principles. A love, desire, passion, or pleasure which arises from this kind of connaturality can also be called connatural; thus Saint Thomas says, "Love of self-preservation, for the sake of which one shuns perils of death, is much more connatural than any pleasures whatever of food and sex which are directed to the preservation of life."[12] By contrast, our supernatural end lies in happiness so radically disproportionate to our inbuilt powers that it can be achieved only by the grace of God in Christ.

Similarly, *connatural operation* is operation that, when unhindered and uninterrupted so that it achieves its proper object, is in accord with the nature of the agent which is acting, or of the principle which is in operation. In this sense Saint Thomas says that pleasure is the result of connatural operation; for example, an animal feels pleasure in the unobstructed attainment of the thing which its sensitive appetite perceives as good.[13]

III

Most of these meanings of connaturality are only casually related to our subject. The meaning most important for our purposes comes into view when Saint Thomas says that something can be connatural to a being insofar as it *becomes natural through habituation,* because "custom is a second nature." What he has in mind here is the way that habits and customs—and, at another level, divine graces—fill in the blanks, so to speak, that the generalities of nature leave undetermined. The result is that we acquire new inclinations to certain things, and come to find pleasure in things in which we did not find pleasure before.[14] There are all sorts of second-nature connaturality, for example the connaturality of the lover with the beloved, whereby our nature adapts itself to the thing that, or to the person whom, we love.[15] In this sense a husband and wife are said to understand each other connaturally.

For purposes of this chapter, the kind of second-nature connaturality that interests us most is the way in which certain aspects of second nature—acquired habits or habitual graces—cooperate with our nature in the sense of completing or perfecting it. For example, a man may take pleasure in giving to others because he has acquired a habitual inclination to liberality.[16] Certain such perfections may be infused by the Holy Spirit; thus Saint Thomas speaks of a "sympathy or connaturality for divine things" acquired through the gift of charity.[17]

The acquisition of second nature in this sense has sweeping effects on us. Saint Thomas thinks that it changes not only our doing—what we call these days our "behavior"—but our thinking and knowing too: what we believe, what we understand, how we judge. This is where we get to the marrow. Saint Thomas says that although man is *made* to be rightly disposed to the universal principles of action, he must *become* rightly disposed to the particular principles of action. The way man is made to be rightly disposed to the universal principles of action is that he has a natural habit, *synderesis*—what this book has called "deep conscience" to distinguish it from *conscientia* or "surface conscience."[18] But the way that man becomes rightly disposed to the particular principles of action is that the action of *conscientia* comes to be shaped by the acquired habits that we have been discussing. Once man has them, says Saint Thomas, "it becomes connatural . . . to judge rightly how actions should be ordered to the end."[19] Saint Thomas is reminding us that we need to distinguish the knowledge of the foundational precepts of good and evil from right judgment about the detailed corollaries of these precepts. We can't not know the goodness of friendship—but we may well fail to know the detailed norms that are necessary to friendship. We can't not know the goodness of loving our children—but we may well fail to know the detailed norms that are entailed by such love.

It is in this sense that Saint Thomas calls acts that are prompted by virtue "connatural to reason."[20] Notice, though, which *aspect* of reason he is talking about: "judgment," not "science." In other words, although the man judges rightly, he may not be able to explain to you why his judgment is right. Yves R. Simon gives a fine example:

> Suppose you are in business, and a would-be partner has a project beneficial to you, to him, and even to the community at large. Now when business projects are so wonderful there is usually something wrong with them. But you cannot see anything wrong, the project appears perfect. The fellow is very smart, it is probably not for the first time that he is telling that story. So you do not see the "gimmick," but you can "smell" the fellow. Indeed, judgments by way of inclination are often expressed by this metaphor. "Are you going to make the deal?" "No." "And why not?" "Because the fellow, excuse me, stinks." There is an inclination in the honest conscience of a man trained in justice which makes him sensitive to the unjust even when he is completely unable to explain his judgment.[21]

The virtuous and experienced businessman in the story is unable to communicate the grounds of judgment, and yet he is right. It isn't that persons who lack the virtues and experience of an honest businessman don't have intuitions about such matters; it is only that their intuitions are unreliable. Another example came to me in a young father's remark that there are certain things about how to love his children that seem obvious now, but that he hadn't an inkling about before he actually had any children. No one could have taught them to him. Yet now that he had submitted to the disciplines of fatherhood they were as plain to him as the sum of two plus three. The virtue of fatherhood had become second nature. But although it was not part of first nature, it was anticipated by first nature, because it perfected, completed, and cooperated with his inbuilt procreative design; it made actual what formerly was merely latent.

This is all perfectly amazing. It works, but no one knows how it works. The young father and the honest businessman aren't simply generalizing on the model of "all crows are black." Nor are they drawing inferences from premises. On the contrary, they acquire some disposition to judge rightly what father-love or honest trade requires, even in novel situations to which their previous knowledge does not apply. It isn't just that judging the right way helps them feel the right way; feeling the right way also helps them judge the right way. We often malign feelings as irrational because we mistakenly view them solely as states of the body. They are more than states of the body; they are states of the practical intellect. Feelings *as such* can be irrational and treacherous, but feelings shaped by connaturality are dependable and reasonable.

Reality seems to require such "intuitive" judgments; as important as demonstrations are, there is something about judgment that "proofs" can never exhaust. I note in passing that this is true even in mathematics. Early in the twentieth century, the mathematician David Hilbert proposed that mathematicians develop an algorithm by which the truth or falsity of any theorem could be shown. Kurt Gödel proved that this is impossible—at least for any theory of numbers complex enough to allow for arithmetic. He showed that, given any set of axioms, however large, there will turn out to be some theorem which is true, but that cannot be demonstrated from the axioms themselves. One may add new axioms in order to prove that theorem, but then there will be some other true theorem that not even the expanded set of axioms suffices to prove. This amazing result cannot be defeated even by the addition of a countably infinite number of axioms; one just has to *see* that certain theorems are true. The meaning of this result is that the recognition of truth is not the same thing as its demonstration. It follows, I think, that the intuition of truth which precedes the attempt at demonstration, and by which efforts to demonstrate are guided, is something more than a sense of how the truth in question *might* be demonstrated; in the domain of the intellect, intuition turns out to have certain rights of its own. If second nature is what makes intuitions reliable, then second nature is even more important than we thought.

The line of reasoning about connaturality that I have been developing may seem to make moral wisdom easy. Everything we know or judge about the good, whether foundational or detailed, turns out to be either first nature or second—either natural or connatural—either something we can't not know, or something that arises from an acquired disposition that cooperates with what we can't not know. Smooth sailing. Or is it?

IV

In fact, the sailing is rather rough. We asked earlier whether something that goes against the grain of higher nature can become ingrained; whether the radically unnatural can become connatural; whether our design is open to what frustrates the purposes of our design. Saint Thomas's answer is yes.

His first point is that something can become connatural to a being in a certain respect, even though it is not connatural absolutely. For example, a human being may be drawn to something, or take pleasure in it, not because of generic human nature, which is good, but because of a *corruption* of nature incident to that being in particular. As he explains,

> [I]t happens that something which is not natural to man, either in regard to reason, or in regard to the preservation of the body, becomes connatural to this individual man, on account of there being some corruption of nature in him. And this corruption may be either on the part of the body—from some ailment; thus to a man suffering from fever, sweet things seem bitter, and vice versa—or from an evil temperament;[22] thus some take pleasure in eating earth and coals and the like; or on the part of the soul; thus from custom some take pleasure in cannibalism or in the unnatural intercourse of man and beast, or other such things, which are not in accord with human nature.[23]

Someone who does suffer such corruption will connaturally think and do and feel in a way that is radically contrary to his connatural good, even to the point of finding his anti-good lovable:

> [W]henever [a man] uses [a] vicious habit he must needs sin through certain malice: because to anyone that has a habit, whatever is befitting to him in respect of that habit, has the aspect of something lovable, since it thereby becomes, in a way, connatural to him, according as custom and habit are a second nature.[24]
>
> And since passion soon passes, whereas a habit is "a disposition difficult to remove," the result is that the incontinent man repents at once, as soon as the passion has passed; but not so the intemperate man; in fact he rejoices in having sinned, because the sinful act has become connatural to him by reason of his habit. Wherefore in reference to such persons it is written (Prov. 2:14) that "they are glad when they have done evil, and rejoice in most wicked things."[25]

Not only can a man come to love what opposes his connatural good—he can come to hate what promotes it. He can learn to loathe the very things that tend to the happiness we humans are fashioned to seek. Evil of some particular kind has become second nature to him even though it is contrary to first nature—but just because it has become second nature to him, he will have difficulty recognizing it as evil. Saint Thomas again:

> Hatred of the evil that is contrary to one's natural good, is the first of the soul's passions, even as love of one's natural good is. But hatred of one's connatural good cannot be first, but is something last, because such like hatred is a proof of an already corrupted nature, even as love of an extraneous good.[26]
>
> Evil is twofold. One is a true evil, for the reason that it is incompatible with one's natural good, and the hatred of such an evil may have priority over the other passions. There is, however, another which is not a true, but an apparent evil, which, namely, is a true and connatural good, and yet is reckoned evil on account of the corruption of nature: and the hatred of such an evil must needs come last. This hatred is vicious, but the former is not.[27]

These reflections qualify the idea that the good is what all things seek. We naturally seek our good, we connaturally seek it even more perfectly, but through unnatural connaturality we may come to despise it. From a Thomistic point of view, when John Milton had his Satan say, "Evil, be thou my good," he was onto something. Does Satan's speech exaggerate the depth of unnatural connaturality? I do not think so. For a single example, consider homosexuality, the first great wedge issue of the twenty-first-century culture wars.

Coffee drinking is unnatural in a trivial and nonnormative sense. To enjoy the stuff, you have to get over your initial innate aversion to the bitter taste. The aversion is functional, because bitter tastes often signal poisons, but the ability to get over it in particular cases is functional, too, because not everything bitter is a poison. By contrast, sodomitical acts are unnatural in a *non*-trivial and *normative* sense. Objectively, there is no way to "get over" sodomy's contradiction of the inbuilt purposes of the sexual powers, or to get over its denial of the natural complementarity of male and female, that thrice-blessed counter to narcissism, which makes each sex know its lack. Yet for all this, sodomy may come to seem lovable, and its most destructive aspects may come to be loved the most. Andrew Sullivan, widely considered a "conservative" proponent of gay liaisons, says that he has never had a stable homosexual relationship, and defends what he calls "the beauty and mystery and spirituality of sex, *including anonymous sex*."[28] One of the most disturbing contemporary trends among homosexual youth is the rise of what is called "bug chasing"—deliberately seeking out HIV-positive partners in hopes of becoming infected.[29] Some years ago in my home city of Austin, Texas, a homosexual performance artist advertised that he would consume human ashes on stage. The meaning of such a performance could hardly be more clear: "Death, I take you into me."

Can *anything whatsoever* become second nature? This side of grace, has unnatural connaturality any limit?[30] Yes and no. On the "yes" side of the ledger is the fact that it is impossible to will evil *qua* evil. We can never will evil as such, but only particular evil, and we can never will it except for the sake of some good. Wrote Saint Thomas:

> Evil is never loved except under the aspect of good, that is to say, in so far as it is good in some respect, and is considered as being good simply. And thus a certain love is evil, in so far as it tends to that which is not simply a true good. It is in this way that man "loves iniquity," inasmuch as, by means of iniquity, some good is gained; pleasure, for instance, or money, or such like.[31]

On the "no" side of the ledger is the fact that so far as we can tell, *any* particular evil can be viewed under the aspect of some good. By telling himself that he deserves a car, Tom can view grand theft auto under the aspect of the good of justice; by telling herself that she is more truly Mark's wife than his legal wife is, Janet can view homewrecking under the aspect of the good of marriage; by telling himself that God is a tyrant, Chad can view alienation from his highest good under the aspect of the good of liberty. Saint Thomas puts the point succinctly:

> [I]n order that the will tend to anything, it is requisite, not that this
> be good in very truth, but that it be apprehended as good.[32]

Then again, on the "yes" side of the ledger, some particular evils are more difficult to view under the aspect of good than others; some rationalizations are harder to choke down. No doubt Carlos can view bug chasing under the aspect of the good of erotic intimacy, but surely this isn't easy for him. But on further consideration, no: A sufficiently perverse will may be more than willing to make the requisite effort. On the other hand, yes: The greater the effort required to choke down the rationalization, the greater the likelihood that the agent will suffer interior conflict afterwards. And yet, no: A will perverse enough to put forth such an effort may also be perverse enough to *deny* the resulting conflict. Finally, yes: If some act or way of life is sufficiently unnatural, then before enough time has passed for it to become second nature, it may simply kill the person who chooses it.[33]

From the point of view of moral rightness, these observations are unproblematic. The fact that something radically unnatural has become connatural doesn't make it all right. From the point of view of moral knowledge, however, these observations pose a terrible problem. When something radically unnatural has become connatural, it is harder to *recognize* it as not-all-right, just because the faculties of reason have become disordered. Nor is it necessary to practice the unnatural deed personally in order to be confused about it; as there are perverse motives to perform certain acts, so there are perverse motives to entertain certain theories about them.

Even so, these disorders do not excuse us from blame, because we ourselves have introduced them into our reasoning faculties. We have *chosen* our rationalizations; we are the authors of our excuses, the devisers of the shams by which we take ourselves in. Even if we have heard them from others, nothing compels us to accept them. On this point, Saint Thomas is unmistakably clear:

Man does not choose of necessity. And this is because that which is possible not to be, is not of necessity. Now the reason why it is possible not to choose, or to choose, may be gathered from a twofold power in man. For man can will and not will, act and not act; again, he can will this or that, and do this or that. The reason of this is seated in the very power of the reason. For the will can tend to whatever the reason can apprehend as good.[34]

As regards the commanded acts of the will, then, the will can suffer violence, in so far as violence can prevent the exterior members from executing the will's command. But as to the will's own proper act, violence cannot be done to the will.

The reason of this is that the act of the will is nothing else than an inclination proceeding from the interior principle of knowledge: just as the natural appetite is an inclination proceeding from an interior principle without knowledge.[35]

In the case of a perverse will, the interior principle of knowledge from which the act of the will proceeds is itself distorted:

[A]ny ... particular goods, in so far as they are lacking in some good, can be regarded as non-goods: and from this point of view, they can be set aside or approved by the will, which can tend to one and the same thing from various points of view.[36]

In short, perverted knowledge beholds real objects—sometimes even real goods—but it views them in false perspective.

V

We have seen that unnatural connaturality introduces disorders into moral reasoning and knowledge. Insofar as it does so, we had better be clear about just what kind of disorders these are. Let us begin with the knowledge of the basics.

We "can't not know" the moral basics; *synderesis* is ineradicable and indefectible. But there is a difference between saying that we can't not know something and saying that we can't deny it; this kind of thing happens often. Take abortion. Saint Thomas believes that the evil of deliberately taking innocent human life is so closely connected with first principles that it is one of those things that we can't not know.[37] But I can pretend that I don't know it. Or I can pretend that I don't know that abortion is deliberately taking innocent human life. Or I can admit that abortion is evil, but pretend not to know that evil may never be done. If I refuse to repent, then I acquire a motive to go on pretending, to make myself stupider yet. If I act on this motive, I succeed even better than I had planned. So far as one can judge, the process is not self-limiting. Its metastatic tendency—or shall I say *connaturally unnatural* tendency—is to spiral further and further out of control.[38]

The disorder in the knowledge of moral details is more subtle, but it is no less grave. The arguments already presented might give the impression that if I have acquired the virtues, then I connaturally understand certain things, while if I haven't acquired them, then I simply don't. If only it were so simple. Actually, the alternative lies not between a virtuously formed personality and a completely unformed personality, but between a virtuously formed personality and a personality which is in some respect formed *contrary* to virtue. In the former case, yes, I connaturally possesses a certain disposition to right judgment. In the latter case, however, I do not simply *lack* this disposition; what I actually possess is a disposition to judge *wrongly*, with the result that I *possess* beliefs that aren't true. Unfortunately, such false beliefs are not self-correcting. In fact they will *seem* to be confirmed by experience, just because they will tend to bring about states of affairs that *make* them seem reasonable. Allow me to illustrate with another instance of unnatural connaturality concerning relations between the sexes.

I once worked in a building in which three late twenty-something, early thirty-something young women served as clerical staff. It so happened that I had to pass through their office quite often, and because of the volume and ceaselessness of their conversation, it was impossible not to notice what they talked about. Their topic was always the same: the fecklessness of men, with special reference to the men with whom they severally claimed acquaintance. These included a husband, at least one ex-husband, two boyfriends, and a string of ex-boyfriends. It amazed me how jaded, how bitter, how dystopian—how Darwinian, so to speak—their conversation was. That the natures of men and of women were essentially opposed, essentially at war, was something they took for granted. In their view, what women wanted was to get married, and as lures they doled out their favors. What men wanted was to enjoy the favors of women without getting married, or, if drawn by some mishap into marriage, to give back as little as possible. Considering the predatory nature of men, why women would want to get married to them at all was a mystery. The conversation was dystopian in another way too. It soon became clear that the third member of the group—the young woman who was married—was not as deeply absorbed in the sexual ideology I have been describing as the two unmarried women were. At times it seemed that she might actually like her husband a little. Unfortunately, the other two young women had stronger personalities than she did, and in many little ways encouraged her to take the same view of her husband that they took of their boy-friends, ex-boyfriends, and ex-husband.

Let no one think that I tell this story against women. As a husband I am all too well aware of my flaws, and as a conscientious father of daughters I know too well the dangers of male predation. Yet the beliefs of the three young women were false. It isn't just that not all men are predators. The error is much deeper, because although the natures of men and women are opposed in their corrupted state, they are complementary in design and in essence. The sexes need each other. There is a kind of incomplete-ness in the nature of each, which only the other can supply; they are *natu-rally* connatural to each other. To be just, I must admit that somewhere far back in the three young women's minds, there must have been an idea of a different sort of relationship between the sexes, a relationship which was collaborative rather than predatory. If they had not conceived such a standard, they could never have seen how their real-life relationships fell short, and their bitterness would be inexplicable. But the beliefs in the fronts of their minds were very different, and unfortunately, they failed to see that these beliefs helped bring about the very state of affairs that they were supposed to be about. You cannot tell predators from nonpredators if you think that all men are predators. You cannot live in a world in which each successful marriage is an encouragement to all others if the specter of marriage so fills you with envy that you want to tear it down. If you act on the conviction that all relations between the sexes are predatory, you will end up in predatory relationships that seem to confirm your belief. So it is that unnatural connaturality feeds on itself.

VI

Perhaps I overstate my case. Consider again the three young women. Didn't I say just now that somewhere far back in their minds, there must have been an idea of a different sort of relationship between the sexes, an idea that served them as a standard? Someone might argue that instead of merely making them bitter about the shortcomings of the relationships they have, this standard might goad them to do better—not only to have better relationships, but to submit to the disciplines that nonpredatory relationships demand and acquire their constitutive virtues.

By the grace of God, this is true. People do try to become whole; even when surrounded by darkness far more profound than what the three young women suffered, they grope toward light. Permit me another illustration. A twenty-year-old woman who said she had been "lesbian-identified" since age thirteen wrote me to say that after several years of being infuriated by publications in which I had argued for chaste and rightly ordered sexuality, she was "throwing in the towel." To explain her change of heart she related the following anecdotes. (1) A lesbian friend had phoned to give her the news that her girlfriend had decided to have her breasts surgically removed. (2) She had visited the website of a lesbian magazine and found an article on how to use needles as an aid to sexual pleasure; the author recommended having benzalkonium chloride towelettes on hand to wipe up the blood. (3) A "straight" friend had written to her, "I have suddenly become sexually brazen, and it scares me a little. . . . I think that it's about time, though, that I stop giving myself guilt trips about it." My correspondent concluded, "When women want to cut off their female organs, when hurting each other with needles is considered a turn-on, and when promiscuous girls feel guilty about feeling guilty (as though they just aren't liberated enough), something has gone terribly, terribly awry."

Change of heart, then, is always a possibility. The difficulty is that moral reform is not simply a process of adding good qualities and subtracting bad ones. This picture is utterly false to human experience. One reason is that bad qualities depend on imperfectly good qualities for their vigor; the more a man imitates virtue, the more harm he can do with his remaining bad ones. Another reason is that we often try to manage our lesser vices by allowing some master vice to check them. If the master vice is weakened, then the lesser ones may run amuck, so we appear to become worse in some respects, even though we are becoming better in another.[39] Aristotle wasn't *wrong* in claiming that there is a natural inclination to virtue; we really are attracted to it. What he overlooked was the difficulty of following this inclination, and the countervailing inclination to vice. Real moral development labors under terrible burdens and paradoxes.

On this point, Saint Thomas is sometimes misunderstood. I mentioned earlier his distinction between our connatural end, to which we are adapted by our natural principles, and our supernatural end, which requires the infusion of additional spiritual principles. A point which is often overlooked is that Saint Thomas regards divine assistance as necessary even for the attainment of our connatural end:

> And because such happiness surpasses the capacity of human nature, man's natural principles which enable him to act well according to his capacity, do not suffice to direct man to this same happiness. Hence it is necessary for man to receive from God some additional principles, whereby he may be directed to supernatural happiness, even as he is directed to his connatural end, by means of his natural principles, albeit not without Divine assistance.[40]

The key is the concluding phrase, "albeit not without divine assistance." Saint Thomas is not distinguishing between a connatural end that we can achieve by ourselves and a supernatural end that can be achieved only with divine assistance; he is distinguishing between two different modes of divine assistance. To achieve our connatural end, we require divine assistance to *support* our natural principles; to achieve our supernatural end, we require divine assistance to *supplement* them so that they transcend their intrinsic limits. The need for extra help is charmingly conveyed by a parable in John Bunyan's *Pilgrim's Progress*. A man attempts to sweep a parlor, but his efforts merely drive the dust into the air, and the room is as dirty as before. After a maid has sprinkled the dust with water, he is able to gather the dust into a pile and get rid of it. Moral discipline is like the broom; divine grace is like the sprinkling of water.[41] Bunyan himself, committed to an un-Thomistic antithesis between law and grace, intended the parable to convey the point that the broom is useless. But the parable is better than he knew. What actually happens is that although the broom is necessary, the sprinkling is also necessary so that the broom can achieve its end. That, I believe, is how Saint Thomas would view the matter.[42]

Speaking of extra help, Saint Paul uses a phrase almost identical to "second nature"—"the new man"[43]—but he means something quite different by it. Up to this section I have been speaking of *mere* connaturality, of the cooperation of nature with habit, of virtue acquired by human discipline. By contrast, Paul is referring to *super*-connaturality, of another kind of discipline, the cooperation of nature with habitual grace. When

Paul says that we must take off the old man and put on the new man, he means that the new man Jesus Christ must be transfused into us, like new blood, or rather that we must be grafted onto him: Our human life not destroyed, but saturated and transformed by the life of God. As Saint Peter puts it, we become "partakers of the divine nature."[44]

Such is the Christian hope. In our present condition, we are at war with our nature, connaturally out of joint with our own design. Our very minds are caught up in the dislocation, for not only do we do wrong, but we call it right. Too often scholars proceed as though the Fall made no difference to their intellectual work. Suffice it to say that it does, for like the redemption of the other goods of nature, the redemption of the intellect is won inch by inch. What would its full term be like? We hardly imagine it, yet we know what it requires: to be "transformed by the renewing of our minds, that we may prove what is the will of God, what is good and acceptable and perfect."[45]

This might be called the divine connaturality, which disposes us not only to judge rightly, but to know as we are known. As Dante wrote, now our minds are but smoke, but one day the smoke will be fire.

5

Accept No Imitations:
Naturalism vs. Natural Law

I

In ethics, there are two ways to take human nature seriously. The first is to regard nature as the design of a supernatural intelligence; you take it seriously because you take God seriously. The other is to regard nature (in a physical or material sense) as all there is. Here you ascribe to matter—or to some property, process, or aspect of matter—the ontological position that theists ascribe to God Himself. Natural lawyers follow the first way; naturalists follow the second. Similar name—radically different meaning.

Nature means something different to the naturalist than it does to the natural lawyer. It has to. He cannot view it as a design, because in his view there isn't anyone whose design it might be. What is, just is. If you accept the principle of sufficient reason, this is rather unsatisfactory, for no one seriously maintains that the universe had to be just the way it is. There might have been fewer stars, or more. There might have been creatures like us, or there might not. There might not have been a universe at all. Nature, then, is a contingent being, not a necessary being like God, and contingent beings need causes. The naturalist rejects this line of reasoning, or at least limits it. He might concede that each thing in nature needs a cause, but he denies that the entire ensemble of things needs a cause. This exception seems suspiciously arbitrary.

It is easy to see how the first approach can ground ethics. If God Himself is the Good—the uncreated source of all being, all meaning, and all value in created things—then inasmuch as his intentions for us are reflected in our own design, in human nature, these intentions are normative.[1] Consider, for example, the inclination to associate in families. This is not the same as a mere desire to do so; indeed, we have conflicting desires, and some people would rather be alone. It would be more accurate to say that we are made for family life, that fitness for family life is one of our design criteria. For humans, then, the familial inclination is a *natural* inclination. When we follow this inclination we are not acting in the teeth of our design, but in accord with our design. Family is not a merely apparent good for us but a real one, and the rules and habits necessary to its flourishing belong to the natural law. Or consider the universal testimony of conscience against murder. This is more than a matter of guilty feelings. No one always feels remorse for doing wrong, and some people never do. Nevertheless, the wrong of deliberately taking innocent human life is acknowledged at all times and everywhere, and this too belongs to the natural law. Notice that both examples concern design. The former concerns the design of the inclinations, as apprehended by the intellect. The latter concerns the design of the intellect itself, for we are so made that there are certain moral truths we *can't not know*.[2]

How the naturalist view could ground ethics is hard to see. If material nature is all there is, then how could actions have nonmaterial properties like right and wrong? How could there be true moral "law" without a lawgiver? Perhaps it would be like the "law" of gravity—a pattern that we cannot help but enact, a force to which we cannot help but yield. But in that case, "you ought to" would mean the same thing as "you do." Stones do not deliberate about whether they "ought" to fall.

II

Some naturalists concede the point, or as we must say here, the pointlessness. William Provine declares that "No purposive principles exist in nature. . . . No inherent moral or ethical laws exist, nor are there absolute guiding principles for human society. The universe cares nothing for us and we have no ultimate meaning in life."[3] Richard Dawkins opines, "The universe that we observe has precisely the properties we should expect if there is, at bottom, no design, no purpose, no evil and no good, nothing but blind, pitiless indifference."[4] According to E. O. Wilson, "Human behavior—like the deepest capacities for emotional response which drive and guide it—is the circuitous technique by which human genetic material has been and will be kept intact. Morality has no other demonstrable ultimate function."[5] Wilson and Daniel Dennett write, "[O]ur belief in morality is merely an adaptation put in place to further our reproductive ends. . . . [E]thics as we understand it is an illusion fobbed off on us by our genes to get us to co-operate (so that human genes survive). . . . Furthermore the way our biology enforces its ends is by making us think that there is an objective higher code to which we are all subject."[6] On the subject of conscience, Robert Wright chimes in, "It's amazing that a process as amoral and crassly pragmatic as natural selection could design a mental organ that makes us feel as if we're in touch with higher truths. Truly a shameless ploy."[7]

The language employed here is astonishing. We are to think of a mindless process as using technique to put things in place. Though it has no intentions, we are to conceive it as enforcing its edicts by fobbing things off on us and using ploys. Though it is incapable of purposes, we are to suppose that it designed us. And though it is insusceptible to moral judgment, we are to be scandalized by its shamelessness. One could almost admire that last equivocation. In the literal sense, of course natural selection is shameless—it is insusceptible to moral judgment and unable to experience such things as shame. The craft of the phrasing is that in another sense, the term expresses a moral judgment. We use it for someone who ought to be ashamed, but is not. And so the very idiom these thinkers choose to tell that God is nonexistent and nature devoid of purpose insinuates, at another level, that nature is full of wily purposes and rules as a crafty, shameless god.

From views like this, it is only a small step to the opinion that a truly authentic morality would be Promethean, setting itself *against* nature's shameless ploy. That's what Dawkins thinks. First he sets the stage: "We are survival machines, robot vehicles blindly programmed to preserve the selfish molecules known as genes." The motto would resemble Rousseau's "man is born free, yet everywhere he is in chains," were it not that Dawkins thinks we are born in chains too. Then he issues the call to arms: "Let us understand what our own selfish genes are up to, because we may then at least have the chance to upset their designs, something that no other species has ever aspired to."[8] *Écrasez l'infâme!* It is all very stimulating, but Dawkins overlooks a little detail. It is one thing to propose freedom to beings capable of freedom, quite another to propose it to those who are slaves by nature. If we really are "blindly programmed" by our genes, then the call to revolt is worse than futile. One might as well expect a typewriter to revolt against the keys.

Perhaps Dawkins is setting his hopes on cultural evolution, for later he suggests that higher-level genetic programs are "open" and do not settle every detail of the way we live. Yet this is hardly a promising gambit, for his discussion of culture merely exchanges one form of determinism for another. As he sees things, our bodies are blindly programmed to preserve the self-replicating molecules called genes, and our cultures are blindly programmed to preserve the self-replicating ideas called "memes." If we take him at his word, then presumably the idea of revolt is merely another of the replicators. In this case he rails against blind destiny just because he is blindly destined so to rail.

Further complicating the story is that from time to time, the very writers who say that naturalism destroys morality have propounded the view that it *implies* a morality. Wilson, for example, believes that we are *morally* obligated to preserve all extant living species. The reasoning seems to be that (1) whatever is, is lovable; (2) the preservation of whatever is, is right; and (3) if we fail to pay sufficient homage to whatever is, there will be retribution. That is not quite how Wilson puts it. Here is how he frames the idea in a newspaper column adapted from his 2002 book, *The Future of Life:*

> "Don't mess with Mother Nature." The lady is our mother all right, and a mighty dispensational force as well. After evolving on her own for more than three billion years, she gave birth to us a mere million years ago, an eye blink in evolutionary time. Ancient and vulnerable, she will not tolerate the undisciplined appetite of her gargantuan infant much longer.

Could it be that he is speaking poetically and does not intend his words to be taken in a moral sense? On the contrary:

> The issue, like all great decisions, is moral. Science and technology are what we can do; morality is what we agree we should or should not do. The ethic from which moral decisions spring is a norm or standard of behavior in support of a value, and value in turn depends on purpose. Purpose, whether personal or global, whether urged by

conscience or graven in sacred script, expresses the image we hold of ourselves and our society. A conservation ethic is that which aims to pass on to future generations the best part of the nonhuman world. To know this world is to gain a proprietary attachment to it. To know it well is to love and take responsibility for it.[9]

The foregoing passage is rather cloudy. For starters, what does Wilson mean by "moral"? Is there an "ought" in there—is he saying anything more than "I have feelings of love, awe, and fear toward nonhuman nature, and I want you to have them too"? Plainly, one can *elicit* such feelings on the part of other people without recourse to an "ought." For example, I might get you to share my fear of environmental disaster by conjuring a vivid image of it. But can one recommend such feelings *as moral* without recourse to an "ought"? To sharpen the point: One sees that Wilson might regard people who fail to share his fear as deficient in *imagination,* but it is hard to see how he could regard them as deficient in *duty.* Duty doesn't look any more like a property of matter than right and wrong do.[10]

Wilson sometimes notices the difficulty. On such occasions he grandly invokes "emergent" properties of matter—properties that appear only when matter is complexly organized. But this is sleight of hand, because he has no idea how complexly organized matter could give rise to such properties either. Finding a property that he cannot account for, he calls it "emergent" and says that he has explained it.

III

A heterogeneous movement, variously styled "evolutionary ethics" and "evolutionary psychology," shares the goal of providing a naturalistic basis for moral judgments, but tries to be more systematic. This new naturalist fashion comes in three overlapping varieties.

The variety closest in spirit to Wilson's own work tries to demonstrate that a moral sense has evolved among human beings because it confers a selective advantage. Consider, for example, the human tendency to help out other people, even at some cost to oneself. At first it might seem that a genetic predisposition for such behavior could never have evolved by natural selection because unselfishness spends resources for nothing; every selfless act reduces the likelihood of passing on the genes that have made one act selflessly. But if the ancestors of human beings already lived in family groups, maybe not.[11] Under those circumstances, the ones most likely to receive aid would be relatives, and for each degree of relationship, there is a certain likelihood that the relative is carrying a copy of the *same* gene. So even though an act of self-sacrifice reduces the likelihood that I will pass on my *own* copy of the gene, it increases the likelihood that my relatives will pass on theirs. If my unselfish act helps a sufficient number of such relatives, then the proliferation of the gene in question is assisted even more than it would have been by selfish self-preservation. This is called "kin selection."[12]

If kin selection really happens, then it might explain the tendency to help out other people. It might even explain why we approve of the tendency. The problem is that it can't explain whether we *ought* to approve of it. After all, the fact that we developed one way rather than another is an accident. We help our kin; some species eat their kin. Someone might reply, "That we *might have* turned out differently is no concern of ours. The fact is that we didn't. Besides, natural selection has determined not only that we are the way we are, but that we're happy about the way we are. We don't need a justification for being pleased!" Not so fast. We may be pleased about our tendency to render aid, but we are not so pleased about its limits. As a matter of fact, many of our tendencies *dis*please us; consider how appalled we are by our propensity for territorial aggression. Now our tendency to territorial aggression and our propensity to be appalled by it must both belong to the genome. What sense could there be, then, in judging between them? Genes provide no basis for judging between gene and gene. The basis of morality must lie elsewhere.

The second variety of evolutionary ethics tries to show that by considering how we came to be, we will learn more about how we are. According to this view, Darwinism reveals the universal, persistent features of human nature. Why it should do so is very strange, because Darwinism is not a predictive theory. It does not proceed by saying, "According to our models, we should expect human males to be more interested in sexual variety than human females; let's find out if this is true." Rather, it proceeds by saying, "Human males seem to be more interested in sexual variety than human females; let's cook up some scenarios about how this might have come to pass." In other words, the theory *discovers nothing*. It depends entirely on what we know (or think) already, and proceeds from there to a purely conjectural evolutionary history.

These conjectures are made to order. You can "explain" fidelity, and you can "explain" infidelity. You can "explain" monogamy, and you can "explain" polygamy. Best of all (for those who devise them), none of your explanations can be disconfirmed—because all of the data about what actually happened are lost in the mists of prehistory. In the truest sense of the word, they are myths—but with one difference, which is this: the dominant myths of most cultures encourage adherence to cultural norms. By contrast, the myths of evolutionary ethicists encourage cynicism about them. Robert Wright is remarkably candid about this effect:

> Our generosity and affection have a narrow underlying purpose. They're aimed either at kin, who share our genes, at nonkin of the opposite sex who can help package our genes for shipment to the next generation, or at nonkin of either sex who seem likely to return the favor. What's more, the favor often entails dishonesty or malice; we do our friends the favor of overlooking their flaws, and seeing (if not magnifying) the flaws of their enemies. Affection is a tool of hostility. We form bonds to deepen fissures. . . .
>
> It is safe to call this a cynical view of behavior. So what's new? There's nothing revolutionary about cynicism. Indeed, some would call it the story of our time—the by now august successor to Victorian earnestness.[13]

An evolutionary ethicist of this second sort does not claim that Darwinism itself provides the foundation for ethics. What it tells us, he thinks, is the general features of human nature with which ethics must somehow come to terms. What ethics we develop to come to terms with them, Darwinism does not decide. Wright's ethics, for example, are utilitarian; he holds that "the fundamental guidelines for moral discourse are pleasure and pain." Given a utilitarian ethics, here is how he explains the usefulness of Darwinism:

> Of course, happiness is great. There's every reason to seek it. There's every reason for psychologists to try to instill it, and no reason for them to mold the kinds of people natural selection "wants." But therapists will be better equipped to make people happy once they understand what natural selection *does* "want," and how, with humans, it tries to get it. What burdensome mental appliances are we stuck with? How, if at all, can they be defused? And at what cost—to ourselves and to others? Understanding what is and isn't pathological from natural selection's point of view can help us confront things that are pathological from our point of view.[14]

If we ask Wright why he *does* favor utilitarianism, he gives the intriguing answer that, once the Darwinist theory gets loose in the world, it becomes harder and harder to find principles on which everyone will agree. All the old ones have been destroyed. We need new ones, but "in a post-Darwinian world," which "for all we know is godless," minimalism rules; fewer principles are better than more. Utilitarianism provides a certain advantage because it has only one—pleasure good, pain bad. Does this *prove* the goodness of pleasure and the badness of pain? No, but we do in fact regard pleasure as good and we do in fact regard pain as bad. "Who could disagree with that?" Wright asks. Like most utilitarians, he is convinced that even people who do not call themselves utilitarians are utilitarians at heart.[15]

The argument is less transparent than it seems to be. In the first place, the kind of minimalism that is likely to strike people as plausible depends on what kind of people they are. In cynical times, when they are well-fed, the One Plausible Principle may seem to be, "pleasure is good." But in violent times, when they are afraid, the One Plausible Principle may seem to be, "death is bad." In fact, this was the very principle propounded by Thomas Hobbes in 1641, in very violent times. Another problem is that minimalism won't get you very far. Hobbes thought his One Plausible Principle was very powerful, but he confused consensus that death is bad with consensus that death is the greatest bad. Though most people do think death is bad, most also think that there are some things worse than death. For that reason, even if they agree that death is to be avoided, they will not agree that death is to be avoided above all things, as Hobbes would have them do.

Utilitarianism runs into similar problems. People may agree with Wright that happiness is good, yet they may not agree with him that happiness is the same as pleasure. (Most of the Western tradition has denied it.[16]) Or they may agree with him that pleasure is good, yet they may not agree with him that pleasure should be pursued as a goal. (The Western tradition has maintained that pleasure is best enjoyed as a byproduct of pursuing other ends; the obsessive search for pleasure dries up the springs of pleasure.) Or they may agree with him that pleasure should be pursued as a goal, yet they may not agree with him that *aggregate* pleasure should be pursued as a goal, as utilitarianism requires. (If torturing one innocent soul would make everyone else much happier, then concern for the aggregate pleasure would require torturing him; in fact it would require torturing him *no matter why* that made them so much happier—even if there were no other reason than that they were all sadists.)

For all that, it is easy to see why naturalists find utilitarianism attractive. I asked earlier, "If material nature is all there is, how could actions have nonmaterial properties like right and wrong?" Confronted with this question, the naturalist has only two ways to proceed. He can straightforwardly deny moral properties, or he can try reducing them to nonmoral properties—which is a more roundabout way to deny them. The only puzzle is why he would want to do either of these things.

The common method of reduction is to explain moral properties in terms of desire. This move has four steps.[17]

Step one is to say that that the right is nothing but what brings about the good as a consequence. To consequentialists, a maxim like "It is wrong to do evil that good may result" means nothing, because apart from results they have no concept of evil or good.

Step two is to say that the good is nothing but the desirable. This is the only unproblematic step in the argument.

Step three is to say that the desirable is nothing but what we actually desire. This definition renders it impossible to make sense of perverse desires, desires we wish we had but don't, or desires we wish we didn't have but do. The utilitarian John Stuart Mill tied himself in knots over the problem.[18]

Step four is to say what it is that we actually desire. According to utilitarians like Wright, this is pleasure. You may think you desire many things—love, skill, friendship, achievement, salvation—but according to utilitarians, you're wrong. They say you desire nothing except as either a part of pleasure or a means to pleasure; hence, the only thing you ultimately desire is pleasure itself. For example, you may think you want dinner, but what you really want is the pleasure of feeling full; knowledge, but what you really want is the pleasure of feeling knowledgeable; love, but what you really want is the pleasure of feeling loved; or God, but what you really want is the pleasure of feeling—well, whatever God would make you feel. It follows that if it were possible to have the pleasures without the things, then that would be just as good. Eat, purge, and eat again. Better yet, drop an electrode into the pleasure center of your brain and forget about everything.

The third and most paradoxical variety of evolutionary ethics proclaims that natural law and naturalism are not at odds after all—that they are getting at the same thing. A dash of Darwin, as it were, makes Saint Thomas Aquinas more powerful and precise. Yes, yes, we must do away with Saint Thomas's silly superstition that a God is somehow behind things and that nature is designed—but the old fellow would have been better off without it.

This kind of evolutionary ethics has been especially popular among conservatives who think they believe in natural law theory but don't notice the sleight of hand. The most vigorous exponent of this "Darwinian" natural law is Larry Arnhart.[19] Arnhart uses the expressions "natural right" and "natural law" interchangeably. Although he borrows liberally from the other two varieties of evolutionary ethics, his approach requires more detailed attention.

IV

The structure of Arnhart's theory is easy to explain. He makes three of the four moves that utilitarians do, differing only as to the fourth.[20]

1. He *tacitly* supposes that the right is nothing but what brings about the good as a consequence, so he is a consequentialist. This critical move is not defended. The unwary reader finds himself joining in the silent assumption that the end justifies the means before he knows what is happening. What is astonishing here is that historically, the natural law tradition has been invoked *against* consequentialism in all of its forms. Yes, the tradition says that good is to be done and that evil is to be avoided, but it has also insisted that some acts are *intrinsically* good and evil aside from all consideration of their consequences. This Arnhart denies, as every consequentialist must. For him there cannot be such a thing as an intrinsically evil act—not even rape or murder. His understanding of the virtue of prudence is that there are no inviolable rules; *everything* depends on circumstances, because circumstances determine results. This utterly obliterates the distinction between the right, pursued by prudence, and the expedient, pursued by craft. Within his theory one can distinguish between socially approved expedience and socially disapproved expedience, but that is not the same thing.

2. He *explicitly* declares that the good is nothing but the desirable; in fact, he asserts and defends the claim repeatedly. Not that it helps much to do so, because this is the only step that is not problematic.

3. He *tacitly* supposes that the desirable is nothing but what we actu-

ally desire. Again no justification is offered, nor discussion of cases that do not seem to fit. For example, what about a masochist who strongly desires "bondage and discipline," but loathes himself for this desire and strongly desires no longer to be burdened by it? On Arnhart's account, we would have to conclude *both* that B&D are desirable for the man, *and* that freedom from such desire is desirable for him. This seems incoherent. A more straightforward view of the matter is that the man *recognizes that what he subjectively desires is not objectively desirable.* It is for precisely this reason that he desires liberation from his burden.

Arnhart does mention one difficult case: that of a person who thinks he wants something, but then discovers that it wasn't what he wanted after all. Unfortunately, the case is equivocal, and Arnhart does not analyze it.

Consider two instances in which I might wish to say that something wasn't what I wanted after all. Instance one: I want to be drunk. As soon as I get what I want, I throw up. I tell myself, "I guess that's not what I wanted after all." This is probably the sort of thing that Arnhart has in mind. Unfortunately, it isn't really true that I didn't know what I wanted. I really did want to be drunk, and I knew it—but I changed my mind.

Instance two: I have a longing for "that unnamable something, desire for which pierces us like a rapier at the smell of a bonfire, the sound of wild ducks flying overhead, the title of *The Well at the World's End*, the opening lines of Kubla Khan, the morning cobwebs in late summer, or the noise of falling waves."[21] Trying to understand what it is that I want, I form one hypothesis after another: "What I *really* want is beauty"; "What I *really* want is the remote and mysterious"; "What I *really* want is ecstatic union with the rest of nature." Pursuing each of these things in turn, I find to my dismay that none of them actually satisfies the longing. Eventually I realize that what I long for is not to be found within the created order at all. What I am longing for is God. This case is different than the other one, because until the end I *really don't* know what it is that I want. Unfortunately, Arnhart has no resources to analyze a case like this, because he does not acknowledge the reality of a Being outside the created order. The closest his classification of desires comes to the longing for God is the "desire for religious understanding," which of course is not the same thing, for religion is not God; not all religions are even about God. Besides, although the equivocal expression "religious understanding" may be taken as referring to the knowledge of the object of true religion, which is God, it may also be taken as referring to the knowledge of the truth behind religious delusion. Thus an atheist, such as Arnhart, who regards material nature as all there is and God as nonexistent, may consider himself to have religious understanding.

4. Not until the step of stating just what it is that we desire does the structure of Arnhart's theory differ significantly from that of utilitarianism. The utilitarian acknowledges only one human desire—pleasure. Arnhart acknowledges twenty, though why Darwinism is needed to discover them is not explained: the desire for a complete life, for parental care, for sexual identity, for sexual mating, for familial bonding, for friendship, for social ranking, for justice as reciprocity, for political rule, for war, for health, for beauty, for wealth, for speech, for practical habituation, for practical reasoning, for practical arts, for aesthetic pleasure, for religious understanding, and for intellectual understanding. No doubt it is better to recognize twenty desires than the One Big Desire of utilitarianism. In the context of Arnhart's theory, however, the list presents difficulties of its own.

The first great peculiarity is that for Arnhart, the general human desires simply *are* the natural laws. As he declares in his discussion of prudence, "The natural desires of human beings constitute a universal norm for morality and politics, but there are no universal rules for what should be done in particular circumstances."[22] The natural law tradition has always rejected such views. To recognize the natural law is not merely to admit that we have certain desires and that it would be unsafe to ignore them; on the contrary, it is to acknowledge certain precepts instructing us in the reasonable response to these desires. Concerning the most basic such precepts, Saint Thomas Aquinas says that they are "the same for all both as to rectitude and as to knowledge," meaning that they are both right for all and known to all, without exception.[23] Speaking for the mainstream of the tradition, he holds that they are well-summarized in the Decalogue, or Ten Commandments, which of course are found in divine law too.[24] For example, there are no exceptions to the precept "you shall not murder."[25] Arnhart denies that there are any such precepts—other than the desires themselves. To take this view is to misunderstand the very concept of law, and confuse prescription with mere inclination.

The reason Arnhart concludes that the natural *desires* constitute a universal norm for morality and politics is that, as we have seen, he thinks of the right as nothing but what brings about the good, the good as nothing but the desirable, and the desirable as nothing but what we actually desire.

From these premises it follow that the right is nothing but what causes what we want. Together with the list of desires itself, this theorem has some very strange corollaries. War, for example, is one of the desires on the list; war is therefore a universal norm for morality and politics. Notice what Arnhart's theory does *not* say here. It does *not* say that war is sometimes an unfortunate necessity for securing justice, as the just war doctrine of the natural law tradition declares. Rather it says implies that war *as such* is a natural law—that it is *good and right in itself*, simply because we do in fact desire war. Arnhart's actual discussion of war softens the point (there is, in fact, a great deal of softening of points in his book), but it follows inescapably from his premises.

Yet another oddity is the tension in Arnhart's theory between general and exceptional desires. In the opening section of the second chapter, Arnhart affirms, "I reject skeptical and solipsistic relativism, which asserts that there are no standards of ethical judgment beyond the impulses of unique individuals." Later in the chapter, in explaining the Big Twenty, he remarks, "In the case of each desire, I speak of what human beings 'generally' desire, because I am speaking of general tendencies or proclivities that are true for all societies but not for all individuals in all circumstances." But although in one sense his theory is based on general desires (for he does in fact generalize about the desires), his fundamental equation between the right, the good, the desirable, and what is actually desired pulls him helplessly in the other direction. For by the logic of the argument, the pursuit of what is *generally* desired is right only for the *generality* of people, those who actually experience them as desires. Should there be someone whose desires are abnormal, he must be viewed as standing outside of our morality; he has his own morality. This is necessarily the case, because what is right *for him* is what brings about the good *for him*, which is the desirable *for him*, which is what *he* actually desires.

This implication becomes strangely clear in chapter 8, which is devoted to psychopaths—those who "lack the social desires that support the moral sense in normal people." Such people, says Arnhart, are "moral strangers." Most of us would simply say that they lack the desire to do right. Because Arnhart *reduces* right to desire, however, he cannot speak this way. In his view, if desire is different for them *then right must be different for them too.* Arnhart says they have "no moral obligation" to conform to what our "moral sense" demands. If we may use force and fear to restrain them, it is not because they are doing wrong, for given their desires, they are doing right. It is merely that, given our own quite different desires, we, too, are doing right in restraining them.

Once this is understood, we can see that many of Arnhart's statements about his theory are misleading. Consider for example the sentence quoted a few paragraphs earlier: "I reject skeptical and solipsistic relativism, which asserts that there are no standards of ethical judgment beyond the impulses of unique individuals." It would be more accurate to say that he accepts solipsistic relativism based on the impulses of unique individuals *and* that he affirms general standards of judgment beyond the impulses of these individuals. On the one hand, psychopaths have a morality of their own which our morality cannot touch; on the other hand, the rest of us are not psychopaths. Nor are psychopaths the only ones who have their own morality. By the logic of the case, *everyone* whose desires are significantly different than the rest of us has his own morality. If the foundational principles of the natural law are "the same for all both as to rectitude and as to knowledge," then Arnhart's theory does not affirm the natural law at all, but rather rejects it.

Nothing in Arnhart's theory is quite as it appears. One of his most vigorously argued theses is that slavery violates natural right. He devotes all of chapter 7 to the subject, warmly endorsing Lincoln's remark that "[i]f slavery is not wrong, nothing is wrong." I have no reason to doubt Arnhart's sincerity. However, his theory cannot support his conclusion. The reason why slavery violates natural right, according to Arnhart, is that it "frustrates the desire to be free from exploitation"—put another way, the desire to enjoy justice as reciprocity (desire number eight out of twenty). But if the right is nothing but what brings about the good, which is the desirable, which is what is actually desired, then the fact that the slaves and the masters desire different things is an insuperable obstacle to the conclusion that Arnhart wishes to draw. He tries to get over the obstacle by emphasizing the social desires that might lead nonslaves to sympathize with the slaves' desire for justice. The difficulty, of course, is that not all nonslaves *do* sympathize with slaves. I believe I am right to say that members of the master class have not generally been known to do so.

The truth is that slavery represents a protracted state of war between the master class and the slave class—and Arnhart seems to forget that he has included war on his list of the twenty general human desires. Although the practice of slavery may frustrate the desire of the slaves for reciprocity, it satisfies the desire of the masters for war, and Arnhart's theory provides no principled basis to judge between these competing desires. As he states in another context, "When individuals or groups compete with one another, we must either find some common ground of shared interests, or we must allow for an appeal to force or fraud to settle the dispute."[26] In slavery, however, there are no shared interests; the interest of the masters is to continue ruling, and the interest of the slaves is to escape. I agree with Arnhart that slavery is against the natural law; I am glad that he reaches a different conclusion than his theory requires. But that does not change what it requires.

The quotation in the previous paragraph is not from either the chapter on war or the chapter on slavery, but from the chapter on men and women. From its context, this is highly revealing. Arnhart criticizes Darwin for giving two conflicting accounts of "the relationship between male and female norms in the moral economy of human life":

> In one account, [Darwin] defends a moral realism that combines typically male norms such as dominance and courage and typically female norms such a nurturance and sympathy, which he presents as complementary and interdependent inclinations of the human moral constitution. In the other account, he defends a moral utopianism that subordinates the male norms to the female norms, and he expands female sympathy into a disinterested sentiment of universal humanitarianism.[27]

But Arnhart also gives two conflicting accounts. The account which he purports to defend is closer to Darwin's first one—that typically male and typically female norms are complementary. The account that actually emerges from his theory is that these two sets of norms are substantially, though not entirely, at war. It is hard to see why else he would conclude his section on male and female complementarity with a paragraph explaining that "deep conflicts of interest between individuals or groups can create moral tragedies in which there is no universal moral principle or sentiment to resolve the conflict." This is, by the way, the same paragraph in which Arnhart offers the comment quoted previously concerning disputes that can be settled only by force and fraud. Perhaps the clearest example of such a dispute turns out to be the conflict between the female desire for a faithful spouse and the male desire for sexual variety, a conflict that is settled—apparently—by fraud.

To defend the idea of sexual complementarity, Arnhart argues (correctly, I think) that even though human males characteristically have a greater desire than females do for a variety of sexual partners, they are actually more satisfied by monogamous marriage than by a life of promiscuous abandon. He does *not* say, however, that males are most satisfied in *faithful* marriage, nor is this the conclusion that emerges from his account of male desire. The Arnhart male will want to be married—but he will also want to cheat now and then, provided that he can get away with it. In the interests of his desire for a stable relationship, he will discipline his desire for sexual variety—but not so thoroughly that he becomes faithful. Since men will desire to cheat occasionally—and since Arnhart takes desire as the measure of morality—he is logically compelled to conclude that, for men, *such cheating is right.* Does he say this in so many words? No, but nothing else could follow from his premises. But wait—what of the opening to the chapter, where Arnhart says that his theory "allows us to recognize and condemn cultural practices that frustrate the natural desires of women"?[28] This statement is not wholly false; Arnhart's theory does allow us to criticize the practice of female circumcision, a subject to which he devotes a number of pages. But his discussion of female circumcision seems little more than a diversion. After all, cheating husbands also "frustrate the natural desires of women," but against the occasional furtive adultery, Arnhart has nothing to say.

The strangest implication of Arnhart's Big Twenty list of desires is that in his determined attempt to make natural law safe for atheists, he is at war with his own theory. Numbers nineteen and twenty on his list of human desires are religious and intellectual understanding—the desire to understand the world "through supernatural revelation" and the desire to understand it "through natural reason." There is no priority here; the two desires are entirely distinct and equally general. If Arnhart means what he said earlier, that "the natural desires of human beings constitute a universal norm for morality and politics," then the implication would seem to be clear: Natural law instructs us to pursue them both. Unfortunately, not only does Arnhart's discussion obscure the point, but by the time the book concludes he is saying something quite different. Here are his words:

> Moved by their desire to understand, human beings will seek the uncaused ground of all causes. This will lead some human beings to a religious understanding of God. It will lead others to an intellectual understanding of nature. Yet, in either case, the good is the desirable. And perhaps the greatest human good, which would

satisfy the deepest human desire, would be to understand human nature within the natural order of the whole.

Instead of being urged to seek both kinds of understanding, suddenly we are urged to seek one or the other. They are no longer presented as either equal or distinct; instead, natural reason is given priority over supernatural revelation, and seems to want to absorb it. This does not wash. If the right is nothing but what brings about the good, the good is nothing but the desirable, the desirable is nothing but what we desire, and we desire *both* supernatural revelation and what reason can learn on its own, then Arnhart's own theory is instructing him to lay aside his atheism and pursue supernatural revelation—but he isn't listening. As Pascal once wrote of cases like this, the heart has its reasons, whereof the mind knows nothing.[29]

From all that has been said, we may conclude that "Darwinian" natural law is entirely at odds with what has traditionally been called natural law. It differs not only in content (no precepts) and structure (consequentialist) but in basic ontology (no lawgiver and therefore no law). In these respects it affirms precisely those tendencies of thought which the natural law tradition has always sought to oppose. If any contemporary scientific movement holds promise for the furtherance of the natural law tradition, it is not the stale dogma of natural selection, but frank recognition of natural design.

6

Thou Shalt Not Kill . . . Whom?
The Meaning of the Person

I

A person seeking to understand the quarrel about "personhood" should not expect to find out about it in the standard legal or philosophical references. Law dictionaries[1] typically define a person as either a "natural" person or human being, the body of a human being, the body and clothing of a human being, or a corporation considered by law as having certain rights of a human being. Very good, but who would guess from such definitions that, according to the U.S. Supreme Court, human beings themselves are not necessarily persons within the meaning of the Constitution?[2] A popular online philosophical dictionary defines a person simply as "an individual capable of moral choice," adding, "Although the details of their theories of human nature differ widely, Descartes, Locke, Kant, and Strawson all accepted a functional description of the person that includes both mental and physical features." As the author goes on to explain, "The attribution of responsibility to a moral agent requires both the ability to choose and an ability to act on that choice."[3] Who would ever glean from these words any hint that one of the most turbulent disputes in contemporary philosophy is *whether* personhood should be defined in merely functional terms?

Muddying the waters is the fact that the English word "person" has an extraordinary range of meaning. Its various senses, both well-known and not so well-known, include a capacity, a human being, a personage of the Trinity, one of a colony of zooids making up a coral reef, an important individual, a class of pronouns, anyone who is rational and self-aware, a role in a play, a form of verb, a public office, a living human body, a "personality," a corporation, or an individual's genitals. Even the magisterial *Oxford English Dictionary*[4] finds itself unable to reduce the varieties of usage to a number less than nine. Without a path through this thicket, the sheer variety of trees gives the dangerous impression that we can make "person" mean whatever we like.

Ironically, this impression works to the advantage of *just one* approach to definition, the approach which holds that a thing is whatever we say it is—a paradox to which we will return. In the meantime, can any thread tie all of the meanings of "person" together?

Surprisingly, yes. The origin of the English word "person" is the Latin word *persona*, which at first meant only a mask used by an actor in a play—hardly auspicious. Yet although this primordial meaning has not survived the rough leap into English, it is the grandfather of all the other meanings that the English word "person" can bear.

II

If we split up and regroup the *OED*'s nine classes of definitions with a view to the twists and turns of trope by which, beginning with the actor's mask, one sense of "person" arises from another, we find just four basic levels of meaning. These form a hierarchy, with all the other uses merely derivative. The tropes on which the ascent through the ladder depends are also four in number: *metonymy*, or the substitution of the whole for a part; *analogy*, or the association of similars; *transferred meaning*, or the replacement of a term by another to which it corresponds; and *hypostasis*, or the substitution of the underlying reality for an outward show. Here is how the hierarchy works.

First rung in the ascent. By *metonymy*, the word "person" can mean not the mask the actor wears but the entire role or character that he assumes. For example, Hamlet is a person of the drama that bears his name. So are Ophelia, Claudius, and the rest of the play's *dramatis personae*.[5]

Second rung in the ascent. By *analogy*, the word "person" can mean not *only* a role or character in a play but *any* role, semblance, guise, character, relation, office, or function—in short, *any* rational function or capacity—in which an individual might act. The role of Hamlet remains a person in the dramatic sphere, but now the office of emperor is a person in the constitutional sphere and the capacity of guardian is a person in the domestic sphere.[6]

Third rung in the ascent. By *transferred meaning,* the word "person" can refer not to the rational function or capacity itself but to the individual who exercises it. This time the "person" is not Hamlet the role, but Sir Laurence Olivier who plays the role; not emperor the office, but Caius Julius Caesar Octavianus who holds the office; not guardian the function, but Aunt Fanny who exercises the function.[7]

Fourth rung in the ascent. By *hypostasis,* the word "person" can mean not the individual who exercises the rational function or capacity but a being of that natural *kind* whose mature representatives *normally do* exercise it, and of which the individual is an instance. In this sense all human beings are persons.[8] To be sure, not all human beings exercise rational capacities; some are too young, too sick, too weak, too hurt, or otherwise indisposed to do so. Yet all belong to the natural kind whose members do exercise such capacities in due course of development, and when no impediment such as sleep or injury intervenes. A human, then, is a person *who belongs to that natural kind,* and he is a person because of what he *is,* not what he does or what he can do. Interestingly, this sense of the word "person" appears in Latin later in time than the third-rung meaning, probably because it is removed by one extra trope from the original meaning of "an actor's mask." However, it makes the jump into English *earlier* in time than the third-rung meaning, probably because—both ontologically and intuitively—it is more fundamental.[9]

With these four rungs of meaning, we have now climbed as high as we can, and they constitute the basic set.

III

Before returning to the personhood debate, let us take a moment to consider the derivative meanings of "person," which are legion.

One way to expand the basic set of meanings is to employ further metonymies, but in different directions than before. If instead of substituting whole for part, we substitute part for whole—moving not upward, so to speak, but downward[10]—then the meanings of the word "person" can be broadened to take in *any part or aspect* of a person. As we saw earlier, for example, the English language permits the "personality" of a person, the body of a person, and even the genitals of a person to be called his "person." The last case is considered a euphemism, but there is no more reason why it should be so considered than that its cousins should be, for it operates on the same metonymical logic.

Another way to expand the basic set is to employ not downward *metonymy* but downward *analogy*. For example, zoologists call the members of colonial organisms, such as corals, "persons" because they act in subrational capacities and relations that *resemble* the rational capacities and relations in which persons act. One of the capacities in which persons act is citizenship; the zooid's role in the colony is supposedly like the citizen's role in the city, so these scientists speak as though zooids were citizens.

A strategy of expansion that resembles the last one is the legal convention by which organizations of individuals who have a common purpose and coordinate their acts—such as governments or business firms—are treated *as though* they could act in the capacities of persons. Such "artificial" persons are never treated as persons in all respects, but only in certain respects, depending on the purposes of those whom the artifice serves. Hence, a business firm may be treated as a person for purposes of contracts and lawsuits, and a government may be treated as a person for purposes of war and diplomacy, but neither is treated as a person for purposes of getting married.

Last but not least, the set can be expanded through mere association. In grammar, for example, we use the word "persons" for the forms and distinctions of verbs and pronouns which *indicate* persons. "First person" denotes the person speaking, "second person" the person spoken to, and "third person" the person spoken of.

IV

To return to the basic set:[11] The question at issue in the debate over "personhood" is which of the four rungs of meaning has ultimate *moral* significance. Which rung denotes a being who deserves our absolute regard? To put the question another way, everyone who is capable of recognizing duties must recognize preeminently the absolute duty expressed in the Fifth Commandment, "Thou shalt not kill"; but *whom* are we not to kill?[12]

The experts of the day reply, "Persons, of course—it is persons who must not be killed." Correct, but to which sense of the term "persons" does this answer refer? No one supposes that the Fifth Commandment is about the first- or second-rung meaning of personhood. If someone said to us, "I am confused about who I am not to destroy—is it Hamlet, or Sir Laurence Olivier?" we would think him a joker. If someone said, "You must not abolish the office of president—it would be murder," we would think him insane. The quarrel lies squarely between rungs three and four.

The Western tradition, including revealed religion, traditional medical ethics, and the common law, favors rung four: Human beings are the ones who deserve our absolute regard;[13] "Thou shalt not kill" means that we are not to take *human* lives. Modernism—including feminism, "bioethics," liberal jurisprudence, and the euthanasia movement—favors rung three: People are not entitled to absolute regard unless they can *do* things like feel, think, have friendships, ponder themselves, and carry out their plans—unless they can exercise capacities like sentience, cognition, self-awareness, sociality, and "full deliberative rationality." Should someone be deficient in these respects, extinguishing him becomes a moral possibility, even if he is human.

Modernists accuse the traditionalists of a superstitious reverence for mere protoplasm. In their view, protecting a fetus or caring for an old woman with Alzheimer's disease is like refusing to leave the house without a rabbit's foot. For their part, traditionalists accuse the modernists of willfull blindness to what even a child can see—that there is something special about a human being no matter what he can do. Human flesh and blood are the pigments by which the Creator painted His image.

There is, by the way, no halfway house. Some people suggest that there is: that although not all human beings are "actual" persons, some of them—for example unborn children—have yet a certain limited value as "potential persons." But this argument makes little sense even from a modernist perspective, because surely, if they ever came into conflict, the higher-ranked interests of actual persons would utterly trump the interests of "potential persons"—and that is just what traditionalists protest. In fact, from the traditional view, the notion of a "potential person" is absurd, for a person is not the kind of thing that one *can* be "potentially." Nonpersons do not turn into persons, any more than characters, given time, turn into actors. Hamlet will never *become* Sir Laurence Olivier. In short, one is either a person or not, just as one is either a human or not. Unborn human beings are not "potential" persons, but *actual* persons loaded with inbuilt potentialities which still await expression.

Another accusation of modernists is that traditionalists are "simplistic" in their black-and-white insistence that intentionally killing an innocent human being is always wrong and should be prohibited by law. Let us look into the accusation a little further. The term "simplistic" means not "extremely simple," but "too simple"—poorer in distinctions than reality is. Of course traditionalists do not make the same distinctions that modernists do; for example, they do not distinguish slicing up the victim of an abortion from knifing the victim of a robbery, or assisting at self-murder from assisting at the murder of another. But traditionalists do make distinctions of their own. One such distinction is that while killing is forbidden, *allowing* to die is sometimes permitted. This does not mean that humane care such as washing or feeding may be withheld or withdrawn. It does mean that a particular medical treatment may be withheld or withdrawn, provided that (a) the patient is dying; (b) his death is imminent; (c) the treatment is of an extraordinary nature; and (d) his death is not the goal of withholding or withdrawing the treatment, but merely one of its possible results. Although these criteria are clear, they are far from simple. For example, extraordinary treatments are defined as those which impose excessive burdens on the patient or fail to offer reasonable hope of benefit, and all traditionalists recognize that judgment is needed to know when that line has been crossed. From this point of view, it would seem that the real simplifiers are the modernists, for they deny that there is any difference between allowing death and causing it in the first place, arguing that if one may ever withhold even the most burdensome treatment, then one may also kill.

Then who dies? Here the modernists split, but none of their criteria bears scrutiny. *Is the individual suffering?* Although not all doctors receive adequate training in palliative care, today almost all physical pain can be rendered bearable. For the rare pain which does resist amelioration, the patient can ask to be sedated. *Is he dying?* The irrational thought behind this criterion is that if we cannot guarantee a person a length of life we think sufficient, he shall not have any at all. *Has his life lost its worth?* That which is in the image of God does not lose its worth because it will never play the piano or because it can no longer use the toilet without assistance; modernism is not theologically *neutral* but committed to a theology that denies that we are made in God's image. *Does he want to die?* Most of those who have lost their desire to live regain it, if only they are treated with compassion. Besides, it is not quite merciful to offer a person death as a reward for internalizing the embarrassment, contempt, and disgust of those around him; some of us would consider it a nasty trick. *Would his death be in the best interests of all concerned?* This is a crafty way of asking whether he has become a nuisance.

The starkest criterion is simply: *Am I willing to take care of him?* Because this one is not often acknowledged, it requires closer consideration. Philosopher Mary Ann Warren is well-known for a defense of abortion that maintains that fetuses may be killed just because they are not moral persons.[14] Her argument is based squarely on a functionalist or third-rung conception of personhood, according to which the capacities "most central to the concept" are as follows:

> 1. Consciousness (of objects and events external and/or internal to the being), and in particular the capacity to feel pain;
> 2. Reasoning (the developed capacity to solve new and relatively complex problems);
> 3. Self-motivated activity (activity which is relatively independent of either genetic or direct external control);
> 4. The capacity to communicate, by whatever means, messages of an indefinite variety of types, that is, not just with an indefinite number of possible contents, but on indefinitely many possible topics;[15]
> 5. The presence of self-concepts, and self-awareness, either individual or racial, or both.

Although Warren says, "[W]e needn't suppose that an entity must have all of these attributes to be properly considered a person," she comes close to saying that the first, second, and third capacities, taken together, are both necessary and sufficient. These capacities look suspiciously like a list of the abilities which would be needed to fight effectively against an enemy; evidently the ancient notion that "might makes right" comes back as "might makes rights."

It is easy to see that if unborn babies may be killed because they fall short of the Warrenite capacities, then a great many other individuals may also be killed for the same reasons—for example, the sleeping, unconscious, demented, addicted, and very young, not to mention sundry others, such as deaf-mutes who have not been taught sign language. Concerning just the very young, Warren has penned a postscript.[16] "Since the publication of this article," she states, "many people have written to point out that my argument appears to justify not only abortion, but infanticide as well." Reading on, we find that she does seem to oppose infanticide, but the interesting thing is *why* she does so. She admits that her argument implies that "[t]he killing of newborn infants isn't murder." However, she insists, "It does not follow . . . that infanticide is permissible," because killing them may be wrong for other reasons than Fifth Commandment violation. As she writes:

> In the first place, it would be wrong . . . because even if its parents do not want it and would not suffer from its destruction, there are other people who would like to have it, and would, in all probability, be deprived of a great deal of pleasure by its destruction. Thus, infanticide is wrong for reasons analogous to those which make it wrong to wantonly destroy natural resources, or great works of art.
>
> Second, most people . . . value infants and would much prefer that they be preserved. . . . So long as there are people who want an infant preserved, and who are willing and able to provide the means of caring for it, under reasonably humane conditions, it is, *ceteris paribus,* wrong to destroy it.

For one already tempted to infanticide, these arguments carry no force whatsoever, for while indicating that *wanted* children should not be killed, they provide no reason why children *should* be wanted. As Warren herself concedes, the thrust of her reasoning is that if society is not willing to care for a child, "its destruction is permissible." Despite her protests, then, it seems that her critics are right after all: She does approve infanticide. "This conclusion," she writes, "will no doubt strike many people as heartless and immoral." Indeed. Whereas in the traditional view, the helpless and unwanted have the greatest claim on our protection, Warren finds that it is precisely the helpless and unwanted who have no claim.

If ever we reach with people in general the point we have already reached with people not yet born—killing them just because they are in the way—then we will have lost everything.

V

A glimpse of what losing everything might mean may be found in the translated Dutch bestseller *Dancing with Mr. D*, a rambling, disjointed journal of a physician's nursing home practice.[17] At the time of its composition, euthanasia was not yet precisely legal in the Netherlands, but was officially tolerated in an ever-expanding set of circumstances. Early in the narrative, author Bert Keizer is called to the bedside of a Mrs. Malfijt, who is choking on her food. There is no use trying to clear the blockage, he says, so rather than help in any way, he fills her veins with morphine. This he calls letting her decide her own course without being harassed from either shore. After fifteen minutes he calls her son to tell him she is dead.

At the end of the passage the reader comes to a full stop, then backs up. Has he just read what he thinks he has? Yes. How can it be explained? It can't; in Keizer's universe, where God is dead and life is meaningless, categories like cruel, mad, and normal can no longer be distinguished. The author gives overdoses of morphine at whim, yet grows furious with relatives of the nursing-home inmates for thinking that euthanasia is easy to arrange. Love for his patients? He declares to a colleague that he has none, but calls it good for the profession to heave a sigh from time to time and say that he does. On this page he mocks his country's official guidelines, which the ignorant in our own country cite as proof that euthanasia can be kept within bounds. On that page he violates his private guidelines, never to kill just for the comfort of the spectators and never to do it in a hurry. Over here he explains the importance of rituals, saying there should be one for euthanasia. Over there he mocks the mourners at funerals, deliberately answering their questions with gibberish. He admonishes one patient for loudly asking about euthanasia in the hearing of others. Yet having been offered some of another patient's shirts, he rummages among them in the very faces of the dead man's former wardmates. He harangues a dying former hippie for not having aborted her only child. Yet he badgers a nurse for refusing on grounds of religious faith to administer a deliberate overdose of morphine to a woman with a broken hip. Because he considers human beings feces—I am merely reporting how he speaks—one can hardly be surprised that he colors all their works with excrement, as when he compares an expiring woman's effort not to retch with the strain of holding in stool. But her death was a good one, he says, because she struggled at the exit.

Perhaps I overreact. Physician Keizer is but a drop in the sea of Dutch medicine. How typical could he be? The defenders of Dutch euthanasia hold that the stories of a social experiment gone berserk have been exaggerated, and that in any case the Dutch medical and legal systems are so different from our own that we have no reason to expect the legalization of euthanasia to have the same results here as it has had there.

These claims are put to the test in a compelling study by psychiatrist Herbert Hendin.[18] Though the executive director of an organization devoted to the prevention of suicide, Dr. Hendin is not a traditionalist. When he arrived in the Netherlands he had not made up his mind whether the law should permit euthanasia and assisted suicide, and he declared in his book that he was still uncertain about the ethics of treatment for people in coma or in dementia. Perhaps for this reason, Dutch doctors and euthanasia advocates were willing to speak more frankly with him than they might have been with someone merely seeking weapons to use against them. In the process they seem to have revealed more than they may have intended, and the longer the author studied "the Dutch Cure" the more horrified he found himself.

Hendin soberly demonstrates that euthanasia and assisted suicide in the Netherlands have resulted in thousands of unjustified deaths *even by the standards and statistics accepted by their advocates.* For instance, most proponents expected the change to increase the ability of patients to make their own decisions, but "[i]n practice," finds Hendin, "it is still the doctor who decides whether to perform euthanasia. He can suggest it, not give patients obvious alternatives, ignore patients' ambivalence, and even put to death patients who have not requested it. Euthanasia enhances the power and control of doctors, not patients." So common had involuntary euthanasia become even before its recent legalization in the Netherlands that many of the Dutch now carry cards to signify that they do *not* want to be put to death without their knowledge and consent.

Especially interesting is the interplay of motives among those who seek suicide, those who assist in it, and those who press for its acceptance. One obvious motive is the need to reduce anxiety about death. Unfortunately, the new mores themselves become the main source of anxiety, so assisted suicide is "the cure that causes another form of the disease." A more surprising motive is the need for connection. Many of those who have assisted in suicide call it the most meaningful thing they have ever done; it gives them a sense of intimacy with another person that they cannot otherwise achieve. Most engrossing is the sheer need for absolution. Accessories to suicide often assuage their uneasiness or sense of guilt by writing about the act, justifying it, and recruiting others to its practice. Of course all of these motives grease the slippery slope. Euthanasia "breeds" euthanasia; even some of those who have participated in it describe it as a contagious disease.

The contrast between the traditional and modernist worldviews could hardly be sharper. Once on a medical ethics panel I remarked that we ought not "play God." My counterpart, a hospital chaplain, declared "of course it's okay to play God; at the hospital we do it all the time."

VI

What does it mean to ask who, or which sense of *person*, is a proper object of absolute regard? Modernists prefer another way of putting the question—"Who is a moral person?"—but although acceptable as shorthand, this phrasing can easily mislead. It gives the impression that everything "moral" is relevant to the question of who deserves absolute regard, and this is not so. Moral rights and moral duties are both "moral," but we are *not* asking, "Who has rights and duties?"

The confusion lies in the duties. Obviously, a moral duty is a rational capacity, and no one can be said to have a duty unless he can exercise or stand in that capacity. Just as obviously, some human beings are incapable of doing so, either temporarily (as in the case of infancy) or permanently (as in the case of dementia). Thus, not all human beings have moral duties. Modernists argue that if not all human beings have moral duties, then not all human beings are "moral persons," and here is where they make their error. Whether one deserves absolute regard has nothing to do with whether he can exercise a duty. The ability to exercise duties concerns a different question altogether—whether he can be held accountable for failing to regard *others* with the regard that they deserve. What it takes to be a proper object of absolute regard is not duties, but *rights*.

I am not speaking here of *objective right,* the property that an action has when it is right, as in "doing the right thing," nor am I speaking of *subjective rights,* faculties or powers of acting in certain capacities or ways, as in "a right to do P." Rather, I am speaking of *claim rights,* valid entitlements, as in "a right to be treated according to Q." Claim rights, such as the right to the protection of the Fifth Commandment,[19] are not a capacity, but a possession; we don't have to be able to exercise them in order to have them. For a claim right to come into play, it is not necessary that I invoke it on my own; it is sufficient if someone would be able to invoke it on my behalf. The inability to exercise rational capacities is therefore a bar to having duties, but not a bar to having claim rights.

Nor are the rights in question *any* sort of claim right. Corporations, or artificial persons, have claim rights, too, but a corporation is not entitled to absolute regard. Its claim rights may be assigned, altered, and abolished according to the needs of the common good, without any wrong necessarily done thereby. They are not inherent to it. To be a proper subject of absolute regard is to deserve immunity from such treatment. It is to have *inherent* rights, rights inherent in one's nature, inherent in what one is. Presupposed in the idea of rights inherent in one's nature is that one *has* a nature, a what-one-is distinct from the present condition or stage of development of what-one-is, distinct from one's abilities in that condition or stage of development, and distinct from how one's condition, stage of development, or abilities are or are not valued by others. In short, a moral person (if the term be used properly) is someone whom it is wrong to use merely as a means to the ends of others. Artificial persons like business corporations are never used *but* as means to the ends of others.

If the warrant for denying the moral personhood of some human beings is that they lack the capacity to exercise moral duties, these considerations are sufficient to defeat it. The case is dead.

In fact the case is worse than dead. As we have seen, the modernist clings to rung three; he defines moral persons exclusively by their functions, by the capacities which they can exercise, by what they can do. But consider. What would have to be true for a functional definition to be appropriate? Putting the question another way, for what kinds of things do we properly employ merely functional definitions?

The answer is that we use functional definitions for *parts* and for *tools*—for objects the identity of which depends solely on their purpose in relation to *something* or *someone else*. A heart is a thing for pumping blood, its identity determined solely by the purpose that it serves in the organism; a screwdriver is a thing for driving screws, its identity determined by the purpose that it serves in our activities. A thing that cannot be used for pumping blood is not a heart, and a thing that cannot be used for driving screws is not a screwdriver. But to see this is to recognize that parts and tools are not intrinsically objects of absolute regard. Neither the heart nor any other part, nor the screwdriver nor any other tool, intrinsically deserves to be regarded in a certain way, as though it were the possessor of its own nature; our regard for such things—in both the sense of *what we take them to be* and the sense of *how much we care about them*—is properly dependent on the purposes they serve for other natures.

Now the same thing is true in the case of third-rung personhood, for persons in any merely functional sense. Their very identity as persons is relative to their capacities, to what we value them for; they *are* their capacities. An actor in a play, *defined functionally,* is valued, not intrinsically, but *for his ability to act;* a ruler of the state, *defined functionally,* is valued not intrinsically, but *for his ability to rule;* and so on. Is this not the whole point of defining him functionally? We are hardly doing more than paraphrasing.

The long and short of it is that to define a person in terms of his functions is not to *qualify* him as a moral person, but to *disqualify* him as a moral person. Someone who can act in rational capacities that are of interest to us, *and whom we do not regard as a person except by virtue of his doing so,* is plainly an object of our regard, not absolutely, but relatively—not for what he is, but for what he can do—not for what he deserves, but for what we respect. At this point I may be misunderstood. The problem is not that we are viewing persons instrumentally, for how their capacities can be "used." That may or may not be what we esteem about their capacities; it doesn't matter. The problem lies in esteeming them solely *for* their capacities, not for themselves. By doing this we reduce personhood to a depot, a warehouse, a bare access point, a location where capacities can be found—which is another way to say that personhood has been annihilated. And so the identification of third-rung personhood with moral personhood does not even rise to the dignity of being wrong. It is incoherent.

Some modernists will bite the bullet and agree with me. They will try to rescue their position not by drawing back, but by pushing further still, becoming *post*modernists. "Very well!" they might say. "Let us grant that the third rung is not enough. Persons, defined only functionally, are not moral persons. But in that case there *are* no moral persons, because the 'human beings' whom *you* call moral persons do not exist. There are no 'natural kinds.' There are no 'natures.' There is no 'what-it-is.' All value is relative because all meaning is relative; all meaning is relative because *every* definition is contrived to the convenience of the definer. The definition of the 'human' is no less contrived than any other."

But alas, this way of thinking escapes one incoherency only to fall into a greater. The former incoherency concerned only how we think of persons. The new one concerns how we think of everything, how we think of reality, how we think of thinking. A condition of being able to say anything meaningful whatsoever is that *not* everything is a creature of our own regard for it. There exist some things that are what they are despite us; they provide the anchors for all other meanings. If all meaning were relative, then even the meanings of the terms in the proposition "all meaning is relative" would be relative. Therefore the statement "all meaning is relative" destroys itself. It is nothing but an evasion of reality.

That seems a high price to pay, even for the privilege of killing people.

VII

A modernist who rejects the greater of these incoherencies is not thereby in the clear; one does not have to believe that all meanings slip away to see the meaning of the person slip away. Though a modernist may keep up the pretense that he is still talking about what persons really are, his method allows him to know only what he wants them to be.

And different modernists want them to be different things. One modernist has greater regard for sentience, another for cognition, another for self-awareness. One thinks the important thing is sociality, another the capacity to make plans. With each different criterion of personhood, a different set of beings is welcomed through the gates of others' regard. This writer says higher mammals are persons, but human babies not. That one says human babies are persons, but Grandma not. The one over there says *some* human babies are persons, depending on whether their mothers think they are.[20]

Inside the gates the contest continues, for functional criteria for personhood are matters of degree. People can be more or less sentient, more or less cognizant, more or less self-aware; they can be more or less adept at sociality, more or less clever at making plans. Plainly, then, they can be more or less abundantly endowed with what modernists call personhood, from which it follows that overpersons must rule and underpersons serve, gradation by gradation, all the way down the line. The conclusion is inescapable; the only question is whom we shall have as our masters. At the top may be those with the most exquisite feelings, with the most complex thoughts, with the keenest sense of self—it all depends.

Tinker, tinker. When else in the history of law or philosophy has it ever happened that a clear principle has been abandoned for one that meant who knows what? The principle of absolute regard for human beings is certainly clear—or was clear, before modernists tried to do for "humans" what they had already done for "persons." In another time and place the tinkering began with tenderhearted doctors, with the notion of *lebensun-*

werten Leben, "life unworthy of life." With us it began with incontinent lovers, for if you are going to separate sex from procreation, then you are going to need a lot of abortions. In both cases things got out of hand, went beyond what the tinkerers had imagined, and for the same reasons. You cannot make moral personhood mean just what you want it to mean and nothing else. The cloth of our common nature is too tightly sewn; it is made of a single strand. Pluck loose one stitch, and the rest unravels too.

No one in that other time and place was able to come up with a criterion that turned the people whom doctors pitied into unpersons but left everyone else as he was. No one in our time has been able to come up with one that turns babies in the womb into unpersons but leaves everyone else as he was. And no one will.

7

Capital Punishment:
The Case for Justice

I

Justice is giving to each what is due to him. So fundamental is the duty of public authority to requite good and evil in deeds that natural law philosophers consider it the paramount function of the state, and the New Testament declares that the role is delegated to magistrates by God Himself. "Be subject for the Lord's sake to every human institution," says Saint Peter, "whether it be to the emperor as supreme, or to governors as sent by him to punish those who do wrong and to praise those who do right."[1] Saint Paul agrees:

> For rulers are not a terror to good conduct, but to bad. Would you have no fear of him who is in authority? Then do what is good, and you will receive his approval, for he is God's servant for your good. But if you do wrong, be afraid, for he does not bear the sword in vain; he is the servant of God to execute His wrath on the wrong-doer. Therefore one must be subject, not only to avoid God's wrath but also for the sake of conscience.[2]

So weighty is the duty of justice that it raises the question whether mercy is permissible at all. By definition, mercy is punishing the criminal less than he deserves, and it seems no more clear at first why not going far enough is better than going too far. We say that both cowardice and rashness miss the mark of courage, and that both stinginess and prodigality miss the mark of generosity; why do we not say that both mercy and harshness miss the mark of justice? Making matters yet more difficult, the argument to abolish capital punishment is an argument to *categorically* extend clemency to *all* those whose crimes are of the sort that would be requitable by death.

I ask: Is there warrant for such categorical extension of clemency? Let us focus mainly on the crime of murder, the deliberate taking of innocent human life. The reason for this focus is that the question of mercy arises only on the assumption that some crime does deserve death. From the perspective of natural law, it would seem that at least death deserves death, that nothing less is sufficient to answer the gravity of the deed. Revelation agrees: As Genesis instructs, "Whoever sheds the blood of man, by man shall his blood be shed, for God made man in his own image."[3] Someone may object that the murderer, too, is made in God's image, and so he is. But this does not lighten the horror of his deed. On the contrary, it heightens it, because it makes him a morally accountable being. Moreover, if even simple murder warrants death, how much more does multiple and compounded murder warrant it? Some criminals seem to deserve death many times over. If we are considering not taking their lives at all, the motive cannot be justice. It must be mercy.

The questions to be addressed are therefore three: Is it ever permissible for public authority to give the wrongdoer less than he deserves? If it is permissible, then when is it permissible? Is it permissible to grant such mercy categorically?

II

Society is justly ordered when each person receives what is due to him. Crime disturbs this just order, for the criminal takes from people their lives, peace, liberties, and worldly goods in order to give himself undeserved benefits. Deserved punishment protects society *morally* by restoring this just order, making the wrongdoer pay a price equivalent to the harm he has done. This is retribution, not to be confused with revenge, which is guided by a different motive. In retribution the spur is the virtue of indignation, which answers injury with injury for public good. In revenge the spur is the passion of resentment, which answers malice with malice for private satisfaction. I am not here concerned with revenge, only with retribution.

Retribution is the primary purpose of just punishment *as such*. The reasons for saying so are threefold. First, just punishment is not something that might or might not requite evil (as, for example, it might or might not rehabilitate the criminal); requital is simply what it is. Second, without just punishment evil cannot be requited at all. Third, just punishment does not require any warrant beyond the requiting of evil, for the restoration of justice is good in itself. True, just punishment may bring about other good effects. In particular, it might rehabilitate the criminal, it might *physically* protect society, or it might deter crime in general. Although these might be additional motives for just punishment, they are secondary. In the first place, punishment might not achieve them. In the second place, they can sometimes be partly achieved even apart from punishment. Third and most important, they cannot justify punishment by themselves. In other words, we *may not do more* to the criminal than he deserves—not even if more would be needed to rehabilitate him, make him harmless, or discourage others from imitation. If a man punches another man in the nose, we may not keep him in a mental institution forever just because he has not yet become kind in spirit, nor may we kill him because we cannot be sure that he will never punch again, nor may we torture him because nothing less would deter other would-be punchers-in-the-nose. For these reasons, rehabilitation, protection, and deterrence have a lesser status in punishment than retribution.

The argument against capital punishment runs as follows: True, the purpose of retribution is served by the murderer's death, but under certain circumstances retribution might interfere with other purposes of punishment. It might prematurely put an end to his rehabilitation; it might undermine deterrence (say, by so angering his friends or compatriots that they, too, commit evils); and it might not be necessary for the physical safety of others. Therefore, it would be better not to kill him, but to protect society by other means—perhaps by locking him up forever. The difficulty with this argument is that it seems to regard the secondary purposes of punishment as sufficient to overturn its primary purpose. Rehabilitation, protection, and deterrence cannot justify doing *more* than what retribution demands; how then can they justify doing less?

III

Fortunately, this is not the end of the story; mercy and justice can, in fact, be reconciled. Let me first consider a false ending to the story that makes their reconciliation seem simpler than it is. This false ending comes from the utilitarian philosophy that has unfortunately come to permeate our society and legal culture.

To the question, "Is it ever permissible to show mercy?" the utilitarian answers "Yes," but in a misleading way because he does not understand what is being asked. A utilitarian says that the only reason to have laws at all is to stop things that make people feel pain and start things that make them feel pleasure. Requiting wrong just because it is wrong will make no sense to him, because he does not believe in *intrinsic* wrong at all. If someone chides him, "Never do evil that good may result," he is confused, because *what results* is the only measure of evil or good that he has. He cannot distinguish retribution from revenge, viewing all punishment merely as an emotional venting which makes people feel better. Not that he objects to it on that account, for in his view, feeling good is all that matters. Over time, though, rehabilitation, protection, and deterrence can make people feel better, too, so the only question is what combination of punishment and remission of punishment makes people feel the best. Therefore, the utilitarian might very well do less to the criminal than he deserves—but for the same reason the utilitarian might do *more* to the criminal than he deserves, for the utilitarian does not grasp the meaning of the verb "deserves."

To the question, "Is it ever permissible to show mercy?" I also answer "Yes," but for a different reason. The faith I hold recognizes the dilemma that utilitarians ignore. Justice is inexorable; evil must be punished. This would seem to make mercy impossible; yet there is mercy. As the psalmist says, "Great is thy mercy, O Lord; give me life according to thy justice."[4] Somehow the irreconcilables meet and kiss.

How can this be? There are two parts to the riddle, one on God's side, the other on man's. On the divine side, the reconciliation of justice with mercy lies in the Cross. God does not balance mercy and justice; He accomplishes both to the full. The reason He can remit punishment to human beings who repent and turn to Him is that the Lamb of God has taken the punishment in their place. His death and resurrection become their death and resurrection, because He identifies with them through sacrifice and they identify with him through faith; the judge Himself steps forward to pay their debt. Divine mercy, then, means two things. One is the divine atonement that makes God's forgiveness possible. The other is the divine patience with which He waits for us to ask for His forgiveness.

Yet whom God loves, He disciplines. For our good, not even divine forgiveness means that the consequences of sin *in this life* are fully remitted. Among these consequences is punishment by human magistrates, who act as God's agents whether they know it or not. The sentences of human magistrates cannot be, and are not meant to be, a final requital of unrepented evil; that awaits the great day of judgment of the quick and the dead. But they foreshadow that final justice, so that something of the retributive purpose is preserved. In the meantime they promote restraint, repentance, and amendment of life. Human magistrates turn out to be not plenary but partial delegates, and not only of God's wrath, but also, surprisingly, of His patience.

All this puts the primary and secondary purposes of punishment more nearly on a level than they would be otherwise—not for God, but for man. Although human magistrates are forbidden to let crimes go unrequited, they do not carry the impossible burden of requiting them to the last degree. For temporal purposes, the retributive purpose of punishment can be moderated by its other three purposes after all. The only purpose that cannot be moderated is the purpose of *symbolizing* that perfect retribution which magistrates themselves do not achieve, for human punishment is a sign of wrath to come.

IV

If criminals in general can sometimes be punished less than they deserve, then perhaps capital criminals can sometimes be punished less than they deserve. The desideratum is when the purposes of punishment can be satisfied better by bloodless means than by bloody ones, so let us consider the four purposes one by one.

"Rehabilitation" refers to the reconciliation of the criminal with man and God. It may seem at first that capital punishment can never aid in rehabilitation, because when the string of life is cut the process of rehabilitation is cut off too. But this is overstated. One part of rehabilitation is cut off, for certainly the dead man is not readmitted to society. But what do the opponents of capital punishment propose as an alternative? For serious crimes and dangerous criminals, they propose life imprisonment, and a man locked in prison for life does not rejoin society either. The real question is not what the prospect of death does to a man's prospect of readmission to society, but what it does to his prospect of the other part of rehabilitation—of change of heart. Here the picture is quite different. "Depend upon it, Sir," said Samuel Johnson, "when a man knows he is to be hanged in a fortnight, it concentrates his mind wonderfully."[5] Indeed there may be many criminals for whom nothing else concentrates the mind enough. By contrast, an offender who is confined in jail for life with no society but that of other criminals is probably more likely to be hardened than reformed. I am forced to conclude that in some cases, the death penalty may contribute to rehabilitation rather than hindering it.

"Protection" refers to the defense of society from the criminal. The restoration of just order is by its very nature a protection of society, a protection of its *moral* order. One might leave the matter there, but there is much to be said even if we consider only physical protection. Some people suggest that, although capital punishment might once have been necessary for physical protection, modern improvements in the penal system make it possible to shield the innocent without killing the guilty. This indeed is the argument of Pope John Paul II in *Evangelium Vitae*, although he states the conclusion in less categorical terms. It is not to his form of the conclusion that I object, but to the more categorical form. What John Paul suggested was that today we may be able to sentence a criminal to life imprisonment with the reasonable certainty that he will not be able to escape. I agree that this is a deeply significant change that may ultimately reduce the weight of the safety question in cases where clemency has been proposed. However, it is difficult to agree that it has reduced its weight already. Today the risk is not so much that dangerous and justly judged criminals will escape from prison; the risk is that we will let them out. It has been long since a "life sentence" meant that the prisoner would stay in prison for the rest of his natural life.

There are several reasons for the erosion of life sentencing, and they tend to compound each other. High crime rates have so swelled the number of inmates that officials find it difficult to feed and house all of them; the pressure to set some free is hard to resist. At the same time, American society finds it increasingly difficult to take right and wrong seriously. Not only does our lax moral attitude contribute further to the high rate of crime, but it generates further pressure to let criminals out of prison. When we do let them out, they are usually more dangerous than when they entered, because of the tips they have learned, the contacts they have made, and the attitudes they have developed among other criminals. An argument is sometimes offered that abolishing capital punishment would foster the virtue of compassion. Conceivably this is so, but in the present moral climate it is more likely to foster that counterfeit compassion which thinks no wrong could be *very* wrong. Should that happen, society would be even more at risk than it is now.

Suppose the unlikely; suppose that somehow we did keep all capital criminals in prison for the duration of their natural lives. Even then the physically protective purpose of punishment would not be fully satisfied. True, a man behind bars no longer endangers society in general. But he endangers other inmates, and he certainly endangers prison staff. Surely they, too, deserve consideration. I am forced to conclude that even today, with our modern penal systems, safety remains an issue. Safety must not trump desert; the risk of future harm to society cannot justify doing *more* to the criminal than he deserves. But in some cases, surely it should keep us from doing less.

V

"Deterrence" refers to the discouragement of crime in general. This is where some opponents of capital punishment claim their strongest ground, for the statistical evidence for the deterrent effect of capital punishment is inconsistent and inconclusive. In his essay "Catholicism and Capital Punishment,"[6] the late Avery Cardinal Dulles suggested a further dilemma. Although grotesque and torturous methods of execution seem most likely to deter, they are incompatible with human dignity. Conversely, those methods of execution that are compatible with human dignity seem unlikely to deter. He concludes that for the means of capital punishment which could actually be used, we probably could not count on a deterrent effect.

For those who view deterrence as the primary purpose of punishment, the uncertainty of capital punishment as a deterrent is the fatal argument against it. For those who view its primary purpose as retribution, however, this uncertainty makes little difference; the mere fact that a deserved punishment does not deter makes it no less richly deserved. But is it possible that high rates of capital punishment would actually *undermine* deterrence, inciting wicked and resentful men to greater evils? We know that banning a favorite vice can have this effect; the prohibition of alcohol, for example, can give drunkenness a certain glamour. But the crimes we class as capital must be prohibited in any case. If there were evidence that punishing them *by execution rather than by bloodless means* incited them, that would certainly be an argument for using the bloodless means. To my knowledge, however, no such evidence has turned up. It seems then that the data on deterrence neither strengthen nor weaken the case for capital punishment.

"Retribution": We saw earlier that although human punishment does not bear the full burden of requiting good and evil, it must hold up requital as an ideal; it must point beyond itself, to that perfect justice of which it is merely a token. Cardinal Dulles agrees, but sees a problem:

> For the symbolism to be authentic, the society must believe in the existence of a transcendent order of justice, which the state has an obligation to protect. This has been true in the past, but in our day the state is generally viewed simply as an instrument of the will of the governed. In this modern perspective, the death penalty expresses not the divine judgment on objective evil but rather the collective anger of the group. The retributive goal of punishment is misconstrued as a self-assertive act of vengeance.

The cynicism that Cardinal Dulles describe is a real and grave difficulty. In general, members of our ruling class no longer believe in those divine decrees of which human decrees are but a hint or shadow, and neither does a large and growing part of the population. More and more our intellectuals agree with the famous statement of Oliver Wendell Holmes that "truth is the majority vote of that nation that could lick all others."[7]

But what is the import of these facts? They do not make it *less* important for our courts to appeal to justice; they make it *more* important. There is a difference between saying that the ideology people hold no longer gives adequate expression to the law which Saint Paul says is "written on their hearts,"[8] and saying that it is not in fact written on their hearts. Even now, people retain a dim idea of desert; the idea "A deserves B for doing C" has not simply become meaningless to them. Besides, were the Roman judges of the first century less cynical than the American judges of the twenty-first? Tiberius Caesar would have been quite comfortable with Holmes's maxim; Pontius Pilate washed his hands of justice, using the question, "what is truth?" not to begin the interview with his prisoner, but to end it. The apostles knew all these things, yet Saint Paul calls the magistrate the servant of God to execute divine wrath on the wrongdoer.

I do not know whether our society can be brought back to believe in a transcendent order of justice, but of this I am certain: if we who recognize this standard do not act as though we believe in it, then we will certainly not persuade others to believe in it. The question to ask about the retributive purpose of capital punishment is this: Is it possible for punishment to signify the gravity of crimes which deserve death if their perpetrators are *never* visited with execution?

That seems unlikely. Consider the deviant who tortures small children to death for his pleasure, or the ideologue who meditates the demise of innocent thousands for the sake of greater terror. Genesis says murderers deserve death *because* life is precious, *because* it is sacred: Man is made in the image of God. How convincing is our reverence for life if its mockers are suffered to live?

VI

Let us consider what objections might be made against our argument to this point. The judicious Cardinal Dulles, to whom my discussion is already indebted, finds less to commend capital punishment than I do. Yet even he does not think that a review of the purposes of punishment is sufficient *in itself* to justify abolishing the ultimate penalty. The crux of his published argument is found, not there, but in four other common objections to the penalty of death: (1) that sometimes innocent people are sentenced to death; (2) that capital punishment whets the lust for revenge rather than satisfying the zeal for true justice; (3) that it cheapens the value of life; and (4) that it contradicts Christ's teaching to forgive. The cardinal calls the first objection "relatively strong;" he concedes "some probable force" to the second and third; and he considers the fourth "relatively weak." Yet, he concludes that "taken together, the four may suffice to tip the scale against the death penalty." Let us revisit these four objections.

Erroneous convictions. Courts sometimes do mistakenly condemn the innocent. Although erroneous conviction is possible in any case, the gravity of the error increases with the severity and irreversibility of the penalty; the penalty of death is certainly irreversible, and it is the most severe that we have in our armory. It would seem that the proper remedy is to require a higher procedural standard in capital cases than in ordinary cases, and to root out the sources of corruption in the system of justice. Indeed, the cardinal acknowledges this point, approving the suggestion that capital punishment would be justified if the trial were held in an honest court and the accused were found guilty "beyond all shadow of doubt." His point is not that this is the wrong criterion, but that it cannot be satisfied, for despite all precautions, errors do sometimes occur.

The difficulty with the argument lies in the notion of guilt "beyond all shadow of doubt." When we say this, do we mean beyond shadow of any sort of doubt, or do we mean beyond shadow of reasonable doubt? In law, the latter standard rules, and surely this is as it ought to be. Anything *might* be doubted, but it does not follow that doubt is always justified by the facts in evidence. The murderer might have told the grocer, doctor, and cabdriver what he was going to do; he might have been videotaped doing it by a newsman, a passerby, and an automatic security camera; he might have boasted about it afterward to a coworker, bartender, and next-door neighbor; and he might have confessed, in the presence of his lawyer, to the arresting officer, the investigating officers, and the court. Yet perhaps someone on the jury has been reading the *Meditations* of René Descartes, and is troubled by the possibility that the sensible world is only an illusion caused by an evil demon or by the nature of minds. If it is, the juror reasons, then none of the witnesses can be trusted. For that matter, neither can the accused; he may have only dreamed the whole murder. True, Descartes concludes that the world is not an illusion after all. But the juror votes for acquittal anyway, reflecting that philosophers sometimes err.

Now the way that the juror reasons about philosophers is very much like how Cardinal Dulles reasons about juries. The cardinal holds that because even honest courts can err, we must not trust any verdict, irrespective of the weight of evidence which supports it. But a doubt which cannot be affected by *any* possible evidence is not a reasonable doubt, nor is it a ground for letting the convict off the hook.

The lust for revenge. Of course it is true that the death penalty might whet the appetite for revenge. It is hard to see, though, why this should be more true of the death penalty than of "locking them up for life." Indeed, it is hard to see why it should be truer of punishment than it is of the other aspects of criminal justice. Seeing policemen on the streets, hearing the testimony of witnesses in court, hearing the judge's solemn charge to the jury—any of these things might whet the appetite for revenge, and no doubt they often do. Should we then abolish policemen, testimony, and solemn charges? Surely not.

Moreover, the love of justice is not the only good impulse that can be twisted toward the wrong. Every good impulse can be, such as love of country, love of family, compassion for those who suffer. The first may be distorted into jingoism, the second into nepotism, the third into mere sentimentality. Even the love of God can be perverted, and when it is, it is a terrible thing. Yet the fact that something right can be perverted does not stop it from being right. As this is true of the other good impulses, so it is true of love of justice.

The cheapening of life. Cardinal Dulles paraphrases the standard argument like this: "By giving the impression that human beings some-times have the right to kill, [capital punishment] fosters a casual attitude toward evils such as abortion, suicide, and euthanasia." He does not con-sider this argument strong. In particular, he observes that many earnest opponents of these other deeds are earnest supporters of capital punish-ment, for they realize that the rights of the guilty and innocent are not the same. He is quite right, and his observation can be paired with another. Many fervent *supporters* of these other deeds are fervent *opponents* of capital punishment. This phenomenon is as common as it is strange. Per-haps it is a form of compensation, as conscience demands its pay: Having approved the private execution of the weak and blameless, the approver now seeks absolution by denouncing the official execution of the strong and ruthless. Whether or not that explains the attitude, at any rate two things are plain. First, it is *psychologically possible* to hold either of the fol-lowing combinations of positions: that it is wrong to kill the innocent but may be right to kill the guilty, and that it is wrong to kill the guilty but may be right to kill the innocent. But second, the *normal moral reason* for upholding capital punishment is reverence for life itself. This is the reason why Scripture and Christian tradition uphold capital punishment, a fact which suggests that if anything, it is not the retention of capital punish-ment that threatens to cheapen life but its abolition.

Christ's teaching on forgiveness. It is true that Jesus taught us to love those who hate us, forgive those who wrong us, and abstain from hypocritical comparisons between ourselves and those who offend us. We must carry out these commands, however difficult they may be. But let us remember that private pardon and civil pardon are different things: The same Lord and God who commands His people to pardon their debtors also gave them Torah, which commands magistrates to call criminals to account. Cardinal Dulles speaks rightly when he says that "personal par-don does not absolve offenders from their obligations in justice." Indeed, he considers this fourth argument against capital punishment "relatively weak" and "complex at best." My only objection to these words is that they are too polite, for the supposition that personal forgiveness implies a requirement for universal amnesty is not merely weak, but altogether mistaken. Taken seriously, it would destroy all public authority, for if punishment *as such* is incompatible with forgiveness, then why stop with capital punishment? Must we not abolish prisons, fines, and even reprimands?

I have heard it asked by fellow Christians, "How dare we play God? How dare we wrest into our own hands the divine prerogative of life and death?" It is a good question. My answer is that we dare not. We dare not wrest into our own hands *any* of the divine prerogatives of justice, whether the deprivation of life, of liberty, or of property. It is a dreadful matter to kill a man, but it is also dreadful to lock him in a hole, away from wife, children, parents, friends, and all that he once held dear in life. It is a fearsome matter to imprison a man, but it is also fearsome to use fines and impoundments to confiscate his worldly goods, which he may have accumulated by honest labor, and which he is counting on for the succor of his family and for the support of his declining years. No, we dare not wrest into our hands any powers over our fellow men. But if God *puts* such powers into the hands of those who hold public authority—what then? Doesn't this alter the picture? How dare we jerk our hands away, hide them behind our backs, refuse the divine commission? For the teaching of Scripture and Christian tradition is just as clear about public justice as it is about personal forgiveness, and the teaching of Christ is that "Scripture cannot be broken."[9] The magistrate is "sent," whether he knows it or not; he is "the servant of God to execute His wrath on the wrongdoer." Yes, we have seen that he is a servant of God's patience, too, but this commission does not cancel the other. However tempered with mercy, public authority remains an augur, a portent, of the wrath that will one day fall upon the unrepentant.

The story has another side as well. To remit deserved punishment too easily is a miscarriage not only of justice, but also of mercy. When a heart is very hard, deserved punishment may sometimes be the only knock strong enough to break the husk and spill out the seeds of repentance. According to our traditions, God Himself uses this method: those whom He loves, He chastens, even perhaps with the prospect of death. If we are to imitate His love, then we must sometimes imitate His chastening, too.

VII

This brief review of the objections to capital punishment has led to the following conclusions. First, in considering whether to grant clemency, the proper question is not whether juries ever err, but whether we have reasonable ground to think that *this particular* jury has erred in fact. Second, any deserved punishment, indeed any element of justice, might whet the impulse for revenge—but when a good impulse is perverted, we should fight not the impulse but its perversion, and so with the impulse for justice. Third, Scripture and Christian tradition uphold capital punishment not in contempt for life, but in reverence for it; it is *because* man is made in God's image that Torah decrees that whoever sheds the blood of man, by man shall his blood be shed. Fourth, although Christ taught personal forgiveness, He never challenged the need for public justice. Official pardon rightly has conditions that personal forgiveness does not. Finally, not only is punishment compatible with love, it is sometimes demanded by it as the only medicine strong enough to do the offender good.

Natural law and Christian tradition have both held that the state has the authority to inflict capital punishment. Although they have also held that in certain cases a deserved punishment of death may be remitted, the grounds for possible clemency are particular, not universal. *Categorical* remission of the penalty, for *all* whose crimes deserve death, contradicts both traditions concerning the duty of the magistrate. It would weaken three of the four purposes of punishment, it would confuse the good counsels of compassion, and it would bring about more harm than good.

What then of *Evangelium Vitae?* I accept the conclusion of John Paul II that "today," cases in which the death penalty is still necessary are "very rare, if not practically nonexistent." Nor do I accept it reluctantly; I wholeheartedly submit to it. However, we must resist the tendency to exaggerate his conclusion by deleting the other five words, leaving the single word "nonexistent."

Some say that because there is a risk of error in both directions, we should prefer to err on the side of mercy. I agree. In individual cases we should indeed prefer to err on the side of mercy. But to err *categorically* is not simply to make a mistake; it is to abdicate from judgment and forsake our bounden duty.

8

Constitution vs. Constitutionalism

I

Lex facit regem. In these three words, Henry de Bracton expressed the essence of constitutionalism. The king is supreme *within* the system of laws but not *over* it; law makes the king, not the king the law.

The aphorism, of course, is not just about kings. It endorses the "rule of law" in opposition to the "rule of men." More precisely, constitutionalism is the principle that the real authority of government, as distinct from its sheer ability to compel, depends not on the personality of the rulers, but on antecedent principles of right. What we commonly call the law—governmental enactments—is not the ultimate ground of right, but an elaboration and specification of these antecedent principles in the light of the circumstances at hand.[1] Because the elaboration and specification of these principles is necessary to the common good, when the enactments that result from them meet certain conditions they "bind the conscience" of the citizens. In other words, they become real obligations. The authority of the government is simply its ability to bind conscience, *subject to these conditions.* Power then is justified by authority, not authority by power.

One would think that a written constitution would provide constitutionalism with its highest and most perfect expression. Of course, not any such document would do. It would have to be simply phrased, properly ratified, publicly promulgated, and compatible with the antecedent principles of right that we have been thinking about. This would enable it to serve as a "higher law"—not in the sense that it replaced these antecedent principles, but in the sense that it regulated all subsequent attempts to elaborate and specify them through ordinary law. Should some rulers declare lawful what the constitution forbade, then other rulers, or perhaps citizens, could appeal to that constitution in opposing them.

This was certainly how the American Founders expected their Constitution to work.[2] As always with big ideas, what actually happened is more complicated. No doubt, having a written constitution does promote constitutionalism in some important respects. However, in other respects it can actually undermine it. Surprisingly, some of the ways in which this can happen were anticipated by critics at the time, especially Brutus, a pseudonymous Anti-Federalist who was probably the New York judge Robert Yates, who had been a delegate to the Philadelphia Convention in 1787.

Probably we don't sufficiently cherish what is good about our Constitution. And yet at the same time, we aren't sufficiently on guard about what is deficient about it either. Even Brutus did not propose doing without *any* written constitution. What he proposed was a greater sensitivity to the dangers of such instruments, and the ways in which they can backfire. Needless to say, his advice was not taken, and perhaps it may be said that thinking about what *might have been* is not much more helpful in statecraft than in love. I think, though, that the Brutusian critique may help us to deal more realistically with the Constitution as it is—the one we must expect to have for a good while longer.

II

As I hope to show, Brutus was an exceptionally acute theorist.[3] However, he was not so talented an expositor and rhetorician as the Federalist writers with whom contemporary Americans are more familiar. James Madison always sets the trees in the context of the forest. Brutus describes the trees, but he leaves his readers to work out the shape of the forest for themselves. It is not that he doesn't see the forest; if he didn't, his pictures of its various localities would not connect up as well as they do. The problem is that he lavishes his powers of portrayal on the localities rather than on the forest as a whole. I hope it will not be presumptuous, then, if I sketch the big picture that all of Brutus's smaller pictures presuppose but which he does not actually paint for us.

Brutus's big picture coincides with Madison's big picture in certain respects, but diverges from it in others. He plainly agrees with Madison that government is both necessary and dangerous. Though indispensable for keeping order, it is also prone to tyranny, because officeholders labor ceaselessly to make themselves more important. Always they seek to expand their spheres of action and enlarge the definitions of their official responsibilities. Human government is always government under the conditions of the Fall.

The disagreement between Brutus and Madison does not concern the identity of this malady, then, but its remedy. Madison had written in *The Federalist* No. 51,

> In framing a government which is to be administered by men over men, the great difficulty lies in this: you must first enable the government to control the governed; and in the next place oblige it to control itself. A dependence upon the people is, no doubt, the primary control on the government; but experience has taught mankind the necessity of auxiliary precautions.

What makes these words interesting is that although the language of "dependence on the people" being the "primary control on the government" conjures up images of direct popular rule, Madison never says that "the people" *as such* are the primary control on the government. No, he says that the government is to "control itself." What he has in mind is checks and balances. The various parts of the government certainly do depend on the people in various circuitous ways, but the crucial thing is not simply that they depend on them, but that they depend on them in such *different fashions,* making it impossible for the government to have a unitary will to oppress them. To put it another way, what makes the government trustworthy is not its similarity to "the people," but the sharpness of the contrast among its own parts. Although each part may reflect some element in the character of the people, there is no part of the government that reflects the character of the people as a whole.

The Madisonian Senate, for example, depends on the considered judgment of the people as filtered through state legislatures interested in protecting their own authority. The House of Representatives, by contrast, depends on the shifting opinions of the people, or to be more exact, on what is left of these shifting opinions after competing factions have cancelled each other out. The presidency depends on the compromise of the various regions of the people, as filtered through the electoral college, and when the college cannot pick a winner, through the House of Representatives. The judiciary depends on the specialized knowledge of those members of the people whose qualities persuade the president to nominate them and the Senate to confirm them. And so on. Direct popular government, had it been instituted, would have been like a mirror that perfectly reflected the people's image. Republican government, as Madison conceived it, is more like a prism that breaks up the light of that image into a multitude of different hues, coupled with a filter that blocks certain hues from passing through.

Brutus is somewhat more sympathetic to popular government than Madison is, and much less sanguine about the possibility of getting the government to "control itself." He does not oppose the idea of checks and balances *per se*. He does oppose the Federalist theory of how checks and balances will work. In the traditional theory of checks, held by most Anti-Federalists, including Brutus, the parties who are checking each other are social classes, and the place where they are checking each other is a single branch of government—the legislature. In the Federalist theory, by contrast, the main parties who are checking each other are the branches of government themselves—legislature against executive against judiciary. Note well that for the Federalist innovation of branch-to-branch checking to work, the Federalists must be right about three things:

> 1. They must be right that just as members of social classes view themselves as vested in the protection and aggrandizement of their classes, so holders of government offices view themselves as vested in the protection and aggrandizement of their offices.
>
> 2. They must also be right that officeholders of different branches view their vested interests in these offices as diametrically opposed, so that the more power and prestige that officeholders in one branch enjoy, the less power and prestige the officeholders in the other branches enjoy.
>
> 3. Finally, they must be right about the inherent advantages that each branch of government brings to the competition, because otherwise the strongest checks will not be awarded to the weakest branches, as they ought to be.

Some Anti-Federalists challenged even the first of these three points of confidence. They refused to admit that self-interest really is actuated just as strongly by office as by social class. Thus Patrick Henry complains in the Virginia ratifying convention, "Tell me not of checks on paper, but of checks founded on self-love."[4] Brutus's approach is quite different. He readily admits the psychological realism of the first point, but he challenges the realism of the other two.

It may seem that I am straying from the original question of how having a written constitution may undermine constitutionalism. Not so. Brutus recognizes that a written constitution is not merely a statement of political ideals, but a legal instrument. It is all well and good to say that the three branches shall be coequal, but legal instruments are normally interpreted by courts. A differently drafted legal instrument might have distributed the power of interpretation among all three branches. It might have identified particular respects in which the legislature, the executive, and the judiciary are each interpreters of the Constitution. What the Constitution actually does, argues Brutus, is just the opposite. Rather than distributing the power of interpretation, it concentrates it in the courts.[5] To make matters worse, he holds, the language by which this is done encourages judges to exercise this concentrated power of interpretation in extravagant ways that bear but a distant relation to what the Constitution actually says.

The Federalists' response to such concerns is that we need not fear the judiciary, because usurping courts will immediately be checked by the other two branches. Brutus has a double response, for the Constitution dramatically misjudges not only where checks are most needed, but also where they will actually be used. In the first place, it assumes that the judiciary will be the weakest of the three branches, when in fact it will be the strongest. In the second place, it assumes that the other two branches will be jealous of its power, when in fact they will collude with it. The consequence of these two misjudgments is that under the Constitution, the legislature, executive, and judiciary will be coequal in name only, and "the real effect of this system of government, will . . . be brought home to the feelings of the people, through the medium of the judicial power."[6] So it is that the very instrument ordained to insure the sober rule of law comes instead to advance the arrogant rule of men—men who hold office as judges.

That is the lie of the forest. Now let us examine the trees.

III

Under the Constitution, Brutus argues, the national courts will be unlike the courts of any other republic in history, endowed with both radical independence and interpretive finality.[7] He does not oppose a moderate judicial independence; in fact, he supports it. Constitutional provisions that prohibit Congress from holding the jobs and salaries of judges for ransom are all to the good. The problem, in his view, is that the Constitution also makes it impossible to remove judges from office for making legal errors. The only grounds mentioned in the Constitution for the impeachment of any official are bribery, treason, and other high crimes and misdemeanors.

Central to his argument is the difference between England and America. Some degree of judicial independence is essential in both regimes. However, the reasons that make judicial independence essential to England have less weight on this side of the Atlantic. The important question about judicial independence is always "independence from whom?" In England, when we speak of the independence of the courts, we mean their independence from the Crown. In America, we mean their independence from Congress.

To be sure, both kings and legislatures desire to increase the powers and prerogatives of their offices. Independence from the latter may therefore seem just as important as independence from the former. According to Brutus, however, such reasoning is specious. Members of Congress will hold their offices only for fixed terms. By contrast, not only does the king hold his office for life, but he transmits it to his posterity. This gives him a far stronger motive to draw power to his office. For this reason, the independence of English courts from the Crown must be very strong indeed, but the independence of American courts from the legislature need not be nearly so strong.

Paradoxically, says Brutus, even though the reasons for judicial independence are less weighty under American than English conditions, the Constitution makes the independence of American judges far greater. For one thing, it is obvious that American judges will have the power of judicial review. English judges have no such power; they may declare the meaning of laws passed by Parliament, but they may not set these laws aside on grounds that they are inconsistent with the English constitution. Additionally, although English judges are accountable for errors in the interpretation of the law to the House of Lords, American judges will not be accountable for errors in the interpretation of law to any tribunal. Consequently, the interpretations they render will be utterly final.

According to Brutus, the consequence of these differences is that whereas English judges are controlled by Parliament, American judges will be supreme. Although the Federalists may have thought that they had learned from the English experience, in fact they had gravely misunderstood it.

IV

In Letter No. 11, Brutus scrutinizes the constitutional language by which the judicial power is characterized. Article III, Section 2, declares without qualification that it extends to all cases, arising *both* under the Constitution *and* under the laws of the United States. Since it is unreasonable to suppose that this language is redundant, these two provisions—"arising under the Constitution" and "arising under . . . the laws of the United States"—must have distinct meanings. In that case, what does it mean to extend the judicial power to all cases arising "under the Constitution"? Evidently, it means that courts will be able to declare what the Constitution *means*. Because the constitutional language is stark and unqualified, we must further assume that this power will be a judicial monopoly, unshared by Congress or the president.

Section 2 also states that the judicial power extends to "all cases," not only in law but in equity. Quoting Blackstone, Brutus defines equity as "the correction of that, wherein the law, by reason of its universality, is deficient."[8] What he has in mind is the fact that every law is a universal rule; it says, "In all cases that fit into category P, do Q." Unfortunately, because of the infinite variability of circumstances, there will always be some cases in the category P where doing Q would achieve a result opposite to, or at least different from, that intended by the legislature. In such cases, a court renders judgment equitably—not according to the words or letter of the law, but according to what the court takes to be the spirit of its reasoning. If we now put the fact that the judicial power extends to cases "arising under the Constitution" together with the fact that it extends to cases arising both "in law and equity," we conclude that the judiciary will be empowered to interpret not only ordinary laws, but also the Constitution itself, not only according to its letter but also according to the spirit of its reasoning. If we put this conclusion together with the fact that the decisions of the court will be final, we further conclude that no one will be able to second-guess the speculations of the courts as to what the spirit of the Constitution may be.

This immensely expands the power of the courts, especially because the structure of the rest of the Constitution encourages the courts to indulge their speculations about the spirit of the document with extravagance rather than restraint. In the first place, the government's powers "are conceived in general and indefinite terms, which are either equivocal, ambiguous, or which require long definitions to unfold the extent of their meaning." In the second place, by suggesting that more power is conveyed than expressed, the necessary and proper clause[9] requires courts to attend not only to the words of the Constitution "in their common acceptation," but also to its "spirit, intent, and design."

Strong as they are, Brutus's arguments seem even stronger today than they did at the time they were written. Historically, references to the spirit of the law in discussions of equity can mean either of two things: the particular intention of the law under examination, or the general intention of fairness that all law is presumed to have. This is why law dictionaries sometimes define equity simply as a set of principles of fairness used in interpreting the law. If we view the particular intention of the Constitution, we find that it was not conceived as an instrument for enforcing fairness in general; rather, it picks and chooses among the kinds and aspects of fairness that it guarantees; the remaining aspects of fairness are left to the solicitude and discernment of ordinary legislators. Today, however, judges treat the Constitution as though it really did guarantee all-around fairness, and that such fairness is to be ensured by their own solicitude and discernment—even when this leads to absurd consequences like reading the principle "one man, one vote" into a document that expressly gives the same number of senators to states of vastly different populations.

V

Brutus's assumptions about the nature of checks and balances directly contradict those of James Madison. To be sure, the Brutusian and Madisonian assumptions do not contradict each other at every point; in particular, both thinkers recognize the deep thirst of officeholders for power and dignity. "It will not be denied," says Madison in *The Federalist* No. 48, "that power is of an encroaching nature." Similarly, says Brutus in Letter No. 11, "Every body of men invested with office are tenacious of power; they feel interested, and hence it has become a kind of maxim, to hand down their offices, with all [their] rights and privileges, unimpaired to their successors; the same principle will influence them to extend their power, and increase their rights." The natural tendency of judges, therefore, is to try to make themselves social umpires, with no limits to the cases and controversies that they can adjudicate.

However, while Madison views the branches as fighting over who gets the biggest slice of a pie of fixed dimensions, Brutus views them as cooperating to get a bigger pie so that all of them may have a bigger slice. To put this another way, Madison thinks in terms of what we now call a zero-sum game. Each gain in the power of one branch diminishes the power of all the others, making the members of each branch natural enemies of the members of the others. By contrast, Brutus thinks in terms of what we now call a positive-sum game. Certain ways of increasing the power of one branch actually *increase* the power of the other branches too, making them natural allies. If Brutus is right, then Madison has made a catastrophic error, for the name of the game is not competition, but collusion. Instead of "obliging the government to control itself," interbranch relations will encourage the government to become ever more powerful.

The pivotal observation in Brutus's argument is that federal courts can hear cases and controversies that would otherwise be reserved for state courts by allowing Congress to make laws on subjects that would otherwise be reserved for state legislatures. Thus, besides the obvious motive to increase their powers directly, judges have a further, though less obvious, motive to increase them indirectly, simply by expanding the power of legislators. One hand washes the other. "Every extension of the power of the general legislature, as well as of the judicial powers, will increase the powers of the courts," Brutus says, "and the dignity and importance of the judges, will be in proportion to the extent and magnitude of the powers they exercise."

In Letter No. 12, Brutus goes on to explain that the collusion of the judiciary with the legislature in increasing the size of the pie is perfectly compatible with an ever-larger *share* of the pie being given to the courts. He is not convinced that courts will be able to tell Congress *directly* what to do:

> Perhaps the judicial power will not be able, by direct and positive decrees, ever to direct the legislature, because it is not easy to conceive how a question can be brought before them in a course of legal discussion, in which they can give a decision, declaring, that the legislature have certain powers which they have not exercised, and which, in consequence of the determination of the judges, they will be bound to exercise.

But he is confident that courts will be able to achieve the *effect* of telling Congress what to do, just because the members of Congress will internalize the principles devised by courts to guide their own decisions:

> These principles, whatever they may be, when they become fixed, by a course of decisions, will be adopted by the legislature, and will be the rule by which they will explain their own powers. . . .
>
> What the principles are, which the courts will adopt, it is impossible for us to say; but . . . it is not difficult to see, that they may, and probably will, be very liberal ones.

The judiciary becomes therefore the practical, if fitful, sovereign, limited mainly by the fact that it can rule on issues only as—and to the extent that—they arise in particular cases.

It might be objected that Congress will *not* internalize the judiciary's explanation of its powers—that this is one of the points at which we should expect Madisonian competition, not Brutusian collusion. However, two centuries of hindsight allow us not only to confirm Brutus's argument but to fortify it. First, constitutional separation of the legislature from the executive makes party discipline in our regime much weaker than in parliamentary regimes. This weakness of party discipline, coupled with the vast increase in the range of the government's activities, makes it impossible for the legislature to fully regulate its own agenda. Positive control over the agenda passes largely to the executive, which finds it easier to seize the initiative; negative control passes to the judiciary, which can overturn laws it does not like. Another fact bolstering Brutus's case is that whereas federal legislators periodically face the electorate, federal judges don't. This makes Congress much more risk-averse than courts are. Rather than resenting the judiciary for taking hot-button issues out of their hands, legislators may be relieved and grateful that someone else has made the decisions for them. Finally, although the public perceives the president and members of Congress as politicians, it tends to view the courts, however unrealistically, as nonpolitical guardians of the Constitution. This makes it still more difficult for any politicians who might wish to resist the puissance of the courts to stir up the political will to do so.

The upshot of all this is that an ever-larger share of the power pie is transferred to the judiciary—and that for a variety of reasons (not least the fact that the pie itself is getting bigger) the other branches acquiesce in the transfer.

VI

We have seen that Brutus thinks the courts will expand their powers indirectly, through expansion of the powers of the legislature. It remains to discuss how he thinks that the courts will expand their powers *directly*, through employment of legal fictions. This technique is so effective, he suggests, that courts in England have been able to use it even in actual defiance of acts of Parliament. How much more effective it may be in America, where no legal barriers stand in the way of its exercise.

His illustrations of the technique are borrowed from William Blackstone.[10] Originally, the court of exchequer was intended for suits by debtors of the king who pleaded that the actions of third parties had made them less able to pay their debts; the court of king's bench, in turn, was restricted to suits by parties who had suffered trespasses, or other injuries, by violence. In passage of time, however, the court of exchequer lost interest in whether the party bringing suit really was a debtor of the king, and the court of king's bench lost interest in whether the party really had suffered an injury by violence. Let the plaintiff only say the words—or file the writ—and his suit would be heard by the court.[11] Brutus expects American courts to follow an analogous strategy to overcome their own jurisdictional limits.

In fact, the Constitution mentions only a single exception to the jurisdiction of federal courts in civil cases: they are prohibited from hearing lawsuits between citizens of the same state, unless the parties claim land under grants of different states. If the federal courts could somehow pack this category of case into their jurisdiction, their civil jurisdiction would be universal. As Brutus explains in Letter No. 12, this would be trivially easy to do. Courts might simply make a routine practice of declaring the parties to be citizens of the same state. If this seems absurd, says Brutus, remember that Article IV, Section 2, guarantees to the citizens of each state all of the "privileges and immunities" of citizens in the several states. If we are entitled to all of the privileges and immunities of citizens in every state, then can we not be regarded as citizens of every state? By this reasoning, the claim of a Virginian to be a citizen of New York would appear perfectly truthful. Even if its falsehood were conceded, if the courts were to allow such a legal fiction, who could contradict them?

The bizarre lengths to which this sort of thing could be taken is suggested by the dissenting opinion of Justice William O. Douglas in the 1972 case *Sierra Club v. Morton*,[12] in which an association of environmental activists sought to halt the construction of a resort in a national park:

> The critical question of "standing" would be simplified and also put neatly in focus if we fashioned a federal rule that allowed environmental issues to be litigated before federal agencies or federal courts in the name of the inanimate object about to be despoiled, defaced, or invaded. . . . Contemporary public concern for protecting nature's ecological equilibrium should lead to the conferral of standing upon environmental objects to sue for their own preservation.

The prospect of vegetables and minerals bringing suit in federal court makes arguments about animal rights seem almost quaint.

VII

Although the members of the *Morton* Court declined to swallow the particular legal fiction suggested by Justice Douglas, it would be a grave mistake to suggest that Supreme Court justices are averse to fictitious claims. For example, a fictitious *history* has been employed to conclude that the First Amendment requires neutrality between religion and irreligion;[13] a fictitious *psychology* has been employed to maintain that the only possible motive for opposing special preferences for homosexuals is animus;[14] a fictitious *embryology* has been employed to insinuate that a child in the womb does not enjoy actual life but only "potential life";[15] a fictitious *classification* has been employed to characterize lethal behavior as reproductive behavior;[16] a fictitious *semantics* has been employed to interpret the constitutional guarantee of "free exercise of religion" as having no necessary reference to religious acts;[17] and along the same lines, a fictitious *grammar* has been employed to treat categorical prohibitions as implying qualified permissions.[18] The use of fictitious suppositions is so pervasive a feature of American constitutional construction that we should no longer speak of actual jurisprudence, but of virtual jurisprudence.

The pivotal moment in the development of virtual jurisprudence was probably *Griswold v. Connecticut*,[19] the 1965 case that established the doctrine of a general right to privacy. Not all of *Griswold's* methods are still used; the importance of the case lies rather in its demonstration of just how much a determined court can get away with. Writing for the plurality, Justice Douglas set loose not just one legal fiction but a battalion of them.

The argument is most ingenious. Certain clauses of the First, Third, Fourth, and Fifth amendments provide, respectively, that citizens may peaceably assemble, that soldiers may not be quartered in private houses during peacetime without the consent of the owners, that unreasonable searches and seizures may not be conducted, and that no one may be compelled to give testimony against himself. Appealing to the Ninth Amendment idea of unenumerated rights, Douglas argued (1) that each of these four provisions protects some aspect of privacy; (2) that by doing so they imply a right to privacy *as such;* and (3) that because this right is general, it encompasses the particular behavior that the statute under challenge had prohibited.

All three claims are specious; here we see virtual jurisprudence at its virtual finest. As to the first claim: The liberty of peaceable assembly guaranteed by the First Amendment is not a private act but a highly public one, connected with petition for redress of grievances. Moreover, the immunity from self-incrimination in the Fifth Amendment prevents government from eliciting confessions through torture; privacy is not the issue in this clause either. As to the second claim: Although the protection against the quartering of soldiers in houses and the protection against unreasonable searches and seizures do have some connection with privacy, neither protection is absolute; the former allows an exception for wartime, the latter an exception for reasonable cause. Moreover, because they protect citizens only against certain kinds of intrusions on their homes, bodies, records, and property, not against all intrusions, it is plainly unreasonable to suggest that they imply a protection of privacy *as such.* As to the third claim: Even if these provisions did imply a generalized right to privacy, the alleged conclusion would not follow. Privacy concerns what other people may do with my property and may know about my affairs. Justice Douglas was not talking about what others may do or know; he was talking about what I myself may do. What he called privacy might better be described as radical self-sovereignty.

VIII

The idea of self-sovereignty is given its purest expression in the 1992 case *Planned Parenthood v. Casey.*[20] By this time the Court no longer finds it necessary to appeal to the Ninth Amendment or allude to "penumbras, formed by emanations." The plurality simply composes a confession of faith:[21]

> At the heart of liberty is the right to define one's own concept of existence, of meaning, of the universe, and of the mystery of human life. Beliefs about these matters could not define the attributes of personhood were they formed under compulsion of the State.[22]

To understand this creedal statement, one must recall what occasioned it. What the Court meant by defining one's own concept of human life was not so much deciding what to think, but deciding what to do: *Because* I have liberty to define my own concept of life, I may kill; I have a private right to use lethal violence for any reason whatsoever against an unprotected class of persons. In strict logic, it would seem to follow that I may kill anyone whomsoever. In fact, it would seem to follow that I may *do* anything whatsoever.

For the time being, the Court restricts its universal permission to the taking of life not yet born. This serves as a salutary reminder of what may be called the first principle of judicial usurpation: Formulae of universal permission never really mean universal permission; they are always instruments for the transfer of the power to prohibit from one set of hands to another. That king who says, "Everything is permitted," must add, "But I decide for everyone what 'everything' includes."

How is it even possible for a confession of faith as chimerical as *Casey's* to seem plausible to educated judges? The plurality had one thing right—all suppositions about what is good and right rest on larger suppositions about the mystery of existence, the mystery of life, and the mystery of human life in particular. If I say that abortion should be illegal because murder violates the law of God, then obviously I entertain suppositions about such things. I suppose that there is a God, that He has a law, that this law ought to be obeyed, that it forbids murder, that abortion is murder, and that He commands human government to back him up on such a point. If instead I say that abortion should *not* be illegal, then obviously I suppose that *either* there is no God—or that even if there is a God, He has no law—or that even if He has a law, it need not be obeyed—or that even if it must be obeyed, it does not forbid murder—or that even if it does forbid murder, abortion is not murder—or that even if abortion is murder, He does not command human government to back him up on such a point. If I seek relief from judgment in the doctrine that the state has neither the right nor the competence to decide such questions, then I deceive myself, for indecision is decision; to say that the state should not pass judgment is merely to suppose that abortion should be legal, thus the state has passed judgment. It is not enough to have no suppositions; at some point there must be a contrary supposition. Although that contrary supposition may be "secular," nonetheless it is a commitment. It is open to certain possibilities about the meaning of existence, and closed to others.

The problem with Casey's "mystery passage" is that it pretends to be equally open to all suppositions about these matters, and it is not. In the name of a universal principle it seems to oppose sectarianism; in reality it is a sectarianism. The relevant distinction for a people constituted as a polity is not between a secular public life and a religious public life, but between a public life informed by a secular religiosity, and a public life informed by that older religiosity which secularism opposes. A particular *kind* of morality and religion can be pushed out of the public realm, but morality and religion *as such* can no more be pushed out than heat can be banished from fire.

But we were discussing the rule of law. The Supreme Court seems to recognize the extraordinary nature of what it is doing, for in the very same decision that it assumes such unprecedented power, it goes to unusual lengths to say that doing so is nothing out of the ordinary. Its argument neatly illustrates the *second* principle of judicial usurpation: In an age when candid monarchy has gone out of fashion, kings cannot be expected to call attention to themselves by announcing that they are the embodiment of the state. Ironically, but inevitably, it is in the very name of the rule of law that the rule of men is proclaimed. As the Court declares, "Our analysis would not be complete without explaining why overruling *Roe's* central holding would not only reach an unjustifiable result under principles of *stare decisis*, but seriously weaken the Court's capacity to exercise the judicial power and to function as the Supreme Court of a Nation *dedicated to the rule of law*."[23]

The opening of this chapter defined constitutionalism as the principle that the real authority of government depends not on the personality of the rulers, but on antecedent principles of right. Governmental enactments are not the ultimate ground of right, but elaborations and specifications of these antecedent principles in the light of the circumstances at hand. Because necessary to the common good, under certain conditions these elaborations and specifications "bind the conscience" of the citizens; that is, they generate a real obligation to obey. The Court's argument is a sort of parody of these ideas. It does not deny them; on the contrary, it nominally affirms them. The twist is that by declaring itself uniquely qualified to interpret these antecedent principles, it puts itself effectively in their place. By so doing, it arrogates to itself the power to bind the conscience of the citizens. In fact, it claims authority to tell them not only what to do, but also when to shut up—for it regards itself as the umpire of national moral controversies.

The Court frames these claims in loftier language, of course, but the meaning is clear enough. Here is where it proclaims the uniqueness of its qualifications to elaborate and specify the antecedent principles of right from which the authority of government arises:

> The root of American governmental power is revealed most clearly in the instance of the power conferred by the Constitution upon the Judiciary of the United States, and specifically upon this Court. As Americans of each succeeding generation are rightly told, the Court cannot buy support for its decisions by spending money, and, except to a minor degree, it cannot independently coerce obedience to its decrees. The Court's power lies, rather, in its legitimacy, a product of substance and perception that shows itself in the people's acceptance of the Judiciary as fit to determine what the Nation's law means, and to declare what it demands.

Here, in turn, is where it declares itself the umpire of national moral controversy, so that, for example, when it tells the proponents of the sacredness of life that the debate is over, they should be quiet and go home:

> Where, in the performance of its judicial duties, the Court decides a case in such a way as to resolve the sort of intensely divisive controversy reflected in *Roe* [v. *Wade*] and those rare, comparable cases, its decision has a dimension that the resolution of the normal case does not carry. It is the dimension present whenever the Court's interpretation of the Constitution calls the contending sides of a national controversy to end their national division by accepting a common mandate rooted in the Constitution.

The Court goes so far as to claim that the measure of the people's fitness to be governed by the rule of law is nothing more than whether the people are willing to agree with what it says:

Like the character of an individual, the legitimacy of the Court must be earned over time. So, indeed, must be the character of a Nation of people who aspire to live according to the rule of law. Their belief in themselves as such a people is not readily separable from their understanding of the Court invested with the authority to decide their constitutional cases and speak before all others for their constitutional ideals.

Confusing this willingness of the citizens to believe as it tells them to believe with its own "legitimacy" as an organ of government, the Court concludes with dark warnings that should its "legitimacy" in this sense be undermined, then so would the country be undermined in its "very ability to see itself through its constitutional ideals." Plainly, the members of the Court can no longer distinguish themselves from the nation; their lawlessness from the law; or their arbitrary will from those principles of right that are antecedent to their own authority, and that limit it.

L'Etat, c'est nous. "We are the State." Such is the unvoiced motto of the monarchs of our day. It was Brutus who saw how such an order of things might come to pass, but it was Bracton who told us how to answer. Against such kings we must say, as he did, *Lex facit regem.* They may believe that they make the law, but it is not so. Law makes the king.

9

Constitutional Metaphysics

I

At the root of a great deal of hostility to natural law is the idea that natural law is "metaphysics." Hardly anyone wants to touch those cooties. Most scholars of law and politics shy from reviving classical metaphysics, even if they are attracted to classical political philosophy. It's an odd attitude to take, because not thinking about metaphysics doesn't mean that one won't have any beliefs about the structure of reality. It only means one will be a slave to these beliefs, because he won't be fully aware that he holds them. They may even be inconsistent and jerk him in different directions.

The protest against metaphysics comes in two forms. One is that we should be dealing with empirical realities, not airy imaginings. Other kinds of scientists are allowed to have facts; so should we. I saw a bumper sticker in a university parking lot one day: "Get out of my way, man, I'm a physicist." We long, perhaps, for the day when we, too, could get away with that: "Get out of my way, man, I'm a political scientist."

The other objection is a little more sophisticated. Admitting that metaphysics *is* about facts—the deepest and most basic facts—it merely holds that the sorts of facts that it deals with aren't available to science. The originator of this argument was the sixteenth-century thinker Francis Bacon. According to the Aristotelian learning of Bacon's day, to understand a thing is to know its four "causes," the four *why*s of it: its material cause (what it is made of, its substratum); efficient cause (what brings it into being); formal cause (its pattern or form, that which makes it the kind of thing that it is); and final cause (the purpose for which it comes into being). Bacon is far from denying the reality of final causes, but he insisted that the only final causes that we can *know* by empirical investigation are the subjective purposes that we ourselves bring to our productions.[1] He reasons that since nature is not our production but God's, its purposes are scientifically inscrutable. Trying to find them out is a fool's errand, distracting us from real science.[2] A century later, Thomas Hobbes draws the dismal implications for statecraft, or tries to. So far as he can tell, politics is *only* about what we want. There is no point in conforming it to the objective moral order, unless by this order we *mean* the pursuance of what we want.

Hobbes couldn't make his thesis fly. He said that men do not agree about the greatest good, only about the greatest evil, death. But it is notoriously obvious that to say that men agree that death is the greatest evil, to be avoided at all costs, is to say they agree that life is the greatest good. Besides, the premise happens to be untrue. All men fear death, but most of us fear other things still more. Because Hobbes hit a snag—I am condensing the story, of course—the fashion now is to say that he and Bacon were not skeptical *enough*. We cannot even recover the purposes that we do bring to our productions. Inquiring into the purpose of a law, a work of literature, or a political regime is just as futile as inquiring into the purposes of things in nature.

But that is the wrong way to proceed. When one has gone down the wrong road, the great thing is not to go further, but to turn around and go back. In fact, we *can* inquire into purposes. Not only can we look into the purposes we bring to things (however tangled and obscure they may be), but we can look into the purposes we find present in them already. Consider the body: Are we really to believe that purposes of the eye, the heart, and the lungs are inscrutable? That the scientist has no means to discern them? That the attempt to do so is a distraction and waste of time, because it would require peering into the mind of God? Your doctor would get a good laugh from that one. In the same way we can consider the purposes of the practical intellect, of the capacity for anger, or of the complementarity of the sexes. Put one way, the problem is that Bacon refuses to admit the significance of organisms. A question like, "what is the purpose of the heart?" makes no more sense to him than the question "What is the purpose of a rock?"

But I say more. Insofar as we are natural beings—beings who did not design themselves but who discover themselves—certain purposes that we did not invent are latent in our very being, in *what we are*. Consequently, the same is true of the things that we do devise, like laws and constitutions. Just because we devisers did not devise ourselves, we find, even in our own productions, that there is more to them than we may have had in mind. For just that reason, I doubt that we can even ask good questions about politics without reviving classical metaphysics.

Or at least reinventing it. Case in point: A colleague shared with me an interesting paper[3] about what he calls "constitutional identity." He means by this term whatever it is that makes a particular kind of regime[4] be what it is and persist over time as the very thing that it is, rather than changing every second into something else. That is an excellent question, but without meaning to be, it is also Aristotelian. At first I was uncertain whether my colleague was trying to say that an "identity" is a formal cause (insofar as it specifies the "what-it-is" of a constitution) or a final cause (insofar as it is not only formal but *formative*, describing the constitution's tendency to persist, resist distortion, and become more fully what it already is latently). But Aristotle struggled with this double kind of cause. In fact, it is something like what he calls an "entelechy"—something that is both a formal *and* a final cause.[5]

Am I barking up the wrong tree in dragging formal and final causes into the matter? Some followers of Alasdair MacIntyre might protest that the home truths of a constitution lie not in its form or finality, but in its story. I answer that this alternative is false. By all means let us tell its story. As I hope that MacIntyre himself would agree, classical metaphysics doesn't mean *not* telling stories; it means looking into them more closely. We tell a thing's story when we tell how it comes to be, how it comes into its own or fails to come into its own, and how it dies or changes into something else. But to ask such questions *is* to ask about forms and finalities. How can we tell the story well, if we refuse to look into them?

II

But I was speaking of entelechies. In his own way, James Madison, who probably did not think of himself as a metaphysician, was concerned about entelechies too. Consider *The Federalist* 51, wherein he argues that "in framing a government which is to be administered by men over men," the great difficulty is that "you must first enable the government to control the governed; and in the next place oblige it to control itself." Anticipating an objection, he says, "[A] dependence on the people is, no doubt, the primary control on the government; but experience has taught mankind the necessity of auxiliary precautions." Chief among these "auxiliary precautions," he argues, is checks and balances, a "policy of supplying, by opposite and rival interests, the defect of better motives."[6]

In Aristotle's terms, Madison was saying that checks and balances, like dependence on the people, are entelechial features of the Constitution. They are formal causes because they characterize what kind of constitution it is; but they are also final causes because they enable it to persist as that kind of constitution rather than suffering a change into something else. We could even say that the boast of the adepts of the Constitution was that the "improved science of politics" had peered more deeply into political entelechy than the ancients had—not necessarily more deeply into the entelechy of a monarchy or an aristocracy, but more deeply into the entelechy of a republic. The ancients had thought that a republic could retain its character through dependence on the people and their virtue alone (they hadn't really thought so, but never mind that now); by contrast, the moderns had discovered that other features are also necessary.[7]

For his part, Alexander Hamilton enumerates five chief discoveries of the improved science of politics: "the regular distribution of power into distinct departments"; "the introduction of legislative balances and checks"; "the institution of courts composed of judges holding their offices during good behavior"; "the representation of the people in the legislature by deputies of their own election"; and "the enlargement of the orbit within which such systems are to revolve."[8] There is one glaring omission. Neither the wisdom nor the virtue of the people and their rulers is on Hamilton's list. This may easily give the impression that Hamilton and his collaborators viewed the Constitution as a purely mechanical contrivance, something that would run as though on autopilot. Not so. Actually, although they did vacillate between somewhat thinner and somewhat thicker views of virtue, they considered both the character and understanding of the people crucial to the entelechy of the republic.

To show that they considered *character* entelechial is easy. They say that it is. Consider just *The Federalist* Nos. 55 and 76:

> As there is a degree of depravity in mankind which requires a certain degree of circumspection and distrust, so there are other qualities in human nature which justify a certain portion of esteem and con-

fidence. Republican government presupposes the existence of these qualities in a higher degree than any other form.

[T]he supposition of universal venality in human nature is little less an error in political reasoning than the supposition of universal rectitude. The institution of delegated power implies that there is a portion of virtue and honor among mankind, which may be a reasonable foundation of confidence.

To show that the Framers considered not only the virtue but the *understanding* of the people entelechial is no more difficult, for they say that too. *The Federalist* 57 calls not only for the virtue to pursue the common good but also the wisdom to discern it;[9] Madison's speech to the federal ratifying convention in Virginia mentions not only the virtue of the community but also its intelligence.[10] We may add to these *The Federalist* 84, where Hamilton says there is no hope for our liberties unless the people have both the right opinions and the right spirit—both sound understanding and the perseverance and zeal to carry it into practice.[11]

III

But wait—what is it that these citizens need an understanding *of*? I have been arguing that, after a fashion, the Framers themselves were doing metaphysics. But we can go further. After a fashion, they even insisted that the people and their rulers themselves do metaphysics. They certainly did not demand that subjects and kings become philosophers,[12] but they did require a certain elevation of common sense about the order of being. For as it turns out, they think the entelechy of the republic depends on the public having a grasp of much more than politics. They also need a grasp of natural law.

This fact may not at first be obvious, because at the beginning of the American republic, the strongest testimony to belief in the natural law comes not from our foundational legal document, the Constitution, but from our foundational political document, the Declaration of Independence. Very well; let us start there. In its familiar "we hold these truths,"[13] God is presented as a Creator who has impressed certain laws onto His creation; the laws of nature are thus His laws, and their authority is His as well. Certain of these principles are called "self-evident," meaning that they are so plain to the mature and disinterested mind that no one can honestly claim not to know them. Notice that I say not merely "claim," but "honestly" claim, because they can certainly be denied. One self-evident yet deniable principle is that all men are created equal, for if all men share the same nature and the same moral capacities, then no man can be the natural servant of another in the sense that a cow or a horse might be. From this fact follows *rights* of a sort that cannot be given up, cannot be taken away, and cannot be destroyed. The words are Thomas Jefferson's, but the argument is John Locke's.[14]

The Constitution's strange silence about natural law does not show that the Framers were in doubt about its reality. Consider for example the famous (or infamous) Ninth Amendment, which states, "The enumeration in the Constitution, of certain rights, shall not be construed to deny or disparage others retained by the people." This statement presupposes not only that some rights are retained by the people, but that we can tell which rights they retain. How are we to do that? There are four possibilities. The first flows from the logic of enumerated powers; the second, from the English common-law inheritance; the third, from original intent, or if you prefer, from original understanding; the fourth, from natural law. Let us consider them in turn.

The first possibility, that the people retain rights to do everything that Congress isn't given power to forbid or destroy, turns things on their head. For the boundaries of the enumerated powers are cloudy, and the necessary and proper clause makes them vaguer still. The Ninth Amendment does not ask us to reason backwards, from what Congress may destroy to what rights people retain; we are to reason forward, from what rights people retain to what Congress may *not* destroy.

The second possibility, that the people retain all of the rights that they have in common law, couldn't be the answer either. Common law can be set aside by statute. One cannot use a tradition that Congress *is* allowed set aside to tell us what rights Congress is *not* allowed to set aside.

The third possibility, that the people retain just those rights that the Framers and ratifiers of the Ninth Amendment had in mind—or that the words of the Ninth Amendment were conventionally taken to mean[15]— fares no better. After all, these were men who believed in an objective moral order. Such an order is not governed by intentions and social conventions about words; on the contrary, they are governed by it.

The only possibility left standing is that the people retain all their *natural* rights. Just as in the Declaration of Independence, we are to assume that these really can be recognized by mature and disinterested minds.

IV

But is that true? Very early in American history, two clashing schools of thought emerged concerning the answer to this question. Although all early jurists *believed* in the natural law, they disagreed about whether judges may declare acts of the legislature void on grounds that they *violate* the natural law. This conflict appears in our case law as early as *Calder v. Bull* (1798), a case involving the meaning and validity of enactments *ex post facto*.[16]

Justice Samuel Chase argues that judges *may* void legislative acts by direct appeal to the natural law, because if they may not, then the legislature will be omnipotent.[17] Justice Samuel Iredell maintains just as firmly that judges may *not* void legislative acts by direct appeal to the natural law, because if they may, then courts will be omnipotent.[18]

With variations, the opposing schools of thought represented by Chase and Iredell have persisted to the present day. It is crucial to understand the nature of the dispute. Chase and Iredell do not give different answers to the question; "may judges void acts of the legislature on grounds that they violate the Constitution?" Both reply, "Yes." They do not give different answers to the question; "is there a natural law?" Both reply, "Yes." They do not give different answers to the question; "is it fitting for the legislature to enact a bill which violates the natural law?" Both reply, "No." Their quarrel concerns the answer to the question; "who has the corrective authority to declare when a legislative violation of natural law has in fact taken place?" Chase replies, "The courts"; Iredell, "Only the legislature." The Constitution does not tell us which jurist is right, the natural law *as such* does not tell us which jurist is right, and tyranny seems to threaten no matter which way the question is answered.

I suspect that this dilemma seems inescapable only because a crucial distinction has been missed by both sides. Natural law thinkers have always recognized a difference between the basic principles of the natural law and their remote implications. Chase seems to have in mind chiefly its basic principles. These are known at some level to everyone, they require no great study to figure out, and only obstinate minds could disagree about them. For this reason, Chase sees no reason why judges should not be able to say to misbehaving legislators, "You know better than that; your unjust act is void." By contrast, Iredell seems to have in mind chiefly the remote implications of the basic principles. These are *not* necessarily known to everyone, they may require a great deal of study to figure out, and even reasonable minds may disagree about them. Since legislators are not limited to the facts of the case at hand, as judges are, legislators have greater facilities for the investigation of such matters. Therefore Iredell sees no reason why judges should be able to second-guess. Each of the two antagonists, Chase and Iredell, makes good sense with respect to the kind of precept he chiefly has in mind. Neither makes good sense with respect to the kind of precept the other chiefly has in mind.

Russell Hittinger helpfully points out that the proper question is not whether courts may ever take lawmaking authority unto themselves in the name of the natural law, rewriting the ordinances of the legislature. To propose such authority is to deny the distinction between legislators and judges. The proper question is whether courts may ever refuse to render judgment according to an enactment of the legislature, when, by the standards of the natural law, the enactment does not rise to the level of true law.[19] I agree. By itself, however, this does not tell us whether Chase or Iredell is right.

If I may propose a solution: Let us say that in a system of divided government with checks and balances, courts *should* be granted authority to refuse to render judgment on grounds that the legislative act violates basic principles of the natural law such as "do not murder" and "punish only the guilty." But courts should *not* be granted authority to refuse to render judgment when the only violations that are alleged concern remote implications of such basic principles.

I do not claim that this is an easy solution—only that it is a sensible solution. One reason it is not easy is that the implications of basic principles may be more remote or less remote; no doubt it would take effort to draw the line well. Another is that human beings are capable of dispute even over the question of which things are reasonably indisputable. These two problems are surely troubling. Notice, though, that the fact that they trouble us does not get us off the hook of judgment. Courts would not be able to avoid considerations of natural law even if they had *no* authority to void acts of the legislature. The fact is that considerations of natural law arise willy-nilly, even in the mere interpretation of legislative acts whose validity is wholly conceded.[20] Although you can replace many undefined expressions by defined expressions, you cannot keep this up until nothing undefined is left. There will always be some rock-bottom undefined expressions in terms of which the rest of the expressions are defined—and *some* of those undefined expressions will inevitably have moral meanings. This fact undermines all versions of legal positivism. It plagues not only the simple "law is the command of the sovereign" versions, but also the more sophisticated "law is a social convention" versions. It afflicts not only those versions that focus on ordinary legal rules, but also those versions that distinguish between these rules and the higher-level rules by which the ordinary ones are established, recognized, or changed. No versions of legal positivism are exempt. The moral of the Chase and Iredell story is that positive, or man-made law, points beyond itself; for much of its meaning, it inevitably depends on the natural law. I defy any legal positivist to show otherwise.[21]

V

To resume the thread of my story, I mentioned two things that make my suggested solution to the problem of judicial discretion difficult. The first, with which we have just been dealing, was the difficulty of drawing the line between the more and less remote implications of basic principles. Allow me to add only one more point, that life is full of messy quags in which lines must be drawn nonetheless. The other was that human beings are capable of dispute even over the question of which things are reasonably indisputable. This, too, is vexing, but from the fact that human beings are capable of dispute over the question of which things are reasonably indisputable, it does not follow that all things are reasonably disputable.

What are we to do at times when our disputes are *un*reasonable? I hope it is not necessary to emphasize that we are in one of those times now. In the previous chapter I mentioned the so-called "mystery passage" of *Planned Parenthood v. Casey:* "At the heart of liberty is the right to define one's own concept of existence, of meaning, of the universe, and of the mystery of human life."[22] What could the authors of the plurality opinion have been thinking to embrace this Harry Potter view that reality is whatever we say it is? Would we employ a carpenter who claimed a right to define his own concept of nails, screws, wood, tools, or the mystery of what makes walls fall down? Please notice that the validity of my complaint does not depend on whether you agree with me about the focus of the dispute in *Casey*, abortion. We need only agree that there is such a thing as reality, and that thinking does not make things so.

Unfortunately, the sort of thing we find in the "mystery passage" is not an oddity. I have already explained how constitutional jurisprudence has got out of hand. Instead let us ask whether we could have avoided coming to this point.

Sometimes it is held that the problem lies in our methods of textual interpretation. The idea is that if only we were "strict constructionists," we would have been all right. This dogma is very Cartesian; it agrees with Descartes that the path to certain knowledge lies in having the right method. It is also, in a sense, very Protestant; it subscribes to the Reformation motto *sola scriptura*, except that the scripture to which it applies the *sola* is not the Holy Bible but the U.S. Constitution.[23] What are we to make of the idea? Certainly fidelity to the Constitution is important, not because the Framers were right about everything (the Anti-Federalist, Brutus, shows us that), but because the law of the regime should not be like ordinary law, mutable at whim. Certainly, too, good methods of textual interpretation can be distinguished from bad ones; good ones would have helped, and bad ones are more popular because they allow judges (and those whom they favor) to do as they please. Even so, no methodology could have kept us from falling into our current slough of despond. If Descartes had been right about the method for dealing with uncertainties, then we would have had more certainties by now. If the Reformers had been right about the *sola*, there would not have arisen so many thousands of denominations, each claiming to follow nothing but *scriptura*.

Would a more "Catholic" approach to interpretation be more helpful? The Catholic Church believes the Bible no less ardently than the Reformers did, but it views the *sola* as a formula for interpretive chaos. Rather than Scripture *alone*, it adheres to Scripture, Tradition, and the Magisterium. Tradition means the teachings handed down from the apostles; we might compare it with the political ideas handed down from the Framers. Scripture means that part of tradition that has been written down; we might compare it with the written Constitution. The Magisterium refers to the teaching authority of the Church as interpreter of Scripture and Tradition; we might compare it with whoever is authorized to interpret the norms of the American constitutional regime.

Let no one denigrate the sheer bulk of these norms. If we distinguish not only between written and unwritten rules, but also between justiciable and non-justiciable rules (rules that are enforceable and are not enforceable in courts of law), then we may think of constitutional "Tradition" as a plane divided into four quadrants, then Quadrant I contains rules that are both written and justiciable (for example, legislation establishing certain courts inferior to the Supreme Court). Quadrant II contains rules that are written, but non-justiciable (for example, the federal guarantee to each of the constituent states a republican form of government). Quadrant III contains rules that are neither written nor non-justiciable (for example, tacit understandings about "how to play the game" and "what just isn't done"). Finally, Quadrant IV contains rules that are unwritten, yet justiciable (for example tacit understandings about what counts as due process of law).[24] Yet our constitutional "Scripture"—the roughly 5,000-word document called the U.S. Constitution—encompasses only a small region intersecting Quadrants I and II.

But ultimately the comparison between political and theological interpretation fails. In the first place, the representatives of our constitutional regime do not agree about who does hold authority to define its norms.[25] In the second place, if some of these norms are unwritten, that does not make interpretation easier; it makes it harder. Finally, not even the strictest "strict constructionist" supposes that the Holy Spirit guides the country's interpretation of her Constitution in the same way that the Church believes He guides her interpretation of the faith. Some would even say that in jurisprudence, the gates of hell have already prevailed, at least against the Supreme Court.

Plainly we need more than a better method of interpreting the text. At the very least—and even here there are no divine guarantees—we need a better grasp on what the text presupposes. That brings us to our final question: why our grasp of natural law is so defective.

VI

One of the most intriguing answers is due to Orestes Brownson, a journalist and Catholic convert who probably had more influence on the nineteenth century's thinking than any other American Catholic.[26] According to Brownson, America's republican institutions are sustained by the spirited belief in natural law, natural justice, and natural reason that gave them birth. But the founding generation were "Protestants of the most rigid stamp,"[27] and Protestantism, he says, is hostile to this founding wisdom: It "asserts the total depravity of human nature, declares all acts done in a state of nature to be sin, and denies nature to make way for grace, and reason to make way for faith."[28]

Brownson embraces the paradox, calling the Founders "bravely inconsequent" and saying that they "builded better than they knew." They "founded the American order, not on their Protestantism, but on the natural law, natural justice, and natural equity as explained by the Church."[29] This paradox has produced mixed results. On the one hand, their institutions, grounded on natural law, encourage the Americans to resist despotism and to recognize the God-given impulse for responsible liberty. On the other hand, their Protestant belief in private judgment leads them to regard every sect as equally good. Having come to view religion with indifference, they fall back on mere nature without help from divine grace. For the same reason, though in practice rather than theory, they place politics above religion.[30]

There is, Brownson thinks, an upside. Having fallen back on mere nature, Americans have paradoxically acquired an interest in that nature; and having, despite their religious indifference, a dim inclination to think that there must be some religious truth, they have paradoxically made themselves receptive to the preaching of the truth not only about nature, but also about grace. Brownson thinks that the embrace of the Catholic faith will rescue Americans from the indifference and despondency left over from the implosion of Protestantism, and that it will complete the robust development of the American character. "[T]he Church of the Future . . . already exists. . . . Between it and our institutions there is no incompatibility, for Catholicity accepts, nay, asserts, the natural law on which our American order is founded."[31]

What are we to say about this conjecture? There is plenty to criticize as to detail. Brownson is certainly less than fair to Protestants; he underestimates the persistence and vitality of the varieties of Protestantism that emerged from the Second Great Awakening, and he does not seem to be aware that there is a long history of Protestant advocacy of natural law. Luther and Calvin themselves believed in it, however uneasily this belief may have coexisted with some of their other beliefs. Echoing Saint Paul, Martin Luther claimed that the Decalogue is "written in the hearts of all men."[32] John Calvin went even further. Although he is often held to believe that fallen man's knowledge of natural law is negligible or nonexistent, that is simply not what he says: "If the Gentiles have the righteousness of the law naturally engraven on their minds, we certainly cannot say that they are altogether blind as to the rule of life. Nothing, indeed is more common, than for man to be sufficiently instructed in a right course of conduct by natural law."[33] In various other works, Calvin finds a natural law basis for the ordinance of marriage, the condemnation of fornication, the esteem due to the capable, the honor due to the old, the prohibition of incest, the help given to the needy, the affection of fathers for their children, the duties of sons toward their fathers (and more generally of children toward their parents), and the even greater duties of husbands toward their wives.[34]

And yet Brownson was right to think the Founders "builded better than they knew." For a variety of reasons, the natural law theories that were known to them had already been flattened and thinned. The Enlightenment philosophers whom they followed thought that they believed in natural law and presented themselves as its adepts, but they were impatient with its metaphysics, ignored its tradition, discarded most of its equipment, and denied its deepest premises. Though they inspired revolutions, over time their theories came to seem more and more implausible, and the very idea of the natural law was eventually dismissed. As Brownson viewed it, the task facing the Americans of his day was to recover the classical natural law tradition without which these insights could be neither elucidated nor preserved. If Americans failed in the task, then not only would the very idea of the natural law be discredited, but their institutions, deprived of their necessary intellectual support, would suffer distortion and decline. This seems to be what is happening.

VII

If our institutions do depend on a grasp of the natural law, then what would this grasp include? By my count, as least four home truths would have to be recovered. After all that I have said about metaphysics, it might be held that I have led the reader on; that these four insights aren't metaphysics after all; that they are merely common sense. But good metaphysics always begins with common sense. All of its equipment is constructed for only one purpose: to illuminate what we already dimly know.

The first home truth is that conscience is a witness to truth. The fashionable theory of our day is that conscience is merely acquired, that we take in whatever we are taught. If this theory is true, then the witness of conscience is discredited. But is the theory true? In one sense, certainly conscience is acquired. The infant babbling at the breast does not know that he ought to be faithful to his spouse. How could he? He does not know that there are such things as "faithfulness" or "spouse." Yet what we do acquire is not just pumped in from outside. We may not be hard-wired with moral knowledge, but we are certainly hard-wired to recognize it. Even the way we teach children depends on deep structure that is present already: "Don't pull the dog's tail. How would you like it if your tail were pulled?"

The second home truth is the designedness of things in general, ourselves included. According to another fashionable theory, "man is the result of a purposeless and natural process that did not have us in mind."[35] If this were true, then conscience would have no authority, and neither would anything else about us. A prudent man might conclude that the best thing to do with his conscience would be to find a way, whether through drugs, surgery, or genetic engineering, to rip it out, because it gets in the way of so many of the things he wants to do. The same would go for anything else about human nature that we happened to find inconvenient. But this is mad.

The third home truth is the actual features of our design. Some of these features show up at the individual level, like the fact that we are persons and not just things, *whos* and not just *whats*. Some show up at the species level, like the complementarity of the sexes, the fact that each needs the other in order to be complete. Some show up at both levels, like the fact that man is a being who desires to know, and that seeking the truth is not just a solitary quest, but requires friendship, both personal and communal. If our institutions stifle any of our design features, we are headed for trouble. Freud spoke of the pathologies that arise from suppressing the "Id," but he didn't know the half of it. Try suppressing conscience, personhood, male-female differences, or the desire to know the truth. Horace wrote, "You may drive out nature with a pitchfork, yet it will always return."[36] The problem is that it may return angry.

That brings me to the fourth home truth, that actions have natural consequences. Even today, we are not so lunatic that we do not perceive any consequences to our actions at all. Our lunacy is of a different kind: We see them, but deny that they are natural. For us, a consequence is always adventitious—something to get around by means of cleverness. In matters personal, the talisman of this outlook is the birth-control pill; in matters political, the policy wonk; and in matters constitutional, the social engineer. We actually consider it more realistic—more base, perhaps, but more secure—to read virtue out of the picture, contriving "systems so perfect that no one has to be good."[37] True realism admits that getting as much mileage as possible from what little virtue there may be is a laudable aim. But trying to do without any virtue at all is an opium dream.

A republican constitution is a difficult and delicate enterprise, requiring a firm hold on the obvious. The most conspicuous mark of the present crisis is how hard it is to notice we are in one. Despite everything, we do notice, so let us hope.

10

The Illiberal Liberal Religion

I

Is it possible that in making a virtue of religious toleration, liberal society actually discourages religion? Let no one jump to conclusions. My answer is neither an unambiguous "yes" nor an unambiguous "no." The question is not to be carelessly dismissed, and it cannot be plainly answered until it is properly framed.

Its importance lies in its challenge to the public self-understanding of liberal society. Religious toleration is not supposed to eviscerate religion; had liberalism been sold to the Western nations on the promise that it would achieve peace among the faiths only by undermining faith, it would have been rejected. But the question is also paradoxical. According to the public relations of liberalism, allowing all of the varieties of faith to flourish together in peace is the very meaning of toleration. If toleration does gut faith, we seem to be left in a logically impossible position, for in that case universal forbearance wreaks universal suppression; the thing that accomplishes the intolerant result is toleration itself.

Paradoxes raise suspicions. Am I just riddle-mongering? On the contrary, the waning of religion seems to be just what some Enlightenment thinkers had in mind all along. Consider for example the hopes and expectations of Thomas Jefferson, who viewed faith as the essence of religion but as a rival to the authority of reason. If all religions were tolerated, he thought, then they would have no grounds on which to compete with each other but reason alone. Inevitably, he believed, rationalistic religions would drive all the others from the market. But by his assumptions, precisely to the degree that religions became rationalistic, they would cease to be religious.[1] Though unstated, the conclusion is plain enough: Religious toleration undermines religion, and that is a very good thing.

What are we to make of this? A coherent idea cannot be at war with itself. If toleration seems to be its own worst enemy, one must suspect that there is something wrong with the liberal understanding of toleration. Alas, there is. Promoters of the liberal project share three faulty premises concerning toleration. All three are tacit, and all three concern the natures of things. The first is that religion is essentially *intolerant;* the second, that liberalism is essentially *tolerant;* the third, that the practice of toleration is essentially neutral—that it accommodates all varieties of belief, suspending judgment as to their merits.

I deny all three premises. For clarity, though, we must slightly modify the form of the opening question. If the premises may be false, then to ask whether liberal society eviscerates religion by *making a virtue* of religious toleration is to give away the game. I propose instead the question whether it eviscerates religion by *enforcing a misunderstanding* of religious toleration. The answer, I think, is yes.

But we are getting ahead of ourselves. Why are the three liberal premises mistaken? Let us consider each one.

II

Is religion essentially opposed to toleration? Every religion proposes certain commitments as supreme and unconditional. These commitments serve as the criterion—the test and measuring rod—for all lesser commitments. For Christianity, the supreme and unconditional commitment is to the God whom Christians believe to have come among us as Jesus, the criterion of fidelity to whom is "faith working in love" (Galations 5:6). For Islam, the supreme and unconditional commitment is to the God whose prophet Muslims believe to be Mohammed, the criterion of fidelity to whom is "submission." Other religions have different supreme and unconditional commitments, with different criteria of fidelity. Normally these commitments cohere with their views of reality. The fact that both of the religions I have mentioned propose gods as their supreme and unconditional commitments should not be taken as implying that all religions propose gods, if one means by "gods" deities or supernatural powers. Unconditional commitments are also made in religions that deny the reality of deities or supernatural powers, such as Theravada Buddhism. One might even ask whether liberalism is in the relevant sense a religion—perhaps an incompletely specified religion—but we must set that question aside for the moment, and return to it later.

The supreme and unconditional character of religious commitment is precisely what gives rise to the liberal hunch that religion is essentially intolerant. God demands adherence, or at any rate, one's supreme and unconditional commitment demands adherence: Well then, failure to adhere to it is intolerable, is it not? Persecution follows, does it not? But it can easily be shown that this inference is a blunder. If we must obey God, then what really follows is that we must obey Him in the way that He desires and directs; if we must adhere to a supreme and unconditional commitment, then what really follows is that we must adhere to it in the manner that its nature requires. What then if God Himself, being who and what He is, detests persecution? Or what if faith, by its nature, is inimical to the forcing of belief? Then, obviously, we must *not* persecute. Persecution for the sake of God would in this case be rebellion against Him; persecution for the sake of faith would be a crime against it.

It may be said that by making such an argument I have already smuggled in a liberal conception of God, a post-Christian conception of the supreme and unconditional commitment. The Christian God does not detest persecution, does He? According to most liberal thinkers, no. The problem with this response is that it puts us in the absurd and unhistorical position of claiming that the Fathers of the Church were not Christians, for they thought God does detest persecution. Nor do the patristic writers argue merely that God detests the persecution *of Christians;* they say that persecution *as such* is repugnant to faith and to the will of God. This argument is elaborated by diverse early Christian figures, just the sort of thinkers whom liberals assume to have been impossible before liberalism. Lactantius speaks well for them all:

> There is no occasion for violence and injury, for religion cannot be imposed by force; the matter must be carried on by words rather than by blows, that the will may be affected. Let [the pagan persecutors] unsheath the weapon of their intellect; if their system is true, let it be asserted. We are prepared to hear, if they teach; while they are silent, we certainly pay no credit to them, as we do not yield to them even in their rage. Let them imitate us in setting forth the

system of the whole matter: for we do not entice, as they say; but we teach, we prove, we show. And thus no one is detained by us against his will, for he is unserviceable to God who is destitute of faith and devotedness; and yet no one departs from us, since the truth itself detains him. . . . Why then do [the persecutors] rage, so that while they wish to lessen their folly, they increase it? Torture and piety are widely different; nor is it possible for truth to be united with violence, or justice with cruelty. [2]

He also responds to the arguments of the persecutors themselves:

But, they say, the public rites of religion must be defended. Oh with what an honorable inclination the wretched men go astray! For they are aware that there is nothing among men more excellent than religion, and that this ought to be defended with the whole of our power; but as they are deceived in the matter of religion itself, so also are they in the manner of its defense. For religion is to be defended, not by putting to death, but by dying; not by cruelty, but by patient endurance; not by guilt, but by good faith: for the former belong to evils, but the latter to goods; and it is necessary for that which is good to have place in religion, and not that which is evil. For if you wish to defend religion by bloodshed, and by tortures, and by guilt, it will no longer be defended, but will be polluted and profaned. For nothing is so much a matter of free-will as religion; in which, if the mind of the worshipper is disinclined to it, religion is at once taken away, and ceases to exist. The right method therefore is, that you defend religion by patient endurance or by death; in which the preservation of the faith is both pleasing to God Himself, and adds authority to religion.

A single counterexample is sufficient to void the opinion that religion is *essentially* intolerant. For good measure, however, let us more briefly survey a few more of the Fathers.

III

We may begin our survey with Hilary of Poitiers and Isidore of Pelusium, whose remarks on toleration are concise and to the point:

God does not want unwilling worship, nor does He require a forced repentance. (Hilary, *To Constantius.*[3])
Since it seems not good forcibly to draw over to the faith those

who are gifted with a free will, employ at the proper time conviction and by your life enlighten those who are in darkness. (Isidore, *Epistles*, 3.363.[4])

Human salvation is procured not by force but by persuasion and gentleness. (Isidore, *Epistles*, 2.129[5])

Tertullian's assertion that ordered religious liberty is a matter of natural right will be especially startling to those who think that such ideas began with the far less stable subjective-right doctrine of John Locke:

It is the law of mankind and the natural right of each individual to worship what he thinks proper, nor does the religion of one man either harm or help another. But, it is not proper for religion to compel men to religion, which should be accepted of one's own accord, not by force, since sacrifices also are required of a willing mind. So, even if you compel us to sacrifice, you will render no service to your gods. They will not desire sacrifices from the unwilling unless they are quarrelsome—but a god is not quarrelsome. (*To Scapula*[6])

For see that you do not give a further ground for the charge of irreligion, by taking away religious liberty, and forbidding free choice of deity, so that I may no longer worship according to my inclination, but am compelled to worship against it. Not even a human being would care to have unwilling homage rendered him. . . . (*Apology*[7])

Certain Old Testament passages may seem to present a problem for the view we have been exploring. Exodus 19:12–13, for example, reads in part, "[W]hoever touches the mountain [of God] shall be put to death; no hand shall touch him, but he shall be stoned or shot; whether beast or man, he shall not live." What about such passages? Gregory Nazianzen is noteworthy for his emphasis on their spiritual meaning, applicable in the age of the Church, rather than their literal meaning, applicable under the special circumstances of the original covenant nation. To be "stoned," in the age of the Church, is precisely to suffer the refutation of one's arguments:

But if any is an evil and savage beast, and altogether incapable to taking in the subject matter of contemplation and theology, let him not hurtfully and malignantly lurk in his den among the woods, to catch hold of some dogma or saying by a sudden spring, and to tear sound doctrine to pieces by his misrepresentations, but let him stand yet afar off and withdraw from the Mount, or he shall be stoned and crushed, and shall perish miserably in his wickedness. *For to those who are like wild beasts true and sound dicourses are stones.* (*Second Theological Oration*, emphasis added[8])

John Chrysostom goes further, making clear that the doctrine he expresses is intended not only for personal but also for civic application:

Such is the character of our doctrine; what about yours? No one ever persecuted it, nor is it right for Christians to eradicate error by constraint and force, but to save humanity by persuasion and reason and gentleness. Hence no emperor of Christian persuasion enacted against you legislation such as was contrived against us by those who served demons. Just as a body given over to a long and wasting disease perishes of its own accord, without anyone injuring it, and gradually breaks down and is destroyed, so the error of Greek superstition, though it enjoyed so much tranquility and was never bothered by anyone, nevertheless was extinguished by itself and collapsed internally. Therefore, although this satanic farce has not been completely obliterated from the earth, what has already happened is able to convince you concerning its future. (*Discourse on Blessed Babylas and Against the Greeks,* Sec. 13[9])

Indeed, so far is Chrysostom from praising civic enforcement of the faith that he considers the Christianization of the imperial government a decidedly mixed blessing:

When a Christian ascends the imperial throne, far from being shored up by human honors, Christianity deteriorates. On the other hand, when rule is held by an impious man, who persecutes us in every way and subjects us to countless evils, then our cause acquires renown and becomes more brilliant, then is the time of valor and trophies, then is the opportunity to attain crowns, praises, and every distinction. (*Ibid.,* Sec. 42[10])

Athanasius argues that by reliance on coercion instead of persuasion, the proponents of the Arian heresy prove that they have neither arguments, confidence, nor divine authority for their beliefs:

Now if it was altogether unbecoming in any of the Bishops to change their opinions merely from fear of these things, yet it was much more so, and not the part of men who have confidence in what they believe, to force and compel the unwilling. In this manner it is that the Devil, when he has no truth on his side, attacks and breaks down the doors of them that admit him with axes and hammers. But our Savior is so gentle that he teaches thus, "If any man wills to come after Me, and, Whoever wills to be My disciple" [Matthew 16:24]; and coming to each He does not force them, but knocks at the door and says, "Open to Me, My sister, My spouse" [Song of Solomon 5:2]; and if they open to Him, He enters in, but if they delay and will not, He departs from them. For the truth is not preached with swords or with darts, nor by means of soldiers; but by persuasion and counsel. But what persuasion is there when the Emperor [Constantius] prevails? or what counsel is there, when he who withstands them receives at last banishment and death? Even David, although he was a king, and had his enemy in his power, prevented not the soldiers by an exercise of authority when they wished to kill his enemy, but, as the Scripture says, David persuaded his men by arguments, and suffered them not to rise up and put Saul to death. But [Constantius], being without arguments of reason, forces all men by his power, that it may be shown to all, that their wisdom is not according to God, but merely human, and that they who favor the Arian doctrines have indeed no king but Caesar; for by his means it is that these enemies of Christ accomplish whatsoever they wish to do. (*History of the Arians*, 4.33[11])

As in the previous passage, so in the following, Athanasius develops his doctrine not in spite of Holy Scripture but because of it:

The other heresies also, when the very Truth has refuted them on the clearest evidence, are wont to be silent, being simply confounded by their conviction. But this modern and accursed heresy, when it is overthrown by argument, when it is cast down and covered with shame by the very Truth, forthwith endeavors to reduce by violence and stripes and imprisonment those whom it has been unable to persuade by argument, thereby acknowledging itself to be any thing rather than godly. For it is the part of true godliness not to compel, but to persuade, as I said before. Thus our Lord Himself, not as employing force, but as offering to their free choice, has said to all, "If any man will follow after me"; and to His disciples, "Will you also go away?" [John 6:67.] (*History of the Arians*, 8.67[12])

Already these quotations supply an impressive armory, and there is yet more in its store.[13] Needless to say, Christians have not always practiced what the Fathers preached. But if the Fathers may be taken as normative

Christians, then the problem is not that the Christian faith is intolerant, but that later Christians have not always lived up to it. Episodes of persecution reflect not the essence of Christianity, but reversions to sub-Christian ways of understanding what it means to adhere to God—ways that fall lower than "faith working through love."

It is not always obvious which episodes in history really did constitute intolerance of the sort reprobated by the Fathers. Consider the case of Augustine of Hippo, reprobated by secularists for having changed his mind about the treatment of the fifth-century heresy of Donatism. According to the conventional account, although at first Augustine favored converting the Donatists through persuasion, he later agreed to coercion because persuasion was not working. The critical question, omitted by this account, is what it is that persuasion was not working *at*. Although, with Augustine's support, the profession of Donatism was indeed made a criminal offense in A.D. 412, what changed Augustine's mind was not that the Donatists refused to accept the Catholic faith, but that in the promotion of their own views they resorted to violence. As he explains in one of his letters,

> Catholics, and especially the bishops and clergy, have suffered many terrible hardships, which it would take too long to go through in detail, seeing that some of them had their eyes put out, and one bishop his hands and tongue cut off, while some were actually murdered. I say nothing of massacres of the most cruel description, and robberies of houses, committed in nocturnal burglaries, with the burning not only of private houses, but even of churches—some being found abandoned enough to cast the sacred books into the flames.[14]

The point here is not that Augustine made the correct prudential judgments about how to deal with such depredations, but that the question about the correctness of his judgments has been framed improperly. The question confronting him was not so much what to do about unbelief, as what to do about ideologically motivated violence. If a comparison with our own day is needed, we may say that from Augustine's point of view, the suppression of Donatism was less like, say, the suppression of Islam than like suppression of the Islamic terrorist organization al-Qaeda.[15]

Suppose all this is conceded. It might nonetheless be objected that the Christianity of the Fathers is only one kind of Christianity, or even that the Fathers were at odds among themselves, so that Lactantius et al. are unrepresentative. I consider these views false, but that is neither here nor there; so far as my general thesis is concerned, they may as well be true. For present purposes, no more is required than that "the Christianity of some of the Fathers" is, even so, a religion. If it is—and if it is tolerant— then it cannot reasonably be maintained that religion is *essentially* intolerant, for we have fortified the counterexample that was already in evidence at the end of the previous section.

Our reasoning so far vindicates the common sense of the matter. Some religions favor toleration, others do not; whether any particular religion favors toleration depends on its other convictions. The idea that only an eviscerated religion can practice toleration would therefore appear to be false. Rather, an eviscerated religion would be one which no longer knew *whether* or *even how* to practice toleration, just because it no longer knew what else, besides toleration, it believed. You cannot know whether God loves or loathes persecution unless you have some idea who He is.

IV

But doesn't the preceding refutation beg the question? For although I have denied that religion is essentially intolerant, I have not yet considered the meaning of toleration itself. If toleration means simply the habit of tolerating, one might even argue that my counterexample fails—that the Christianity of the Fathers is *not* tolerant. After all, the Fathers do not tolerate everything. True, they deny that force may be used to keep people from believing in Christ (or for that matter Jove), but they do not deny that force may be used to keep them from, say, committing rape or murder. They make distinctions. In fact, every religion makes distinctions. It tolerates some things; it refuses to tolerate others. Is it not then inadequate to say that some religions are tolerant while others are not? Should we not say that *none* of them are tolerant, because each refuses to tolerate *something*?

But surely this would be a futile way to understand toleration. By such a standard *no* societies or systems of belief would be tolerant—neither those that call themselves religious, nor those that deny being religious. A distinction that fails to distinguish has no point. If the term "toleration" is to be useful, it must denote a property that some societies or systems of belief possess, but that others do not.

Fortunately, the term is not really useless. No one actually does use it in the way just described; no one calls a society or belief system intolerant just because it refuses to countenance rape or murder. And why not? Evidently because we do *not* take toleration to mean merely tolerating. We take it to mean tolerating the things that ought to be tolerated. Rape and murder are not among them.

Taken by itself, the statement invites misunderstanding. If someone announces, "toleration is the habit of tolerating *just those things that ought to be tolerated*," it may sound as though he means "toleration is the habit of tolerating *just those things that are good and right*." But this was not what toleration meant to Lactantius; he did not think that believing in Jove was good and right, yet even so he execrated using violence to stop people from believing in Jove. Toleration does not mean the habit of tolerating just those good things that must be tolerated because they are good; it means the habit of tolerating even those bad things that ought to be tolerated despite being bad.

But how is one to know which bad things to tolerate? And why should one ever tolerate a bad thing anyway? The latter question unlocks the former. As it happens, suppression of given evils may itself bring about certain evils. Prohibition, for example, brought some good things, but also black markets, official corruption, and a lessening of respect for public authority. See, for example, Saint Thomas Aquinas:

> [A]s Augustine says, human law cannot punish or forbid all evil deeds: since while aiming at doing away with all evils, it would do away with many good things, and would hinder the advance of the common good, which is necessary for human intercourse.[16]

> [L]aws imposed on men should also be in keeping with their condition. . . . Now human law is framed for a number of human beings, the majority of whom are not perfect in virtue. Wherefore human laws do not forbid all vices, from which the virtuous abstain, but only the more grievous vices, from which it is possible for the majority to abstain; and chiefly those that are to the hurt of others, without the prohibition of which human society could not be maintained: thus human law prohibits murder, theft and such like.[17]

One must therefore consider not only the evil of the thing suppressed, but the evil brought about by suppression itself, which may sometimes be worse. The conclusion: Certain bad things (not all of them) are to be tolerated because the nature of the good itself requires doing so. It follows that in order to know which bad things to tolerate, one must know the true nature of the good.

By the way, the fact that I have mentioned consequences—what suppression "may itself bring about"—does not make the argument "consequentialist." Contrary to the consequentialist view, in which no act is intrinsically evil and the decision about whether to do it depends only on results, some things really are intrinsically evil—they are not to be done for the sake of anything whatsoever. The counsel "let us do evil so that good may result" is to be reprobated. Even so, it is only in the light of the good that we are able to see *which* things are not to be done even that good may result. Toleration, then, has not just a single but a dual function. It protects greater ends against lesser ends, but it also protects ends against mistaken means—means which intrinsically undermine the ends to which they are supposedly devoted.

And this is precisely the view of Lactantius and his colleagues. The pivot of his argument is the remark "as they are deceived in the matter of religion itself, so also are they in the manner of its defense." Just so: The proper manner of defending the good depends on the nature of the good. In Lactantius's discussion, the good in question is adherence to the truth about God. This good commends itself to the mind because it proceeds from the Author of the mind, but it must be accepted voluntarily, because love by its nature is voluntary and because it is precisely *as* love that it makes its claim on us; for God is love, and we are made in His image. It follows from the nature of such a good that the proper method of conversion is not force, but persuasion. Yet nothing about the nature of this good prohibits the use of force to suppress rape and murder. In fact, force should certainly be used for such purposes—in due measure and by public authority—because not all uses of force are intrinsically evil, and because protecting the life and dignity of innocents is a consideration of higher order than letting outlaws do as they will.

The foregoing line of reasoning aligns perfectly with what we know about the rest of the moral virtues. Just as the virtue of courage lies not in mere bravery but in being brave for the right reasons, in the right way, at the right time, about the right objects, and toward the right people, so also the virtue of toleration lies not in merely tolerating, but in tolerating for the right reasons, in the right way, at the right time, about the right objects, and toward the right people. Courage is to merely being brave as toleration is to merely putting up with things. Moreover, in both cases there is error on both sides of the mean. A man is not properly called courageous for dashing into a collapsing building to save the pencil sharpener; nor is he properly called tolerant for putting up with perjury or theft.

To be a good judge of "the right reasons, the right ways, the right times, the right objects, and the right people," one must recognize and judge well about the good. A person who is fundamentally in error about goods and evils may be brave about many things, but he will miss the mark of courage; he may put up with many things, but he will miss the mark of toleration.

I opened this section by conceding that there was something question-begging in my use of the Fathers to refute the idea that religion is essentially intolerant. We may now be more precise about what that begged question was. A given religion can be properly tolerant if, and only if, it has a sound understanding of goods and evils. For if it does not, it will spend much or even most of its time either tolerating what should not be tolerated, or failing to tolerate what should be. It may be indulgent, repressive, or sometimes the former and sometimes the latter, but the virtue of proper toleration will elude its grasp. So the begged question in my discussion of the Fathers was *whether they were right about the nature of the good in question.*

I think, of course, that they were. But how are we to know? Neutralism is utterly useless here. The only way to know which bad things should be tolerated is to judge rightly about goods and evils. There is no shortcut; one must be willing to do the work. For example, *does* the truth about God commend itself to the mind, and *must* the love of God be voluntary to be truly love? The practice of proper toleration is not a substitute for true beliefs about such matters, but presupposes them. It doesn't get us off the hook of moral judgment, but puts us on it.

Among other things, the inescapability of judgment forces us to rethink liberal views about the relation between faith and reason. Granted that the instrument of judgment is reason, even so the object of faith is one of the things that we must reason well about. This difficulty is not merely theoretical. Consider the highly practical problem of a child who is hemorrhaging to death. The parents, who are Jehovah's witnesses, refuse blood transfusion in the conviction that it violates the Old Testament prohibition of consuming blood. May the public health authorities administer a transfusion anyway?

Convinced that faith and reason have nothing to do with each other—that the notion that they might somehow cooperate is simply false—liberals try to settle the question of transfusion in ways that suspend religious judgment. For example, they may justify the decision to administer the transfusion by arguing, "This decision isn't about whether the parents' religion is right, but about saving the life of the child." Alas, the very judgment that the decision "is about" saving the child's this-worldly life presupposes that the parents are wrong, for they think it is about life eternal. In turn, liberals might justify the decision *not* to administer the transfusion by arguing, "This isn't about whether the parents' religion is right, but about religious liberty." Unfortunately, the argument is no more neutral here than in the former case. No one holds that *every* act is protected by the shield of religious liberty; we do not admit a religious liberty to bomb the subway. What the liberal is claiming here is that the decision of the parents to refuse blood transfusion for their child is one of the things protected by the shield. But to reach this conclusion, one must suppose either that the parents are right about the will of God, or that, even though they are wrong, it is not the case that God authorizes the public health authorities to override parental judgment on such a point. These suppositions are plainly religious. The fact that the latter is negative rather than affirmative—"it is not the case that"—does not render it agnostic; it *claims to know* that a certain view is contrary to the facts.

We see again that toleration is never neutral; commitment on a series of religious questions is necessary even to flesh out religious liberty. When liberals think that they are suspending religious judgment, they are merely hiding their commitments in the fog.

V

The second liberal premise was that liberalism is essentially tolerant, by nature favorable to toleration. I have spoken of liberalism, but the term is misleadingly used in various senses, so let us sort them out. First, it can mean a set of social and institutional arrangements, including government of laws rather than men, distinction of the roles of church and state, respect for the dignity of persons and of their forms of association, broad representation, protection of property and contracts within the limits of the common good, a vigorous civil society, and a shared understanding that actions not expressly forbidden by law are permitted by law.

Second, the term can mean any of various systems of belief by which such arrangements are in part or in whole defended. Theories that are liberal in this sense differ not only in the ways that they justify such arrangements, but also in the ways that they interpret them. Consequently, they may generate quite different practical implications. Consider the deep contrasts among Locke's *Letter on Toleration,* Mill's *On Liberty,* and the Second Vatican Council's Declaration on Religious Liberty, *Dignitatis Humanae.*

Third, the term can mean a particular family of such theoretical defenses. In recent times these theories have been more or less neutralist. Their name is legion, but the most conspicuous examples at the moment are the doctrine of John Rawls's *A Theory of Justice* (1971) and the doctrine of his later *Political Liberalism* (1993).[18] Remembering our criterion—"more or less neutralist"—the former approach qualifies for family membership by way of its "thin theory of the good," the latter by way of its notion of liberalism as "political, not metaphysical" and its aversion to "comprehensive doctrines." Liberals in this third sense tend to be historical imperialists; they read the older writers as foreshadowing themselves. A good example is the way the current majority of the U.S. Supreme Court reads its own religious neutralism back into the First Amendment religion clauses. As applied to most of the older writers, such readings seem curious and chimerical, though in a few cases they may be more or less accurate. It is crucial to notice that the criterion of liberalism in this third sense is intellectual, not terminological. Whether one uses the *term* "neutrality" is neither here nor there. The important thing is the persistence of a certain underlying idea—the idea of suspending judgment among truth claims, of refusing to weigh, consider, or even distinguish among them, of making fundamental choices while somehow remaining uncommitted as to the larger issues in which they are implicated. The language of "neutrality" may pass out of fashion; in various misleading ways, the languages of "rights," "choice," "liberty," "autonomy," "equality," "nonjudgment," or "nondiscrimination" may be used in its place, but a neutralist by any other name would smell the same.

Fourth and last, liberalism can mean any society that lives in the shadow of the third kind of liberalism, in the sense that its social and institutional arrangements are formed under it, governed by it, or subject to pressure from it. Arrangements that are liberal in this fourth sense may or may not claim historical descent from arrangements that are liberal in the first sense, and they may or may not actually resemble them. In the local case—the contemporary United States—they do claim descent, but the degree of resemblance is a matter of bitter dispute.

I have nothing to say against liberalism in the first sense, or in general, in the second; these senses are simply not my subject. My concern lies with liberalism in senses three and four: with neutralism, and with societies that live in its shadow. Hereafter, I employ the term "liberalism" only in this manner.

We return to the question whether liberalism (as so construed) is essentially tolerant. One way to take the query is to ask whether liberalism lives up to its own notion of toleration, that is, neutrality. The other is to ask whether it lives up to what I have called proper toleration, that is, tolerating just those bad things that ought to be tolerated. One notion requires suspension of judgment, the other requires its exercise.

Taking the question in the former way: Does liberalism live up to neutrality? The answer is no, because neutrality is logically impossible. It is not a bad idea; it fails to rise to the level of an idea. One must choose *what* to tolerate, *what* to accommodate, *what* to encourage—and choice, by its nature, is never neutral. To offer but a single example, consider the controversy over what is sometimes called "gay marriage." Advocates say that marriage law should be neutral, and surely traditional law violates this criterion. It discriminates; it officially endorses a vision of marriage as the family-forming institution, worthy of protection and definition because it nurtures the young and keeps the wheel of the generations turning. Yet opening the state's definition of marriage to homosexual liaisons would be no less discriminatory among visions of the good than keeping it closed. It would repudiate the traditional vision, endorsing in its place a different one. To reply, "Yes, but even so, men and women could still get married and have children" is to confess ignorance of how social institutions work. Laws, like ideas, have consequences. The effects of the change in marriage law would ripple outward, first through family law, then through families, as people realized that in the view of the custodians of public order, the vital thing to consider is no longer the interests of children, but the sexual convenience of grown-ups. There is no neutral way to define an institution. Whatever definition we adopt, someone's ox is gored.

As we have already seen in another context, liberals resist such conclusions, offering a variety of arguments to show that choice really can be neutral. Such arguments have in common that they all try to get something from nothing. If we really were neutral about goods and evils, then among other things we would be neutral between belief in the goodness or badness of toleration itself. That is worth thinking about. Another good exercise is pressing the liberal theorist about *why* neutrality is right. Almost always, he replies that neutrality promotes, or at least expresses, some substantive good such as peace, prosperity, mutual respect, or the chance to discover the truth. Is it not plain that to propose such a good as the reason for neutrality about good is not to be neutral about good? Some neutralists try to get out of the trap by suggesting that the reason for neutrality is to be found not in our judgments about good *per se*, but in the fallibility and uncertainty of such judgments. But this escape is blocked, for if we considered all such judgments *equally* fallible, then we would be uncertain about our judgment that toleration is a virtue. We may as well admit that when we practice toleration, we do so not because we are in doubt, but because of what, despite our doubts, we are not in doubt about.

Another neutralist gambit is to admit that we cannot be neutral about everything at once, but suggest that at least we can be neutral about some things—we can be neutral between A and B for the sake of X, even while conceding that we are not neutral about the goodness of X. For example, I might argue that the reason for religious toleration is securing the peace. "Plainly I am not neutral about the goodness of peace," I might say, "but can't I, for the sake of peace, be neutral among religions?" No. The fatal consideration is that not all religions agree in holding peace in high esteem. To propose toleration *for the sake* of peace is anything but neutral between religions that cherish peace and religions that despise it; it privileges the claims of religions that cherish it. To speak more generally, to say, "Toleration is right because of the goodness of X" implicitly treats religions that believe in X differently than religions that do not. This holds true even if X happens to be toleration—that is, if we say, "Toleration is good, not for the sake of something else, *but in itself.*"

Earlier in this section we saw that the question whether liberalism is essentially tolerant may be taken in two ways. We now have the answer to the first version of the question: Does liberalism live up to its own neutralist notion of toleration? The answer is no. No belief system could, because neutrality is incoherent; when liberalism claims to be neutral about goods and evils, it is not telling the truth.

If liberalism does not live up to its own notion of toleration, might it, despite itself, live up to proper toleration? (To put the question another way, if liberals are not really being neutral, then what are they doing?) Deciding what to tolerate logically necessitates moral judgment; like everyone else, liberals exercise judgment. The crux of the matter is that unlike everyone else, they exercise it without admitting that they are doing so—certainly not to others, perhaps not even to themselves. Could they, nevertheless, be judging well?

Let us first observe that this self-imposed blinkering of judgment is strange and contrary to nature. All men by nature desire to know, says Aristotle, and he is right. Considering that human beings are designed with a natural interest in how things stand in reality, the curious neutralist reluctance to face the question of the true and the good requires explanation. Strong countermotives must be at work, competing with the longing for truth. And so it is in fact. Certain such motives are merely confused; others are simply bad. To be sure, confused or bad motives add nothing to the demonstration that neutralism is in error, but they do help explain why neutralists so often argue irrationally. Let us consider them.

One example of a confused motive for avoiding the question of truth is fear that some people will resort to violence and persecution in its name. Because history exhibits so many religious wars and violations of conscience, many people leap to the naïve conclusion that religion *as such* is a cause of such things. It may not occur to them that some people may resort to violence and persecution in the cause of any good one can name, even peace. It may also not occur to them that if we want to know whether someone is prone to violence or persecution, the important question is not whether he ardently believes something, but exactly what it is that he ardently believes.

Another example of a good-but-confused motive for avoiding the truth question is the conviction that moral and religious truth is wholly opaque and inaccessible to reason. In a muddled way, people convinced of the futility of reason may consider themselves driven to neutralism just because there seems no rational alternative. Such views are widely shared not only among atheists, who disavow faith,[19] but among fideists, who misconceive it. In many cases, it is not so much that they reject the classical view—that the grace of rightly ordered faith imparts greater clarity, stability, penetration, and scope to the operation of reason—as that they have never heard of it.

A *bad* motive for avoidance is what might be called disguised dictatorship. A dictator is someone who can impose his own social, moral, or religious judgments on others without having to justify them. One might think that in a republic this would be impossible to do, but not so; it is easy. The simplest way to impose such judgments is simply to deny that they are judgments. After all, which of the following strategies is more common among abortion proponents? To say, "I support the private use of lethal violence against innocent and helpless human beings, and here are my reasons"? Or to say, "I'm not the one imposing a moral judgment, the other fellow is—I'm for choice"? The latter, of course. What such slogans accomplish is the power to legislate a particular morality in the name of not legislating morality. This is disguised dictatorship.

But I digress. The *point* at hand is that although, like the rest of us, liberals exercise moral judgment, they exercise it without admitting that they are doing so. The *question* at hand is whether they exercise it rightly. And the answer to the question is this: *Just because* they do not admit that they are doing so, they cannot do so rightly.

Why is this the case? Surprisingly, the answer sounds almost liberal: because, in a certain sense, they are "cramming their morality down our throats." I should not wish to be misunderstood here. It would be foolish to suggest that no one may ever "impose judgments" on anyone else. If that were the case, there could be no laws whatsoever. But we should certainly demand, as an element of proper toleration, that we have enough respect for the good of truth, and for the dignity of other persons, to tell our neighbors the true grounds of the judgments that we wish to impose upon them. Once they are out in the open, they can be respectfully debated. Neutralism makes all this impossible, by denying that it is exercising judgment. To put this another way, any theory of what should be tolerated presupposes standards about what is really good and evil. The problem with liberalism of the neutralist sort then is not that it has such standards, but rather that it has only ad hoc standards that it doesn't admit to having. According to the more ancient standards defended here, one of the things that proper toleration requires is transparency; but liberalism *cannot* be transparent about its standards, because it is theoretically committed to denying that it has any. Though it may make a great show of debate, its debates are factitious; they are shadowboxing. The substance is offstage: "Pay no attention to that man behind the curtain."

Concerning toleration, then, liberalism fails in two ways. In the first place, it fails to live up to its own neutralist notion of toleration. No belief system could do so; one cannot "live up" to an incoherency. In the second place, it fails to live up to what I have called proper toleration, which takes as its criterion objective good. This is because, through its programmatic commitment to concealing the real basis of its choices, it puts itself at odds *at least* with the goods of transparency, truth, and human dignity—whatever the real basis of its choices may be.

These are not contingent failures, which might be corrected; they are essential failures, which arise from the nature of the beast. Far from being essentially tolerant, liberalism is essentially estranged from the proper grounds of judgment as to what must be tolerated and what must not. We now consider the consequences.

VI

Liberalism of the neutralist sort undermines religion, not by making a virtue of religious toleration, but by enforcing a deadly misunderstanding of it. No comfort can be drawn from the fact that it is incoherent, for this does not prevent it from having powerful effects on popular culture. Three popular attitudes prevail in liberal society; we may call them the three-legged stool. The first leg of the stool is the belief that the meaning of toleration is tolerating: the more you tolerate, the more tolerant you are. The second leg is the idea that the best foundation for toleration is to avoid having strong convictions about good and evil: the more you doubt, the more tolerant you are. Third is the attitude that if you cannot help having strong convictions, then the next best foundation for toleration is refusing to express or act upon them: the more pusillanimous you are, the more tolerant you are.

Practiced consistently, each of these attitudes explodes itself. If you really believe that the meaning of toleration is tolerating, then you ought to tolerate even intolerance. If you really believe that the best foundation for toleration is to avoid having strong convictions about good and evil, then you should try not to harbor the strong conviction that intolerance is bad. If you really believe that when you do have strong convictions you should refuse to express or act upon them, then your belief in toleration should be a dead letter; it should be one of the things you are pusillanimous about.

If these attitudes cannot be practiced consistently, then how can they be said to be powerful? Because they *can* be practiced inconsistently—selectively—as weapons for demonizing opponents. For the liberal, too, has strong convictions; it is just that his convictions are not the ones that he thinks one should not act upon. Consistency would require that if it is intolerant to prohibit the abortion of babies in the womb, then it must also be intolerant to prohibit their protection; if it is intolerant to believe in the natural law, then it must also be intolerant to be offended by people who do; if it is intolerant to act on the conviction that marriage is a union of a man and a woman, then it is intolerant to act on the conviction that it isn't. By contrast, selective neutralism remembers itself only long enough to condemn the party who holds the traditional view.

Why can't the traditionalist simply point out the inconsistency? He can, and among honest and rational people this goes a long way. The problem is that the neutralist variety of liberalism conditions people to certain forms of irrationality. There are two kinds of error. Some errors are merely contrary to the facts, like believing that the moon is closer to the earth than it is; reasonable people can have a talk about that. Other errors are contrary to reason, like denying the principle of noncontradiction; you cannot have a reasonable talk about whether the principle is true with a person who refuses to admit that "true" and "not true" exclude each other. Neutralism is an error of the latter kind, not the former. It supposes that there can be judgment without judgment. Since no valid argument can produce such a conclusion, the neutralist is at best confused, and at worst driven by unworthy motives.

But can't two play at that game? Why can't the traditionalist be the man behind the curtain? I do not propose, I only ask. Why can't he be the one who inconsistently and selectively uses the language of neutrality for non-neutral ends? Well, it happens. Some slip into the habit without meaning to; others are more deliberate. There is even such a thing as a conservative neutralist, as witness the British philosopher Michael Oakeshott.[20]

However, neutralism cannot easily be employed by just anybody. One might think that it could be, because neutralism has no fixed shape of its own; you can't pin it down. That is the point, is it not? Considered more closely, however, neutralism turns out to be easier to pin down on one side than on the other—for although one cannot easily say what it is for, one can easily say a good deal about what it is against. What is the explanation of this paradox? As we saw earlier, neutralism is *essentially* at odds with the goods of transparency, truth, and human dignity, just through its programmatic commitment to concealing the real basis of its choices. It doesn't matter whether it intends to be at odds with them; it is. But these goods are central to the Western tradition. In conscience, no one who believes in them can be a neutralist. For all who believe in these goods—conspicuously, traditionalists—neutralism is therefore a betrayal.

There is another reason why the neutralism of, say, an Oakeshott could never be as influential as the neutralism of, say, a Rawls—a deeper reason. In an odd sort of way, neutralism is more easily adapted to revolt than to defense, to attacking traditions than to conserving them. After all, though neutralism is not averse to moral and religious judgments *as such*, it is intensely averse to judgments that can be *recognized* as judgments, to judgments that look like what they are. Now traditional judgments, just because they are traditional, are also widely known; they cannot be disguised. Even if their proponents try to spin them as neutral (as some inevitably do), few people are taken in. By contrast, moral and religious judgments that rebel against tradition can easily be dressed up as neutral—just because they are in rebellion. How can they *be* judgments, the question runs, if they *set us free* from judgments?

Such reasoning may be fatuous, but it is also well-nigh irresistible. Take sex. "Fidelity is good" is a judgment, and, being traditional, it looks like one. "Promiscuity is better" is also a judgment, but, being opposed to the traditional one, it doesn't look like one. Or take God. "God deserves obedience" is a judgment, and, being ancient, appears to be just what it is. "Nobody can even know whether there is any God" is just as much a judgment, and a much more demanding one, for one would have to know a great deal about God to know what one could *not* know about Him; but, being in rebellion against the ancient judgment, it appears to be something other than it is. Insofar as the liberal movement was born in revolt against the age-old judgments, it is easy to see why this quirk, this duality of appearance, is so convenient. Nonjudgmentalism is a kind of sucker punch.

The chief way in which liberalism undermines religion, then, is that both religious and antireligious citizens internalize the nonjudgmentalist attitude. For antireligious citizens, the psychological cost of doing so is low, because they do not recognize their own judgments as judgments. They blithely criticize the faithful for consciously doing what they themselves do constantly, necessarily, and unawares. Unfortunately, for religious citizens, who do recognize their judgments as judgments, the psychological cost of nonjudgmentalism is much higher. Their sentiments may line up with proper toleration; if they have an intellectual grasp of the matter, their minds may line up with it too. In this case religion may remain strong. Unfortunately, if they do *not* have an intellectual grasp of the matter, then living as they do in a liberal culture, they will probably confuse proper toleration with mere neutrality—they may mix up judging well with suspending judgment. In this case, of course they go on judging, but they feel guilty about doing so. Their judgments about nonjudgmentalism condemn their judgments about everything else. Liberals call them fanatics; they worry that maybe they are.

We are now in a position to return to a question broached earlier, but put off till now: whether liberalism itself is a religion. It is in the nature of religions, I suggested, to propose certain commitments as supreme and unconditional. Whatever proposes such commitments is (in the relevant sense) a religion. The sole fact that liberalism is against what it recognizes as religious need not prevent it from being a religion—provided that it does not perceive what it is.

Then is it one? The answer is "yes"—but with strange qualifications. If we do call liberalism a religion, we must call it an incompletely specified religion, one which tends to become more complete, but which at the same time fights this very tendency. In the days of its youth, it is characterized not so much by what it is for as by what it is against. As time goes on, it becomes more and more committed to its secret love, like a river flowing downward toward a quag. Not just by its initial revolutionary urge, but even more by its subsequent choice of neutralist apologetics, it gravitates toward a view that could never have seemed attractive without help—the view that the great moral evil is moral order, and the great moral good, moral chaos. Even now, for liberalism to admit this love would be suicidal. The game would be over. In order to hold power, it promotes and yet denies its own self-dissolving commitment; it drapes itself with words that our ancestors gave other meanings, words like "liberty," "equality," or "choice." Since it no longer has any principled way to decide *which* liberties, equalities, or choices to embrace, the drapery conceals less and less. But the less it hides, the more tightly liberals hold onto it, like girls in short skirts who keep trying to cover up their thighs.

That is the real significance of the *Casey* plurality's "right to define one's own concept of existence, of meaning, of the universe, and of the mystery of human life" (and my excuse for returning to it yet again). This proclamation is every bit as religious as the Nicene Creed, a veritable anthem of nonjudgmentalism—yet what a judgment! Have I blown up the Oklahoma federal building? According to my concept of existence, maybe those people weren't real. Have I tortured and raped the woman in the next-door apartment? According to my concept of meaning, maybe her suffering wasn't meaningful. Have I gathered some buddies and kicked a homeless man into a coma? According to my concept of the mystery of human life, maybe he didn't have a life. Don't forget, I have a *right* to my definitions. Everything is permitted, nothing denied, for I am the center of the universe that I define.

Such is the logic of liberalism, but the Supreme Court resists logic, as liberalism always must. It hoards its elixir carefully; the acid of nonjudgmentalism may be uncorked from time to time, but only to dissolve the judgments of someone else. This raises the interesting question of how long a universal solvent can be bottled up. Eventually it melts through the cruet.

VII

Suppose the conclusions of this essay are accepted. What follows? What is the alternative to liberalism? Liberals conjure up the bogeyman of a confessional state. In reality, a certain sort of confessional state is just what liberals want, and very nearly have: a *liberal* confessional state, which, being liberal, pretends to be something else.

We are not used to speaking of liberal states as confessional states, because expressions like "confessional state" were coined in the days before camouflage. The term, however, fits. Consider again John Rawls, for example, who proposes what is called "public reason" as a binding norm for all public discussion. One would expect such a term to mean freedom to reason in public; actually it means limits on the reasoning allowed there. In the state that Rawls desires, no one would be permitted to make arguments that depend on a "comprehensive" theory, or at any rate, no one would be permitted to base policies on them. A "comprehensive" theory turns out to mean any considered view of reality which admits that neutrality is impossible and therefore tries to supply more adequate reasons for doing things than liberals can supply. Prohibited from offering more adequate reasons, the citizens of the liberal state would be limited to incomplete and inadequate reasons. To be sure, they would be allowed to base their policy proposals on any views of reality that they might wish—but only so long as these views were not *recognized by liberals* as views of reality. In other words, citizens would be allowed to appeal only to those views that liberals—by virtue of refusing to admit that they were views—deemed acceptable.

But a state can be "confessional" in more than one sense. Just now we have been using the term for a state that circumscribes public reasoning within the limits of the official state religion of liberalism. Rather than allowing citizens to reason for their views of reality, it limits the views of reality from which they may reason about other things. Insofar as it regulates confessions, this is plainly one kind of confessional state, but let us consider others.

Classification might begin with the observation that the constitution and laws of every state are based on certain fundamental commitments. At the moment we are not considering what a given state's commitments happen to be (whether they are high, like the good of the commons, or base, like the greed of the high), but what it does about them. We might call a state that acknowledges and solemnizes its fundamental commitments a *declaratory* confessional state. Because it makes laws, and because laws direct behavior, a state that is *merely* declaratory certainly coerces citizens to act in certain ways, but it does not coerce them to believe in the commitments on which this coercion is based. Such a state may also be either *weakly* or *strongly* declaratory. If the former, then it identifies its fundamental commitments, but declines to identify the sources from which they are derived. If the latter, then it identifies both its fundamental commitments and their sources.[21]

A *coercive* confessional state is a different sort of fish. It does coerce the citizens to believe in a certain way—or at least to act as though they did. For example, it might punish belief in nonapproved religions, or prohibit proselytizing for them. If this state is liberal, it will probably be more subtle. For example, the U.S. Supreme Court declares that laws motivated by religious purposes are invalid,[22] but does not consider secularist ideologies as religious.[23] Thus a law motivated by, say, sheer dogmatic hedonism might be upheld, but a law motivated by belief in a providential God could never be. No doubt with an eye on the judiciary, self-described secular humanists have flipped on the question of their own religious identity. There have been three "humanist manifestos," issued in 1933, 1973, and 2000.[24] The first proclaimed that secular humanism is a religion; the second was silent about the matter; and the third *denied* that it is a religion, scolding those who say it is. Bosh; of course it is.[25] This is a good time to remember a point discussed earlier. Willingness to coerce people to accept one's beliefs is not a measure of how fervently one believes, but of *what* one believes. A religion convinced, with Hilary of Poitiers, that

God does not want unwilling worship, cannot coerce belief, at least not without betraying its commitments. A religion convinced, with Osama bin Laden, that Allah urges death to all infidels, certainly will. For its own reasons, so will liberalism.

One is tempted to think of the different kinds of confessional states as forming a progression: first nonconfessional states, then weakly declarative confessional states, then strongly declarative confessional states, and finally coercively declarative confessional states. Listing them this way is misleading, for a confessional state can be coercive without being declaratory. Such is the liberal state, for under the auspices of neutralism, it insists that it has nothing to declare. Rather than a progression, then, what we have is a two-by-two table:

Nonconfessional states: Confession neither declared nor coerced	Type A confessional states: Confession declared but not coerced
Type B confessional states: Confession coerced but not declared	Type C confessional states: Confession both declared and coerced

Though claiming to seek a nonconfessional state, in fact liberalism seeks a Type B confessional state, for it uses state power to discriminate among confessions while pretending to be neutral among them. At the time of its founding, the American republic was a Type A confessional state, for it frankly declared its commitments but declined to compel belief in them. The Constitution, our founding legal document, was only weakly declaratory, but the Declaration of Independence, our founding political document, was strongly so. Not only did it identify commitments to natural law and natural rights, but also it identified their source, for it said that "the laws of Nature" were the laws of "Nature's God." Though it did not go so far as to identify this God as the God of a particular historical religion, its view of Him was creational, monotheistic, moral, and providential,[26] and together these four qualities also entailed a high view of human worth. All of this aligned closely with biblical religion.

Of course the Founders knew that not all religions impute these four qualities to God. Most, in fact, do not. Yet within the bounds of public order, those which did not would also enjoy free exercise. There might arise points at which religions of the former and latter sorts would conceive public order differently. No doubt, in such a case the Founders would have hoped that the former would prevail. Even so, the latter would be free to press their case. Precisely this liberty to press their case would be denied *all* religions under liberal strictures like "public reason"—just because they are religions.

Since liberalism seeks a confessional state, the question: "Would the alternative to liberalism be a confessional state?" must be reframed. The right way to put it is like this: "Will we have the kind of confessional state that we have historically enjoyed, which is declaratory but not coercive—or will we have the kind that liberal thinkers now seek for us, which is coercive but not declaratory?" In this country, for the foreseeable future, the chief danger to religious toleration arises not from our avowed religions, but from the unavowed and illiberal religion of liberalism itself.

Afterword

The Architecture of Christian Citizenship:
Two Stories with Basement and Mezzanine

I

According to a certain old idea, there are two different levels of human goods, natural and supernatural. That picture is not bad for starters, but the architecture of good turns out to be more complicated. In particular, much goes on between and beneath the two stories. The interests of this book—some may say its obsessions—lie mostly there.

To gain perspective, we need to go still further back and change the metaphor. Let us speak not of a house, but of a city. Historically, thinkers of my communion have adopted all manner of attitudes toward temporal and political life. At the poles, some withdraw from the City of Man altogether, or try to. Others seek to dissolve themselves into it, like sugar into lemonade. How should they view the earthly city, a community whose laws regulate not only themselves, but others too?

Aristotle claims that the City of Man is a "perfect community," a comprehensive partnership in the good life, ordered by justice. In this view, citizenship is the status which gives a person the privilege of full participation in that partnership. For scholars of public life like me, this is the gold standard. I don't mean that Aristotle is right; I mean that the old pagan provided the backdrop for all subsequent discussion of the question. One may disagree with him, but one cannot ignore him and still be a participant in the conversation.

If one does disagree with him, there are two main ways to do it. One is the way of classical liberalism, according to which the city is not really a partnership in the good life but merely a sort of treaty among individuals not to interfere unnecessarily with the *private* pursuit of the good life. Although the city's authorities may use coercion to enforce the treaty, they have no other business. The problem with this view is that the most important human goods are not purely private; they all implicate other people. To be enjoyed at all, they require traditions and institutions; institutions require protection by law; and in order to provide this protection, lawgivers must make up their minds what these institutions are. Consider marriage. Laws that conceive it as monogamous put polygamy at a disadvantage; laws that conceive it as polygamous put monogamy at a disadvantage; and laws that attempt to be open to both monogamy and polygamy conceive it, in effect, as polygamous. There is no such thing as a neutral conception of marriage; there is no such thing as neutrality, period.

As I suggested in Chapter 10, this is one of the reasons why even our so-called liberals are not really liberal any more. The rights talk of some people has turned into a justifying script for gross interference with rights as understood by other people. The right to marry is weirdly offered as a reason for defining out of existence the very institution to which one is demanding a right of entrance. A spin is applied to religious liberty so that it turns into a reason for interfering with the liberty of parents to ensure the religious education of their children. The right to enjoy life is flipped into a right for others to euthanize me when they think my life is no longer sufficiently enjoyable. In all such conflicts, the real difference of opinion is not about whether rights should be protected, but about what rights there are. Behind this disagreement lies an even deeper one, about the nature of the good life that true rights exist to protect.

So in the end, the liberal challenge to the Aristotelian view is not very interesting, except as all mistakes are interesting. The more interesting challenge is the Christian one. Christians are participants not in one but in two partnerships in the good life; they are subjects of both the City of Man and the City of God. Our primary citizenship is in the latter. The phrasing is Augustine's, but the idea is apostolic. "We must obey God rather than men," Saint Peter declares; "our commonwealth is in heaven," Saint Paul announces; and the author of the letter to the Hebrews reminds us that we are "strangers and exiles on the earth" who desire "a better country, that is, a heavenly one."[1] Yet we have real duties to the earthly city. Paul instructs, "Let every person be subject to the governing authorities. For there is no authority except from God, and those that exist have been instituted by God." Peter agrees: "Be subject for the Lord's sake to every human institution, whether it be to the emperor as supreme, or to governors as sent by him to punish those who do wrong and to praise those who do right. . . . Honor all men. Love the brotherhood. Fear God. Honor the emperor."[2]

Where does this leave Aristotle? From the point of view that I have just described, the earthly city—the only city that he knew—is certainly important in some way, but it is not a comprehensive partnership in the good life after all, just because it fails to "comprehend" the goods of the heavenly city. Not only does it not provide for them, but it cannot provide for them. Within the limits of Aristotle's understanding, it cannot even be friendly and cooperative toward these goods, because the heavenly city is a rival. After all, earthly politics as conceived by Aristotle is the master art of the good, and the heavenly city challenges this mastery.

I do not claim that Aristotle is wholly without resources for understanding the problem. In the first place, he recognizes that because the human good is multifaceted, the earthly city is not a first-order partnership in the good life, but only a second-order partnership. I mean that it is a partnership of partnerships—an association of various smaller associations, like families, each of which has first-order responsibility for particular aspects of the comprehensive good. Aristotle knows that among these first-order partnerships are religious associations. His recognition that the city is only a second-order partnership is what distinguishes the Aristotelian view from totalitarianism; in this way he (partly) anticipated what later came to be known as the principle of subsidiarity.

Moreover, in a certain way, even Aristotle's philosophy concedes that the earthly city falls short of being a *fully* comprehensive partnership in goodness. In his view, the highest good attainable to man is the good that belongs to philosophy—the intelligible good, the apprehension by the intellect of the principles of being, of matters that transcend the merely human. However, the attainment of this high good seems to him to require detachment from preoccupation with the everyday aspects of the good life. For this reason, it resists the various blandishments of politics and business. The result is a permanent tension between the city, which seeks to co-opt the philosopher, and the philosopher, who seeks to understand the city without loving it.

But these resources are not enough. In the end, Aristotle simply does not have all of the equipment he needs to understand what the heavenly city is up to. To begin with, the Church is not like other first-order associations, because the first-order goods for which it cares transcend the first-order goods for which the other associations care. Take marriage, a covenant between a man and a woman, the first concern of which is children. The Church is also a covenant, but between man and God, the first concern of which is the grace of redemption. To be sure, marriage may be *taken up* into the economy of grace, and this is its greatest glory; Saint Paul rhapsodizes about it, regarding the relationship of husband to wife as a sacramental sign of the relationship of Christ to the Church.[3] But the Church, unlike marriage, is not a preexisting form of association taken up only afterward into the economy of grace. It is like them in being an association, and it certainly has prerequisites in the social nature of man; these facts are important. Even so, it is a *new kind* of association. Apart from grace it would not exist at all. It is not a natural institution, but a divine initiative that more and more penetrates mere nature.

Yes, but didn't we say that Aristotle makes room in the earthly city for religious associations? We did, but the Church is not simply a religious association in the Aristotelian sense. Aristotle thinks of religion strictly as a civic function—as a telling of stories that aren't really true and a performance of rituals that aren't really efficacious, but which do have the merit of taming the divine madness among inferior people who are incapable of philosophical contemplation, rendering that madness amenable to the city's purposes. By contrast, Christianity resists being tamed; it cannot be reduced either to a mere civic function on the one hand, or to a mere philosophy on the other. Indeed, it speaks of a God who judges the cities, who mocks the pretensions of those whom the world may call philosophers, and who, in the torrent of His inexorable love, desires for us goods we have never imagined, we may yet be unable to desire, and which, in our present state, we would tremble to conceive.

How should Christians respond to the deficiency of Aristotle's view of the City of Man, and to the corresponding flaws in his view of citizenship? According to a certain minority view (versions of which have influence on both the religious left and the religious right[4]), the facts of the matter demand of us a total rejection of the earthly city, an immediate submission to the unmediated rule of God. We are citizens of heaven only, not of earth.

But this minority view suffers several fatal defects of its own. In the first place, it is unrealistic about the way that God's rule works. The rule of God is never unmediated. By the divine condescension, it is a *participated* theonomy,[5] a rule in which we are expected to cooperate rationally and with understanding, an understanding that manifests the inbuilt order of the created human intellect and of the rest of the human faculties. God could have arranged matters so that we never had to deliberate about how the general principles of good should be applied to the day-to-day problems of the City of Man. Evidently, He did not. He could have just jerked us around. Instead, by creating us in His image, by illuminating our intellects, by making us deliberating beings, He drew us a little into His wisdom.

In the second place, the minority view is unrealistic about the Fall. In this world, men who make themselves mouthpieces of an unmediated rule of God always turn out to be the mouthpieces of other gods. They are imams, not prophets; the prophets work differently. Not even Moses, the great prophet of the Torah of God, was an exception to this rule. Rather he was its highest confirmation, for he was not instructed by God to bypass mediating institutions, but to build them up. What else is Torah but such an institution? God could have ruled without rules, by moment-to-moment commands. Instead he gave a law. Neither was it an arbitrary law, but a law that made sense to men already, because of the way that they were made. "And what great nation is there, that has statutes and ordinances so righteous as all this law which I set before you this day?"[6]

Finally, although the minority view appeals to revelation, it obstinately ignores the fact that revelation contradicts it. Earlier I quoted the words of Saint Paul: "Let every soul be subject unto the higher powers. For there is no power but of God: the powers that be are ordained of God" (Romans 13:1). If Paul is right, then paradoxically, God's rule *makes use* of earthly rule; the eternal wisdom is reflected even in the order of human government. The "higher powers" of earth are not evil in themselves, but fallen, like the rest of creation. What they need is not dishonor, but the right kind of honor: the kind that keeps open the door to their redemption.

The standard Christian correction of Aristotle is much different than the heterodox variant that I have just criticized. We are to picture the goods offered to man as a two-story house, of which the first floor is constituted by the goods of nature, the second by the goods of grace. Nature itself is a kind of grace—the "first" and irrevocable grace of creation, as

Russell Hittinger, following Lucidus, reminds us[7]—but here we are speaking of the grace of redemption, the grace that comes after. Notice that I call this view a correction of Aristotle, not a total repudiation of his thought. It is what Aristotle might have said had he known the gospel of Christ. Something of his view of the city survives the burning fire of the gospel, for although the earthly city's partnership in good no longer looks *absolutely* comprehensive after correction, it still appears *relatively* comprehensive—comprehensive relative to the natural goods, which, by God's providential government of all things, present to us a certain integrity of their own. Does this claim merely baptize Aristotle, or is it compatible with the Christian tradition? Of course it is compatible. As the psalmist says, God has made a covenant with day and night; things don't just "happen," they happen according to a certain order, an order of time, causality, and finality or purpose. Crops are sown, grow, and are reaped. The young are given in marriage and have young of their own, who in turn are given in marriage. Kings and magistrates enact laws and judge their nations. From this point of view, we can respect the authority of the earthly city over its own domain without allowing it to assert mastery over heaven's. At least in principle, we can square our duties to the heavenly and earthly cities after all. "Render to Caesar the things that are Caesar's, and to God the things that are God's."[8] Of course the things that are Caesar's are ultimately God's too, and Caesar had better remember it; nevertheless, it pleases God Himself to rule in this two-story way.

Or it seems to.

II

In a few moments I will suggest an amendment of the two-story view, but let me first turn to the other facet of the question: What may Christian citizens demand of the earthly city, a city whose laws regulate not only themselves, but nonbelievers too?

A good first approximation to the answer is that we *may* demand civic enforcement of the natural law, but that we *may not* demand civic enforcement of the divine law. The former is the law of God as reflected in the arrangements of creation, while the latter is the law of God as more perfectly reflected in the arrangements of salvation.

According to this first approximation, the reason we may demand civic enforcement of the natural law—of its foundational precepts, and with respect to the common good—is that they are already matters of both common knowledge and common concern.[9] As Saint Thomas Aquinas says, they are "the same for all, both as to rectitude and as to knowledge."[10] All natural law thinkers agree that this knowledge includes inviolable goods like marriage, formal norms like fairness, and everyday moral rules like "do not murder." At some level, everyone knows them. There is a difference between knowing something and acknowledging that you know it, but given knowledge, it isn't unreasonable to demand acknowledgement. Deep down, even the murderer knows the wrong of murder. One does not have to be a Christian to know it; these truths are common ground.

By contrast, the reason we may *not* demand civic enforcement of the divine law is that the knowledge of it depends on the gift of faith. Yes, it may be true that deep down even murderers know the wrong of murder, but can we honestly say that the proud know that the meek will inherit the earth? That the comfortable know that mourners will be comforted? And what about the rich—do they really know that the kingdom of heaven belongs to the poor? Probably not! Therefore, the divine law belongs to the regimen of the City of God, not the City of Man—of the church, not the state.

The reason this account is a good first approximation to the truth is that it honors the two-story architecture of the goods that are offered to man, and at the same time the limits of our natural faculties. Yet to praise it as an "approximation" is to imply that it is not the *whole* account of the matter. What is wrong with it?

The answer is that although the two-story picture I have sketched is correct as far as it goes, it is not quite complete. Taken by itself, it fails to do justice to the *dynamic* elements of good and privation of good—of how the good is affected by salvation history. It reflects neither the full impact of the Fall, nor the full action of God's mercy. There is no need to throw out the two-story building diagram. Beneath and between the two floors, however, we need to draw in a basement and a mezzanine.

Let us begin with the basement. Man after the Fall is injured even in the enjoyment of the natural goods. Yes, the natural law is common ground, but because our shoes are wet with the dew of our evasions, this common ground is slippery and hard to stand on. Consider again the institution of marriage. It is a natural institution, a procreative partnership, the right ordering of which is not just a mystery of faith (as even many Christians mistakenly think), but something ordinary human reason can perceive. Something like a true account of it—though perhaps only a thin one—is weakly acknowledged in all or almost all societies.

But does every society live up to it? Scarcely any does, and our own sophists roundly deny it. Denial takes extravagant and irrational forms. Take for example the argument that irresponsible sex "doesn't hurt anyone." Two generations into the sexual revolution, after a full harvest of poverty, disease, divorce, mistrust, fatherlessness, teen violence, and increasing violence against children, we should know better. One full generation after *Roe v. Wade*, we should know better still. In order to normalize incontinence, we had to normalize murder. In order to normalize one kind of murder we had to normalize others. We are now poised for yet another spin of the sexual revolution that started it all. Already, children have oral sex on school buses. Professional journals praise pedophilia, calling it "intergenerational intimacy." Legal scholars call for recognition of "polyamory." Under such circumstances, it may seem utopian to demand robust civic enforcement of the natural law. That is the ideal, but in practice, most of our energy will go toward robust amelioration of its most grievous and damaging violations. We are not even on the first story of the building. We are in the basement.

Not everyone is in the basement proper. Even now, most people are somewhere on the stairs between the basement and first floor. Perhaps we can persuade some of them to climb up to a higher stair. Perhaps we can persuade others not to slouch down to a lower one. The design of creation works in our favor, because the lower the stair, the more dismal it is, and the higher the stair, the more joyful. The malice of sin works against us, because although it is impossible to will anything whatsoever except because it seems good to us, it is all too easy to insist on enjoying the good in ways that violate its character and bring us to ruin. It is even possible to regard ruin itself as good. Not that it can be regarded as good in itself—but to regard it as a deserved self-punishment, or as a way to make other people sorry, or as an end to some present unhappiness, is well within the range of human possibility.

The fact that the house has a basement has long been recognized. Saint Thomas Aquinas comments that sin, though literally unnatural, becomes, in a way, *connatural* to the person who is habituated to it. He quotes Scripture: "They are glad when they have done evil, and rejoice in most wicked things."[11] Yet the basement has never been fully explored in the natural law tradition, and there are at least four reasons for this neglect. First, the mystery of sin is not wholly analyzable; second, looking too much into dark corners is perilous in itself; third, the development of theoretical immoralism has taken place with such rapidity in our time that most Christian thinkers have not fully caught up; and fourth, appropriate responses to public vice depend as much on prudence as they do on sound principles.

Concerning the need for such prudence, Saint Thomas Aquinas says that "laws imposed on men should also be in keeping with their condition," leading them to virtue gradually rather than all at once, because imperfect men whose favorite vices have been forbidden will despise sound precepts and "break out into yet greater evils." This is no small problem. Quoting again from Scripture, he says that trying to accomplish too much through law, too fast, is like violently blowing one's nose; it brings out blood.[12]

III

But enough of the basement. Let us turn to the mezzanine. We have seen how the earthly city, when left to itself, slips below even the level of natural good. This is not the whole story, because God never does leave it to itself. By His mercy, the natural goods are shot through not only with the grace of preservation, but with anticipations of the grace of redemption. At times these anticipations allow the earthly city to live, to a degree, above itself.

Even less is known about these bright mysteries than about the dark mystery of sin, but something is known about them, and they have their own relevance to Christian citizenship. A certain Godward longing is built into the human heart, a natural desire for something that nothing in nature can fulfill. As the author of Ecclesiastes writes, "He has put eternity into man's mind, yet so that he cannot find out what God has done from the beginning to the end." There is nothing surprising in the fact that the pagans whom Saint Paul addressed at Athens knew there is a God; so much could be inferred just from the Creation.[13] Much more surprising is the fact that they knew that none of their gods was *this* God. So sure of it were they that they had erected an altar to "an unknown god."[14]

An indistinct, inbuilt sense of awe clings to the mystery of human life itself. The revealed truth that man is the image of God seems unknown beyond the Bible's sphere of influence; nonetheless, some dim sense of the sacredness of human life is found everywhere, and this toehold in our intuitions is the very thing that makes the doctrine of the *imago Dei* so compelling once it is heard. Death doesn't merely frighten or disappoint us; it strikes us as sacrilege, as desecration. Why should it strike us so, unless it is really true that we are made in the image of our Maker?

There are a great many things of this sort, natural premonitions of supernature. Consider the sense of beauty. Dogs don't contemplate sunsets; bees are attracted only to the brightness of flowers, not to their loveliness, and only for the sake of the pollen. Natural selection cannot account for the power to be shaken by glory. Yet we have it; why? Or consider the impulse of wonder. There might, to be sure, be survival value in seeking to know how things happen, but we humans don't just try to find out their causes; we demand to know what they *mean*.

Such premonitions not only dispose us to seek something above nature, they move us to seek something *within* nature that is really a supernatural gift. Consider what I said earlier in the book about the purposes of marriage. Two are natural: the good of procreation, and the good of loving union within the procreative partnership. But to Christian marriage, a third is superadded by grace: the good of sacramental participation in the union of Christ with His Church. That is why, when grace entered the world, the dignity of marriage became immeasurably greater than it had ever been. Century by century, though slowly at first, this strange upheaval gathered force. Not even the very corruption of nature could defeat it; base metal was transmuted into gold. Knighthood passed from the world, but for a time even husbands thought of chivalry. Marriage became *romantic*.

Considering this history, one would think that the moment a culture lost its faith, the moment marriage lost its sacramental grace, the echoes of that grace would die too. Marriage would instantly revert to its former pagan state, if not sink beneath it. We no longer live in a culture of faith, and that is exactly what is happening. Even so, the reversion has not been *instant*. Three generations into the so-called death of God, two generations into the sexual revolution, one generation into pop-culture nihilism, even now, most people still want sex to mean something. They may no longer know how to recognize that meaning, but they are disappointed when they don't. The echoes of sacramental grace have not yet died away. Why haven't they? That is a mystery. In what medium are they reverberating? No medium but nature is left. Ah, but that is my point. Nature was made to anticipate grace; erotic nature is no exception. There was always something more to eros than mere sex could fully explain; even the pagans suspected that. Even in its shame, so powerfully does nature point beyond itself that the strings of the lute preserve a faint memory of lost music.

When the heavenly city bears faithful witness to the earthly, it prolongs and amplifies that reverberation, sharpening the longing for the music itself. This possibility transforms Christian citizenship. It turns out that keeping the earthly city out of the basement is not our only work after all. We may be able to uplift its imagination by singing the music of higher things than it has heard of.

Any man may apply for dual citizenship in the City of God, but the City of Man cannot simply turn itself into the City of God, and the echo of grace is not the same as grace itself. This side of death, moreover, "the line dividing good and evil" will continue to cut through the heart of every human being. Even so, the City of Man might come to reside in the mezzanine. Arguments might become accessible to some of its residents that were previously beyond their reach. They may come to hold loftier conceptions than they formerly held, even of the merely natural goods. They may begin to glimpse in them lights, shimmers, flashes, that they had never caught before. Eventually they may even see them *nearly* as they really are: not healed of all privation, not yet taken up into grace, but truly illuminated by it.

This book has been written in the hope that in a small way (all books are small ways) it may help to bring this about.

Appendix

A Note on Natural Law Theories

It would be too much to expect that this book would make for light summer entertainment, like the latest novelistic sizzler. On the other hand, one shouldn't have to be a specialist in order to read it. For general readers, as well as for students, let me offer just a few words about the meaning of natural law. Since the tradition encompasses more than one approach to the subject, it might be good to add a few more words about how these approaches are related.

Natural law theories share a conviction that the most basic truths of right and wrong—I don't say all the details—are not only right for everyone, but at some level known to everyone by the ordinary exercise of reason. They are an heirloom of the family of man. Of course, to say that they are at some level known to everyone is not to say that they are consciously admitted by everyone, and there's the rub. Any moral theory that fails to take account of excuses, rationalizations, and self-deceptions will badly misunderstand the human condition. Even so, natural law is real. To the mature mind, in fact, the thing itself is obvious, though the theories that thinkers develop about it may not be obvious at all.

Natural law is really natural because it is embedded into the structure of creation, especially *human* nature, which includes the structure of the human mind. Because it really obligates—in the ancient expression, it "binds in conscience"—it is also really law. The natural law tradition is closely associated with the jurisprudential view that any human "law" that is incompatible with these basics is not a law in the full sense of the word, but only an enacted fraud. As my choice of words suggests, most natural law thinkers have also maintained that the authority of the natural law is rooted in the goods of the created order, which are rooted in turn in the uncreated goodness of God. However, just because natural law really is natural, it provides a sort of common ground among those who are willing to recognize the obvious.

This classical view of natural law is a "thick" view, and it is also the mainstream of the tradition. It is not just a teaching of one faith, although, of course, my own faith is deeply committed to its exploration. Among those who seem, or claim, to be speaking of natural law, thinkers like Aristotle, Cicero, Aquinas, Suarez, Hittinger, and John Paul II are all more or less congenial to the thick view; thinkers like Hobbes and Pufendorf are more or less hostile to it; and thinkers like Grotius and Locke are ambivalent.

Although even non-classical theories of natural law agree about the content of the moral basics—there is no mystery about things like honoring your parents, not cheating, and not murdering—natural law thinkers explore them in different ways. As epitomized by Saint Thomas Aquinas, classical approaches weave together at least four different kinds of consideration (although the enumeration of them is mine, not his): (1) The deep structure of practical reason, classically called *synderesis*, which I have sometimes called deep conscience; (2) the sheer designedness of human beings, along with what follows from this fact; (3) the details of this design, along with the purposes and meanings embedded in it; and (4) the natural consequences of doing wrong, always recognizing that an intrinsically evil act would still be evil even if no evil consequences ensued.

Non-classical natural law theories emphasize one or two of these four considerations over the others. Perhaps the sharpest contemporary disagreement among natural law theorists concerns whether the second and third considerations (sometimes called natural teleology) are valid at all. In keeping with the classical tradition, I maintain that all four considerations are both valid and necessary, and that any which are pushed out the front door tend to creep in again through the back door. At the same time, I recognize that the alternative, "basic goods" approach, which tries to reconstruct natural law theory on the basis of the first consideration alone, has made several real contributions, and I have not hesitated to make use of them where they seem helpful. For example, I have incorporated elements of John Finnis's analysis of "one-flesh unity" into my own discussion of the natural teleology of sex, even though Finnis does not regard it as teleology.

Certain differences among natural law writers lie not so much in theory as in emphasis. For example, it was once customary to nourish those seeking to become lawyers on highly general Latin maxims of practical reason, such as *consuetudo est altera lex*, custom is another law; *delegatus non potest delegare*, a delegate cannot delegate; *nemo debet esse judex in propria causa*, no one can be judge in his own cause; and *nemo tenetur ad impossibile*, no one is required to do what is impossible. Such maxims were also quoted in judicial decisions. This approach is sometimes called "maxim jurisprudence," as though it were a particular kind of jurisprudence. Really it is not a kind of jurisprudence, but a kind of education and a kind of legal idiom—concededly friendly to natural law, but not a distinctive theory of natural law.

For classical thinkers, who recognize natural teleology, one of the most controversial and exciting recent events has been the suggestion of Karol Wojtyla, known to the world as John Paul II, that the constitution of the human person includes not only certain inbuilt purposes but also certain indwelling meanings. As this book makes clear, I accept the suggestion, although it raises fundamental questions which philosophy has hardly begun to address. One is the relation *between* the inbuilt purposes and the indwelling meanings. Another is the criteria for distinguishing between those meanings which really do dwell in our acts and powers, which we discover, not invent—and on the other hand the various other meanings with which we try to invest our acts and powers, sometimes harmoniously, sometimes not. The next generation of thinkers will have plenty of work to do.

Notes

Preface

1. I agree, of course, that a bad man may do a good thing for a bad motive—a theme alive in Christian political thought since Saint Augustine's discussion of "glorious vices" that imitate virtues in Book 5, Chapters 12–21, of *The City of God.* For a discussion of the possibilities and limits of the various strategies that philosophers and statesmen have developed for trying to get a better government than we deserve—for trying to uphold justice and the common good when there is not enough virtue to go around—see Chapter 4 of J. Budziszewski, *The Revenge of Conscience: Politics and the Fall of Man* (Dallas: Spence Publishing, 1999). A version of the chapter is available online as "Politics of Virtues, Government of Knaves." http://www.firstthings. com/article.php3?id_article=4465.

2. In this book, whenever the term "revelation" is used without qualification it refers to direct or special revelation, what God has revealed to the community of faith. By contrast, general revelation is what God has revealed to the entire human race through the grace of creation, including the resources of intellect and conscience. The euphemism of what the mind can know "by itself" or "without help" thus really refers to what the mind can know without *extra* help.

3. George W. Carey, "The Philadelphia Constitution: Dead or Alive?" in Mitchell S. Muncy, ed., *The End of Democracy?* Volume II (Dallas: Spence Publishing, 1999), 248.

4. Though often confused, neutrality and objectivity are not the same thing; in some respects they are diametrically opposed. Neutrality, if it were possible, would mean

having no commitments. By contrast, objectivity is shot through with commitments—to the reality of the world outside our minds, to the possibility of discovering truth about it, to the norms of discussion and inquiry which promote such discovery, and to the truth of whatever else must be true for these possibilities to be true.

5. G. E. M. Anscombe, "Modern Moral Philosophy," *Philosophy* 33:124 (1958): 1–19.

6. Another influential version of this argument was offered by Alasdair MacIntyre in *After Virtue: A Study in Moral Theory* (Notre Dame, IN: University of Notre Dame Press, 1981).

7. See for example Richard Dawkins, *The God Delusion* (Boston: Houghton Mifflin, 2006), Daniel C. Dennett, *Breaking the Spell: Religion as a Natural Phenomenon* (New York: Viking, 2006), Sam Harris, *The End of Faith: Religion, Terror, and the Future of Reason* (New York: W. W. Norton & Company, 2004), and Christopher Hitchens, *God Is Not Great: How Religion Poisons Everything* (New York: Twelve, 2007).

8. For a few diverse examples, see Robert M. Adams, *Finite and Infinite Goods* (Oxford: Oxford University Press, 1999), William A. Dembski, *The Design Inference* (Cambridge: Cambridge University Press, 1998), Alvin Plantinga, *Warrant and Christian Belief* (New York: Oxford University Press U.S.A., 2000), and Richard Swinburne, *Is There a God?* (Oxford: Oxford University Press, 1996.)

Chapter 1

1. Joseph Cardinal Ratzinger, in *God and the World: A Conversation with Peter Seewald* (San Francisco: Ignatius Press, 2002), 51–52, 161.

2. This expression, with its overtones of Luke 2:34, was also a favorite of John Paul II, and the title of one of his books.

3. Joseph Cardinal Ratzinger, *Introduction to Christianity* (New York: Herder and Herder, 1970), 19.

4. G. K. Chesterton, *Heretics* (New York: John Lane Co., 1905), 305 (Chapter 20).

5. Emphasis added.

6. I borrow this striking expression from Russell Hittinger, who is not responsible for the use (or abuse) to which I put it.

7. Thomas Hobbes, *Leviathan: Or, the Matter, Form, and Power of a Commonwealth Ecclesiastical and Civil*, Part I.

8. *Crazy*, lyrics and music by Willie Nelson (1961).

9. Such as it is, my answer to the puzzle rests on the fact that in order to reach a comparative appraisal of different goods, the mind turns now to the right, now to the left, suspending consideration of each good in turn in order to contemplate the other. This very power of suspending consideration allows us to prolong the suspension beyond the needs of deliberating, willfully short-circuiting the appraisal that is supposed to result. Like Scarlett O'Hara, we say, "I'll think about that tomorrow."

10. Thomas Aquinas, *Summa Theologica* (hereafter ST), I–II, Q. 90, Art. 4.

11. Thomas Aquinas, Commentary on Aristotle's *Physics*, II.

12. For brief discussion of the other kind of legal positivism, which regards law as a social convention, see Chapter 9, note 20, and text.

13. This statement is not intended as shorthand for an account in which nature is normative because God commands that it be normative (and could have commanded that it not be). Rather, the created good is normative because it is rooted in the uncreated Good who created it. For all we know, God could have created a different nature, but He could not have willed that we dishonor or disregard the structures of good contained in the nature that He did, in fact, create.

14. For quotations, see "Creation Reveals God and His Love, Says Benedict XVI: Comments on Psalm 135(136) at General Audience," Vatican City, November 9, 2005, Zenit (www.zenit.org/english/visualizza.phtml?sid=79681).

15. I adapt these two conditions from Robert C. Koons, *Realism Regained: An Exact Theory of Causation, Teleology, and the Mind* (Oxford: Oxford University Press, 2000). The change lies in the second of the two conditions: Rather than requiring that the fact that P brings about Q be part of the *efficient cause* of P, I say that it must be part of the *explanation* of P, leaving open the possibility that final cause is a fundamental and irreducible category of explanation, a possibility which Koons also now accepts (personal communication).

16. See Peter Geach on predicative vs. attributive adjectives in "Good and Evil," *Analysis* 17 (1956), 32-42. "Red" is predicative; it means the same thing no matter what kind of thing we are talking about. By contrast, "fast" is attributive; what it means depends on what kind of thing we are talkinga about. As Geach points out, "good" is attributive and depends on the function of the thing.

17. Paraphrasing George Gaylord Simpson, *The Meaning of Evolution*, rev. ed. (New Haven: Yale University Press, 1967), 344–45.

18. Thomas Aquinas, ST, I–II, Question 94, Article 4.

19. Acts 14:16–17, RSV.

20. Psalm 19:3–4, RSV. I return to these four witnesses in the conclusion of Chapter 9.

21. See Thomas Aquinas, ST, I, Q. 79, Art. 13.

22. Romans 1:20, RSV.

23. Unfortunately, the same cannot be said of *conscientia*, which is why we must distinguish between well-formed and poorly-formed consciences.

24. As well as many other things, in particular the *embodied* character of all *human* rational being.

25. Galatians 6:7.

26. John Locke, *First Treatise of Government*, secs. 53 and 86, and *Second Treatise of Government*, secs. 4–6 and 54; see J. Budziszewski, *Written on the Heart: The Case for Natural Law* (Downers Grove: Intervarsity Press, 1997), 104–105.

27. See Germain G. Grisez, *The Way of the Lord Jesus*, 3 vols. (Quincy, Illinois: Franciscan Press, 1983–1997); John Finnis, *Natural Law and Natural Rights* (Oxford: Oxford University Press, 1980); Germain G. Grisez, John Finnis, and Joseph M. Boyle, "Practical principles, moral truth, and ultimate ends", *American Journal of Jurisprudence* 32 (1987), 99–151.

28. In speaking of "depravity" I am not embracing Calvinism. The Calvinist mistake is to think that we are *totally* depraved. If we were totally depraved, then we could

not be depraved at all; bereft of all good, we would lack even the good of existence. Augustine's insight is more profound. Evil is a deficiency, a privation, a perversion; the only way to get a bad thing is to take something good and mar it. In order to be marred, it must be still there.

29. Eileen L. McDonagh, *Breaking the Abortion Deadlock: From Choice to Consent* (Oxford: Oxford University Press, 1996), 6, 11–12, 36, 176–77, 188.

30. Warren D. Hern, M.D., "Is Pregnancy Really Normal?" *Family Planning Perspectives* 3:1 (January 1971). The full text of the article is available at the website of his abortion facility, http://www.drhern.com.

31. Dante Alighieri, *Inferno*, Canto III. My quotation is from the translation of John Ciardi (New York: Penguin, 1954, 1982), 42, lines 16–18.

Chapter 2

1. Matthew 22:35–40.

2. John Rawls, *Political Liberalism* (New York: Columbia University Press, 1993).

3. J. Bottum, "The Pig-Man Cometh," *The Weekly Standard* (October 23, 2000, © News America Incorporated); paragraph divisions suppressed.

4. I am adapting the formal analysis of purpose developed by philosopher Robert C. Koons. See Chapter 1, note 15.

Chapter 3

1. Second Vatican Council, *Gaudium et Spes*, Sec. 22. Although I am quoting a Catholic source, much the same problem faces Protestants.

2. John Paul II, *Memory and Identity: Conversations at the Dawn of a Millennium* (New York: Rizzoli International Publications, 2005), 110–11; emphasis added.

3. *Gaudium et Spes*, ibid.

4. Ecclesiastes 3:11.

5. Encyclical letter *Spe Salvi* (2007), Sec. 2.

6. Deuteronomy 4:8, RSV.

7. Romans 2:14–15, RSV, changing plural verb to singular.

8. From time to time even those who do try to rely on reason "alone" recognize this fact. For discussion, see J. Budziszewski, "Second Thoughts of a Secularist" (review of Guenter Lewy, *Why America Needs Religion: Secular Modernity and its Discontents* (Grand Rapids,: Eerdmans, 1996)), *First Things* 72 (1997): 42–43.

9. If we follow Thomas Aquinas, ST I–II, Question 94, Article 2, we might say that marriage and sexuality pertain to the second of the three facets of human nature. Insofar as we are rational, animate beings, we may be regarded from the perspective of what we share (though in a distinctly human way) with all beings whatsoever, of what we share (though in a distinctly human way) just with all animals, or of what we share (though in a distinctly human way) just with all rational creatures. To the first facet belong those precepts that concern the inclination to self-preservation; to the second, those that concern the inclinations to such things as sexual intercourse and procreation; and

to the third, those that concern the inclination to such things as social communion in the knowledge and pursuit of the truth, especially the truth about God. Because revelation illuminates the whole of human nature, not merely facet two, we could equally well consider how it shines upon facets one and three.

10. *Summa Theologica* (henceforth ST) I–II, Question 100, Article 1.

11. ST I–II, Question 100, Article 11.

12. ST, I–II, Question 94, Article 4.

13. Julius Caesar, *The Gallic War,* 6.16.

14. Ibid., 6.23.

15. ST I–II, Question 91, Article 4.

16. Proverbs 8:22–23, 30–33, 35–36.

17. *Emunot Ve-De'ot* 3.2, quoted in David Novak, *The Image of the Non-Jew in Judaism: An Historical and Constructive Study of the Noahide Laws* (New York: Edwin Mellen, 1983), 224.

18. *Moreh Nebukhim* 3.48:598–599, quoted in Novak, 248.

19. *Abot* 3.2, quoted in Novak, 72.

20. Psalm 50:10, RSV.

21. ST, Question 91, Article 2: "Now among all others, the rational creature is subject to Divine providence in the most excellent way, in so far as it partakes of a share of providence, by being provident both for itself and for others. Wherefore it has a share of the Eternal Reason, whereby it has a natural inclination to its proper act and end: and this participation of the eternal law in the rational creature is called the natural law."

22. Psalm 8:4–5, RSV.

23. Malachi 2:15–16a, RSV.

24. When I speak about this subject before groups, I am sometimes asked by feminists, "If pleasure is not the purpose of the sexual powers, then what is the purpose of the clitoris?" The error of the question lies in tearing things out of their contexts. Actually the exercise of every voluntary power is pleasurable. The purpose of the organ in question is not pleasure *as such,* but to make the procreative act pleasurable, which is not the same thing.

25. Genesis 1:27, RSV.

26. ST, III, Question 16, Article 12, Reply to Objection 2.

27. Some translations of the Bible obscure this point by misrendering *sarkos,* "flesh," as "sinful nature."

28. Matthew 19:8, RSV, emphasis added.

29. Hints of the idea run through the Old Testament in the recurring motif of the covenant people as an unfaithful bride who will one day be restored. See Isaiah 54, Jeremiah 3:20, 31:32, Ezekiel 16, 23, Hosea 2; an allegorical interpretation is also traditionally given to the Song of Songs.

30. The preposition is *eis.* Paul's statement that he speaks *eis* Christ and the Church is variously translated—*in* Christ and the Church, *about* them, *of* them, *concerning* them, *regarding* them, *with application to* them, *in reference to* them.

31. See verse 31, where Paul quotes Genesis 2:24.

32. Perhaps we may think of it like this. Supernatural grace leaves a trace in nature,

much like the miracle by which Jesus turned water into wine. Wine is still water, but it is not mere water; it is water *plus.* Yet although wine exceeds the nature of water, it is not contrary to the nature of the water. And though water, by nature, could not have converted itself into wine, nevertheless water, by nature, is open to being converted into wine.

33. As Reginald Garrigou-Lagrange explains more precisely, human nature has been endowed by the Creator with "the obediential potency, by which the creature is capable of elevation to the supernatural order." This potentiality is "passive," a potentiality to receive the actuality in question, rather than "active," a potentiality to produce it. Reginald Garrigou-Lagrange, *Reality—A Synthesis of Thomist Thought* (St. Louis: Herder, 1950), Chapter 55, "The Twenty-Four Thomistic Theses." The text of the chapter is available on the internet at http://www.thesumma.info/reality/reality56.php. For the *locus classicus*, see Thomas Aquinas, ST, III, Q. 11, Art. 1.

34. Sociologist Mary Eberstadt holds that the common notion that religious people are more likely to marry and have children may have it backward; in fact, she writes, those who marry and have children are more likely to be religious. Richard John Neuhaus rightly remarks that her insight instantiates the saying that nature is a preparation for grace. Mary Eberstadt, "How the West Really Lost God," *Policy Review* 143 (June/July 2007), http://www.hoover.org/publications/policyreview/7827212.html; Richard John Neuhaus, "The Public Square," *First Things* 175 (August/September 2007): 71–72.

Chapter 4

1. Republic III, 395d: "Or have you not observed that imitations, if continued from youth far into life, settle down into habits and second nature in the body, the speech, and the thought?" Trans. Paul Shorey, in Edith Hamilton and Huntington Cairns, eds., *The Collected Dialogues of Plato* (Princeton, NJ: Princeton University Press, 1961), 640.

2. ST I, Q. 93, Art. 6, ad 3.

3. ST I, Q. 108, Art. 1, ad 3.

4. ST II–II, Q. 101, Art. 3.

5. ST I–II, Q. 26, Art. 1, cor., and ad 3. See also I–II, Q. 26, Art. 2 and I–II, Q. 31, Art. 8, ad 2. For a more subtle problem relating to the connatural inclinations of bodies, see Supp., Q. 84, Art. 3

6. ST I, Q. 55, Art. 2, cor., and ad 2; I, Q. 57, Art 1, ad 3; Q. 58, Art. 1; and I, Q. 94, Art 3, obj. 1. Compare Supp., Q. 96, Art. 9.

7. ST I, 86, Art. 4, ad 2; and I–II, Q. 31, Art. 7, obj. 1.

8. ST I–II, Q. 32, Art. 8; II–II, Q. 84, Art. 2; and II–II, Q. 96, Art. 1. See also II–II, Q. 23, Art. 2; II–II, Q. 175, Art. 1; II–II, Q. 180, Art. 5, ad 2, and Art. 8, obj. 3; II–II, Q. 183, Art. 1, ad 1; and III, Q. 11, Art. 3, ad 3, Art. 5, and Art. 6.

9. ST I, Q. 94, Art. 2, ad 2. Compare I–II, Q. 28, Art. 3; and I–II, Q. 31, Art. 7, obj. 1.

10. ST II–II, Q. 168, Art. 2.

11. ST, Q. 62, Art. 3.

12. ST II–II, Q. 142, Art. 3, ad 2; see also II–II, Q. 150, Art. 3, ad 1; II–II, Q. 151, Art. 2, ad 2; II–II, Q. 153, Art. 4; II–II, Q. 155, Art. 2, ad 5; and II–II, Q. 162, Art. 6, ad 1.

13. ST I–II, Q. 31, Art. 1, ad 1; I–II, Q. 32, Art. 1, sed contra and ad 3; I–II, Q. 32, Art. 6, obj. 2; and Supp., Q. 70, Art. 3.

14. ST I–II, Q. 32, Art. 2, ad 3; I–II, Q. 32, Art. 8, ad 3.

15. ST I–II, Q. 32, Art. 3, ad 3.

16. ST I–II, Q. 32, Art. 6, resp.; see also II–II, Q. 139, Art 1. For a more subtle question, involving pleasure in habitual acts of bravery, see II–II, Q. 123, Art. 8, obj. 1.

17. ST II–II, Q. 45, Art. 2; II–II, Q. 45, Art. 4; compare Supp., Q. 95, Art. 5.

18. *Synderesis,* or deep conscience, is the natural habit of knowing the first principles of practical reason; *conscientia,* or surface conscience, is the act of applying such knowledge to particular instances. Though surface conscience can err in particular cases, deep conscience is ineradicable and indefectible. See esp. ST I, Q. 79, Arts. 12 and 13; I–II, Q. 19, Arts. 5–6; I–II, Q. 94, Art. 1; I–II, Q. 96, Art. 4; II–II, Q. 47, Art. 6; and Supp., Q. 87, Arts. 1 and 2. See also *Disputed Questions on Truth,* Q. 16–17.

19. ST I–II, Q. 58, Art. 5; see also II–II, Q. 45, Art. 2; II–II, Q. 47, Art. 15.

20. ST I–II, Q. 70, Art. 4, ad 1.

21. Yves R. Simon, *The Tradition of Natural Law: A Philosopher's Reflections,* trans. Vukan Kuic, ed. Russell Hittinger (New York: Fordham University Press, 1965, 1992), 128.

22. That is, from an imbalance of humors.

23. ST I–II, Q. 31, Art. 7.

24. ST I–II, Q. 78, Art. 2. See also Q. 94, Art. 5, ad 1.

25. ST II–II, Q. 156, Art. 3.

26. ST II–II, Q. 34, Art. 5, ad 2.

27. Ibid., ad 3.

28. Emphasis added. The remark is contained in a letter from Sullivan to *Salon* magazine, defending his book *Love Undetectable* (New York: Alfred A. Knopf, 1998) against criticisms by other gay-rights advocates. The letter, published on December 15, 1999, is available at www.salon.com/letters/1999/12/15/sullivan/index.html. Sullivan's reputation as a "conservative" defender of sodomy arises from the argument of his earlier book *Virtually Normal* (New York: Alfred A. Knopf, 1995) that the extreme instability of homosexual relationships is due to social disapproval; if only homosexuals could "marry," they would become more faithful to each other. But in his final chapter, he lets the cat out of the bag. It turns out that he doesn't expect gay "marriage" to change homosexual behavior so much as to change heterosexual behavior. According to Sullivan, social approval of homosexual liaisons would be good for straight culture because it would teach straights to accept infidelity: As he puts it, there is "more likely to be a greater understanding of the need for extramarital outlets between two men than between a man and a woman."

29. See Gregory A. Freeman, "Bug Chasers: The Men Who Long to Be HIV+," *Rolling Stone* 915, February 6, 2003. The opening sentences of Freeman's article are illuminating: "Carlos nonchalantly asks whether his drink was made with whole or skim milk. He takes a moment to slurp on his grande caffe mocha in a crowded Starbucks, and

then he gets back to explaining how much he wants HIV, the virus that causes AIDS. His eyes light up as he says that the actual moment of transmission, the instant he gets HIV, will be 'the most erotic thing I can imagine.'" Freeman's article has been widely criticized in the homosexual media for reporting an alleged statement by Bob Cabaj, director of behavioral-health services for San Francisco County and past president of both the Gay and Lesbian Medical Association and the Association of Gay and Lesbian Psychiatrists, to the effect that 25 percent of newly infected homosexual men fall into the category of bug chasers—a statement that Cabaj now denies making. But although activists and public-health professionals debate how prevalent the phenomenon may be, few deny its reality.

30. I am grateful to Lance Simmons for provoking me to address this question.

31. ST I–II, Q. 27, ad 1. See also ST I, Q. 100, Art. 2, "nothing is desired or loved but under the aspect of good."

32. ST I–II, Q. 8, Art. 1.

33. I owe this last reminder to Michael Sherwin.

34. ST I–II, Q. 13, Art. 6.

35. ST I–II, Q. 6, Art. 4; see also I–II, Q. 13, Art. 6.

36. ST I–II, Q. 10, Art. 2.

37. More precisely, that we all have the "habit" of knowing; see note 18.

38. I discuss this aspect of the problem further in *What We Can't Not Know: A Guide* (Dallas: Spence Publishing, 2003), Chapter 7.

39. Here I draw help from Saint Augustine, who wrote ten chapters about how the vice of glory could simulate virtue; see *The City of God,* Book V, Chapters 12–21. For further discussion, see J. Budziszewski, "Politics of Virtues, Government of Knaves, *First Things* 44 (1994): 38–44, reprinted as *The Revenge of Conscience: Politics and the Fall of Man* (Dallas: Spence Publishing, 1999), Chapter 4.

40. ST I–II, Q. 62, Art. 1.

41. John Bunyan, *The Pilgrim's Progress,* ed. J. B. Wharey (Oxford: Oxford University Press, 1928; first published 1678).

42. This provides another reason not to separate Saint Thomas's philosophy from his theology. See esp. ST I–II, Q. 109, Art. 6., cor. and ad 2, Art. 8, and Art. 10; I–II, Q. 111, Art. 2; II–II, Q. 137, Art. 4.

43. Ephesians 4:22, 24, following the Greek, *kainon anthropon.*

44. ST, Q. 62, Art. 1, quoting 2 Peter 2:4; see also I–II, Q. 68, Art. 2; I–II, Q. 109, Art. 7, ad 3; and II–II, Q. 10, Art. 4, ad 2.

45. Romans 12:2, RSV.

Chapter 5

1. The idea of a divine authority behind the natural law is often misunderstood. Some people imagine that if God had ordained that we rape instead of marry, murder instead of cherish, hate Him instead of love Him, then such things would be right. The absurdity of this idea is considered an objection to God's authority. What the objection overlooks is that a being capable of commanding such things would not be

God. God is neither constrained by nor indifferent to the good; He *is* the good, the uncreated good in which the goodness of created being is grounded.

2. For discussion, see J. Budziszewski, *What We Can't Not Know* (Dallas: Spence Publishing, 2003), chapters 4–5.

3. William B. Provine, "Scientists, Face it! Science and Religion Are Incompatible," *The Scientist* (September 5, 1988), 10–11. See also William Provine, "Evolution and the Foundation of Ethics," *MBL Science* 3:1 (1988): 25–29, reprinted in Steven L. Goldman, *Science, Technology, and Social Progress* (Bethlehem, PA: Lehigh University Press, 1989).

4. Richard Dawkins, *River Out of Eden* (HarperCollins: New York, 1995), 132–33.

5. Edward O. Wilson, *On Human Nature* (Cambridge, MA: Harvard University Press, 1978), 176.

6. Michael Ruse and E. O. Wilson, "The Evolution of Ethics," *New Scientist* 108:1478 (October 17, 1985): 51–52.

7. Robert Wright, *The Moral Animal: The New Science of Evolutionary Psychology* (New York: Random House, 1994), 212.

8. Richard Dawkins, *The Selfish Gene* (Oxford: Oxford University Press, 1989), 3.

9. Edward O. Wilson, "What Is Nature Worth? There's a Powerful Economic Argument for Preserving Our Living Natural Environment," *San Francisco Chronicle*, Opinion, 5 May 2002, adapted from Edward O. Wilson, *The Future of Life* (New York: Knopf, 2002).

10. Neither does imagination, but we may leave this question for another time.

11. There is a danger of circularity: Unless they had already developed the tendency to mutual aid, why *would* they have lived in family groups?

12. William D. Hamilton, "The Evolution of Altruistic Behavior," *American Naturalist* 97 (1963): 354–56, and "The Genetical Evolution of Social Behavior," *Journal of Theoretical Biology* 7 (1964): 1–52.

13. Wright, 313–14.

14. Ibid., 211–12.

15. Ibid., 332–33.

16. Pleasure is not the good as such, but the enjoyment of something else that is good (such as friendship). Moreover, although one can hardly be considered happy if he experiences no pleasure, one can experience a great deal of pleasure and yet not be happy. Mortimer Adler puts it nicely in the introductory chapter to *The Time of Our Lives* (New York: Fordham University Press, 1970): Happiness is having a good life; pleasure is just having a good time.

17. For more detailed discussion of the significance of these four steps for utilitarianism, see J. Budziszewski, *Written on the Heart: The Case for Natural Law* (Downers Grove, IL: Intervarsity, 1997), chapters 10–12.

18. See his essay "Utilitarianism."

19. Larry Arnhart, *Darwinian Natural Right: The Biological Ethics of Human Nature* (Albany, NY: State University of New York Press, 1998). See also Larry Arnhart, Michael J. Behe, and William A. Dembski, "Conservatives, Darwin and Design: An Exchange," *First Things* 107 (November 2000): 23–31; and Larry Arnhart, "Evolution

and Ethics: E. O. Wilson Has More in Common With Thomas Aquinas Than He Realizes," *Books & Culture* 5:6 (November/December 1999): 36.

20. See note 17. John Hare pursues a similar line of reasoning in his paper "Evolutionary Naturalism and the Reduction of the Ethical Demand," presented at "The Nature of Nature: An Interdisciplinary Conference on the Role of Naturalism in Science," Baylor University, April 2000. Because Hare's purpose in writing is somewhat different than mine, he does not comment on the confusion between naturalism and natural law, nor does he draw out the parallel between Arnhart's theory and utilitarianism. However, he vigorously criticizes Arnhart for what he calls the "double identity" of equating the good with the desirable and the desirable with what in fact is desired (my steps two and three), and our arguments coincide at several points.

21. C. S. Lewis, *The Pilgrim's Regress,* preface to 3rd ed., xii. Lewis's analysis of the experience is illuminating.

22. Arnhart, 1998, Chapter 2.

23. ST, I–II, Q. 94, Art. 4.

24. Ibid., Q. 100.

25. Not all of these basic and exceptionless precepts are "first" principles; for example, each of the precepts of the Decalogue is derived either from the still more basic precept to love God or the still more basic precept to love one's neighbor. Nevertheless, each of the precepts of the Decalogue binds without exception.

26. Arnhart, 1998, Chapter. 6, section on "The Moral Complementarity of Male and Female Norms."

27. Ibid.

28. Ibid., introductory section.

29. Blaise Pascal, *Meditations,* Aphorism 277.

Chapter 6

1. *Merriam-Webster Dictionary of Law* (Springfield, MA: Merriam-Webster, 1996) and Daniel Oran, *Oran's Dictionary of the Law,* 3rd ed. (Albany, NY: West Legal Studies, 2000).

2. The Constitution uses the word "person" in Art. I, Sec. 2, Cl. 2 (qualifications for representatives); Art. I, Sec. 3, Cl. 3 (qualifications for senators); Art I, Sec. 2, Cl. 3 (apportionment); Art I, Sec. 9, Cl. 1 (migration and importation); Art. I, Sec. 9, Cl. 8 (emolument); Art. II, Sec. 1, Cl. 2, and the superseded Cl. 3 (provisions for electors); Art. II, Sec. 1, Cl. 5 (qualifications for president); Art. IV, Sec. 2, Cl. 2 (provisions for extradition); Art IV, Sec. 2, Cl. 3 (superseded fugitive slave clause); and in the Fifth Amendment; Twelfth Amendment; Fourteenth Amendment, Secs. 2, 3; and Twenty-Second Amendment. According to the Court's holding in *Roe v. Wade,* 410 U.S. 113 (1973), Sec. IX, *none* of these references "indicates, with any assurance, that it has any possible pre-natal application"; this despite the fact that unborn human beings clearly fall within the definition of human beings or "natural" persons. Here the Court assumes that a word in the Constitution should not be assumed to mean what it means elsewhere in law or common usage *unless the Constitution says that it does.* It

would seem more rational to assume that it means what it means elsewhere in law or common usage *unless the Constitution says that it does not.* That is also the traditional practice: "But when the word 'Persons' is spoken of in legislative acts, natural persons will be intended, unless something appear in the context to show that it applies to artificial persons." John Bouvier, *Bouvier's Law Dictionary,* 6th ed. (Philadelphia: Childs and Peterson, 1856), definition of "person."

3. The *Dictionary of Philosophical Names and Terms,* an online reference tool maintained by philosopher Garth Kemerling at http://www.philosophypages.com/dy.

4. J. A. Simpson and E. S. C. Weiner, eds., *Oxford English Dictionary,* 2nd ed. (Oxford: Clarendon Press, 1989).

5. An instance of use in this sense: "The persons of the drama belong rather to the world of imagination than of reality," [1895] (*OED*).

6. An instance of use in this sense: "They sustain the persons of intercessors," 1560 (*OED*), spelling modernized.

7. An instance of use in this sense: "The bequest did not spring from a parent or person standing in the place of a parent," [1827] (*OED*).

8. So are the Persons of the Trinity. Indeed, it seems likely that the idea of the human person descended from the idea of the divine Persons, rather than the other way around. "So God created man in his own image, in the image of God he created him; male and female he created them" (Genesis 1:27, RSV); "[w]hoever sheds the blood of man, by man shall his blood be shed; for God made man in his own image" (Genesis 9:6, RSV).

9. An instance of use in this sense: "The Fifth Commandment is that thou slay no man. . . . And also here is forbidden unrightwise hurting of any person" 1340 (*OED*); spelling modernized, capitals added. Obviously, the passage regards "person," and "man" in the sense of human being, as interchangeable.

10. This type of metonymy is also called *synecdoche,* but by other writers *metonymy* and *synecdoche* are used as synonyms.

11. This section and the next include paragraphs adapted from my essay "Playing God," *National Review* 49:13 (July 14, 1997), 45–47 (a review of Bert Keizer, *Dancing with Mr. D: Notes on Life and Death* (New York: Nan A. Talese/Doubleday, 1996); Herbert Hendin, M.D., *Seduced by Death: Doctors, Patients, and the Dutch Cure* (New York: W. W. Norton, 1997); Wesley J. Smith, *Forced Exit: The Slippery Slope from Assisted Suicide to Legalized Murder* (New York: Times/Random House, 1997); M. Scott Peck, M.D., *Denial of the Soul: Spiritual and Medical Perspectives on Euthanasia and Mortality* (New York: Harmony/Crown/Random House, 1997); and George E Delury, *But What If She Wants to Die? A Husband's Diary* (New York: Birch Lane/ Carol, 1997)).

12. Killing is traditionally taken in the sense of murdering; thus a good paraphrase is "thou shalt not deliberately take innocent life." In this case the question becomes "*whose* innocent life are we not to take deliberately?"

13. I am not here considering spiritual persons, such as angelic persons and the Persons of the Trinity (although they are fourth-rung persons too), simply because they do not belong to our subject. Notwithstanding the "God is dead" movement of the

1960s, the contemporary controversy is not about whether we may kill God, but about whether we may kill the very young, the very old, and the very weak—human beings whose rational capacities are suspended, impaired, or undeveloped.

14. Mary Ann Warren, "On the Moral and Legal Status of Abortion," *The Monist* 57:4 (1973). For the view that Warren is challenging, see John Noonan, "Deciding Who Is Human," *Natural Law Forum* 13 (1968).

15. The communicative criterion may seem puzzling. For an illustration of how it might fit into a broader theory, see Bruce A. Ackerman, *Social Justice in the Liberal State* (New Haven, CT: Yale University, 1980). According to the author, we are not at liberty to kill someone who has the capacity to engage in "neutral dialogue," because he can argue back; by contrast, abortion is all right because the victim is not capable of dialogue. Analogously, we may intervene in families that bring children to adulthood without the capacity for "liberal citizenship"; but if they never reach adulthood in the first place, the problem apparently disappears.

16. Mary Ann Warren, "Postscript on Infanticide," in Sue Dwyer and Joel Feinberg, eds., *The Problem of Abortion*, 3rd ed. (Belmont, CA: Wadsworth Publishing, 1997), 71–74.

17. For citation, see note 11, above.

18. Ibid.

19. I am using Augustine's division of the Decalogue, used by Catholics and some Protestants, which places the prohibition of murder fifth on the list. To forestall confusion it should be mentioned that another division, found in Origen, Philo, and Josephus, and more familiar to other Protestants, splits the first commandment into two but combines the last two commandments into one, placing the prohibition of murder sixth.

20. "I've always been a classic liberal. I believe in freedom in its broadest sense. . . . I frankly think the soul or personage comes in when the fetus is accepted by the mother." Abortionist James McMahon, as quoted in "The Abortions of Last Resort: The Question of Ending Pregnancy in Its Later Stages May Be the Most Anguishing of the Entire Abortion Debate," *Los Angeles Times Magazine*, February 7, 1990, cited in Faith Abbott, "The Abortionist as Craftsman," reprinted in *Human Life Review* 22:1 (Winter 1996): 24.

Chapter 7

1. 1 Peter 2:13–14, RSV.

2. Romans 13:3–5, RSV.

3. Genesis 9:5–6, RSV.

4. Psalms 119:156, RSV.

5. G. Kirkbeck Hill, ed., *Boswell's Life of Johnson: Including Boswell's Journal of a Tour to the Hebrides and Johnson's Diary of a Journey into North Wales* (New York: Macmillan, 1887), Vol. III, 167.

6. Avery Cardinal Dulles, "Catholicism & Capital Punishment," *First Things* 112 (April 2001): 30–35. I am using the unpaginated web edition at http://www.firstth-

ings.com/article.php3?id_article=2175. All quotations from Cardinal Dulles are from this article.

7. Oliver Wendell Holmes, "Natural Law," 62 *Harvard Law Review* 40 (1918): 40. Though Holmes writes that he is reporting a sentiment of his youth, he reports it in order to approve it.

8. Romans 2:14–15, RSV.

9. John 10:35, RSV.

Chapter 8

1. Specification of these principles means more than simply declaring what would have been right even in the absence of enacted law. The enacted law in our country specifies that in the interests of safety, automobiles on two-way roads must drive on the right, not the left. Even apart from law, citizens would have been obligated to drive safely. However, they would not have been obligated to drive on a particular side.

2. I employ the uncapitalized word "constitution" to refer to a kind of political order, but the capitalized word "Constitution" to refer to the document titled *The Constitution of the United States.*

3. Though not on all subjects. For example, his resolute opposition to standing armies seems even more naïve now than at the time he wrote.

4. Speech at Virginia Ratifying Convention, June 9, 1788, reprinted in Herbert J. Storing, ed., *The Complete Anti-Federalist*, 5.16.14.

5. Later, President Abraham Lincoln disagreed; see Chapter 9, note 24.

6. Brutus [pseud.], *New York L.J.* 1787–1788, Letter No. 11.

7. Brutus's argument is first sketched in Letter No. 11, and elaborated in Letter No. 15 (ibid.) It may fruitfully be contrasted with the argument of Alexander Hamilton in *The Federalist*, No. 78.

8. William Blackstone, *Commentaries on the Laws of England*, Introduction, Section 2, quoting Hugo Grotius, *On the Law of War and Peace*, Book 2, Chapter 16, Section 26, which in turn relies on Aristotle, probably either *Nicomachean Ethics*, Book 5, Chapter 10, or *Rhetoric*, Book 1, Chapter 13.

9. Article I, Section 8, final clause.

10. The first is discussed in Letter No. 11, the second in Letter No. 12.

11. In one medieval case, a plaintiff wroth about having been sold watered wine alleged that the merchant had watered it "with force and arms and against the peace of the King, to wit with swords and bows and arrows." *Rattlesdene v. Gruneston*, Y. B. Pasch. 10 Edw. II pl. 37, 140–41 (1317) (Selden Soc.), cited in Eben Moglen, "Legal Fictions and Common Law Legal Theory: Some Historical Reflections," 10 *Tel-Aviv University Studies in Law* 35 (1991).

12. 405 U.S. 727 (1972), at 742.

13. "The wholesome 'neutrality' of which this Court's cases speak thus stems from a recognition of the teachings of history that powerful sects or groups might bring about a fusion of governmental and religious functions or a concert or dependency of one upon the other to the end that official support of the State or Federal Government would be

placed behind the tenets of one or of all orthodoxies. This the Establishment Clause prohibits. And a further reason for neutrality is found in the Free Exercise Clause, which recognizes the value of religious training, teaching and observance and, more particularly, the right of every person to freely choose his own course with reference thereto, free of any compulsion from the state. This the Free Exercise Clause guarantees." *Abington School District v. Schempp*, 374 U.S. 203 (1963), at 221. Notice that the Constitution is inconsistently said to require neutrality between religion and irreligion because it recognizes the value of religion but not irreligion.

14. "[T]he amendment seems inexplicable by anything but animus toward the class that it affects"; later in the same case, "laws of the kind now before us raise the inevitable inference that the disadvantage imposed is born of animosity toward the class of persons affected." *Romer v. Evans*, 517 U.S. 620 (1996), at 631, 633.

15. "With respect to the State's important and legitimate interest in potential life, the 'compelling' point is at viability. This is so because the fetus then presumably has the capability of meaningful life outside the mother's womb." *Roe v. Wade*, 410 U.S. 113 (1973), at 163.

16. "[F]or two decades of economic and social developments, people have organized intimate relationships and made choices that define their views of themselves and their places in society, in reliance on the availability of abortion in the event that contraception should fail. The ability of women to participate equally in the economic and social life of the Nation has been facilitated by their ability to control their reproductive lives." *Planned Parenthood v. Casey*, 505 U.S. 833 (1992), at 856.

17. "Our cases do not at their farthest reach support the proposition that a stance of conscientious opposition relieves an objector from any colliding duty fixed by a democratic government." *Gillette v. United States*, 401 U.S. 437 (1971), at 461 (emphasis added). Notice that the statement of the Court goes far beyond the mere assertion of a tacit condition that religious conduct be confined within the bounds of good order.

18. "The essence of all that has been said and written on the subject is that only those interests of the highest order and those not otherwise served can overbalance legitimate claims to the free exercise of religion." *Wisconsin v. Yoder*, 406 U.S. 205 (1972), at 215. According to this alleged interpretation of the First Amendment, even "legitimate" claims to the free exercise of religion can be overbalanced by "interests," not defined in the Constitution, which judges consider sufficiently important. Yet the First Amendment states that "Congress shall make *no* law . . . prohibiting the free exercise of religion" (emphasis added). Again notice that the statement of the Court goes far beyond the mere assertion of a tacit condition that religious conduct lie within the bounds of good order.

19. 381 US 479 (1965).

20. *Planned Parenthood v. Casey*, cited in note 16.

21. I intend the expression literally; see Chapter 10.

22. *Casey*, at 851.

23. Emphasis added.

Chapter 9

1. "It is a correct position that 'true knowledge is knowledge by causes.' And causes again are not improperly distributed into four kinds; the material, the formal, the efficient, and the final. But of these the final cause rather corrupts than advances the sciences, except such as have to do with human action." Francis Bacon, *Novum Organum* ("The New Organon") 2.2. On the Continent, a similar claim is made later in the writings of Giambattista Vico.

2. "For the handling of final causes, mixed with the rest in physical inquiries, hath intercepted the severe and diligent inquiry of all real and physical causes, and given men the occasion to stay upon these satisfactory and specious causes, to the great arrest and prejudice of further discovery." Francis Bacon, *De Augmentis Scientiarum* ("The Advancement of Learning") 2.7.7.

3. Gary Jeffrey Jacobsohn, "Constitutional Identity." *Review of Politics* 68 (2006), 361–97.

4. As in the previous chapter, I employ the uncapitalized word "constitution" to refer to a kind of political order, but the capitalized word "Constitution" to refer to the document titled *The Constitution of the United States*.

5. I say "something like" rather than "exactly like" because although political communities are natural in the sense that it is natural for human beings to form them, they cannot be natural in the way that, for example, our bodies are natural, and their entelechies are derivative and imperfect. The reason lies in the relation between whole and part. An arm is a part of the physical body and nothing more. By contrast, a person is more than a part of the body politic, and cannot simply be absorbed into its process. Even so, the body politic *has* a process, and we can speak of it—carefully and analogically—as entelechial.

6. *The Federalist*, J. and A. McLean edition, 1789.

7. As we saw in Chapter 8, critics of the improved science of politics, like Brutus, complained that its adepts had not peered into the entelechy of a republic as deeply as they thought.

8. *The Federalist*, No. 9.

9. "The aim of every political constitution is, or ought to be, first to obtain for rulers men who possess most wisdom to discern, and most virtue to pursue, the common good of the society; and in the next place, to take the most effectual precautions for keeping them virtuous whilst they continue to hold their public trust."

10. "Is there no virtue among us? If there be not, we are in a wretched situation. No theoretical checks, no form of government, can render us secure. To suppose that any form of government will secure liberty or happiness without any virtue in the people is a chimerical idea. If there be sufficient virtue and intelligence in the community, it will be exercised in the selection of these men; so that we do not depend on their virtue, or put confidence in our rulers, but in the people who are to choose them." Quoted in Herbert J. Storing, *What the Anti-Federalists Were FOR* (Chicago: University of Chicago Press, 1981), 72.)

11. His specific example is liberty of the press. "Who can give it any definition which

would not leave the utmost latitude for evasion? I hold it to be impracticable; and from this I infer that its security, whatever fine declarations may be inserted in any constitution respecting it, must altogether depend on public opinion, and on the general spirit of the people and of the government."

12. As Madison remarks in *The Federalist*, No. 49, "The reason of man, like man himself, is timid and cautious when left alone, and acquires firmness and confidence in proportion to the number with which it is associated. When the examples which fortify opinion are ancient as well as numerous, they are known to have a double effect. In a nation of philosophers, this consideration ought to be disregarded. A reverence for the laws would be sufficiently inculcated by the voice of an enlightened reason. But a nation of philosophers is as little to be expected as the philosophical race of kings wished for by Plato. And in every other nation, the most rational government will not find it a superfluous advantage to have the prejudices of the community on its side."

13. "When in the Course of human Events, it becomes necessary for one People to dissolve the Political Bands which have connected them with another, and to assume among the Powers of the Earth, the separate and equal Station to which the Laws of Nature and of Nature's God entitle them, a decent Respect to the Opinions of Mankind requires that they should declare the causes which impel them to the Separation.

"We hold these Truths to be self-evident, that all Men are created equal, that they are endowed by their Creator with certain unalienable Rights, that among these are Life, Liberty and the Pursuit of Happiness. . . . "

14. "[M]en being all the workmanship of one omnipotent, and infinitely wise maker; all the servants of one sovereign master, sent into the world by his order, and about his business; they are his property, whose workmanship they are, made to last during his, not one another's pleasure: and being furnished with like faculties, sharing all in one community of nature, there cannot be supposed any such subordination among us, that may authorize us to destroy one another, as if we were made for one another's uses, as the inferior ranks of creatures are for ours." John Locke, *Second Treatise of Government*, 2.6. Other parts of the argument probably come from Jean-Jacques Burlamaqui, *Principles of Natural and Political Law*.

15. I am here distinguishing between original intent and original understanding. See Antonin Scalia, *A Matter of Interpretation: Federal Courts and the Law* (Princeton, NJ: Princeton University Press, 1997). Justice Scalia is a proponent of the latter.

16. 3 U.S. 386 (Dall.) (1798).

17. "I cannot subscribe to the omnipotence of a State Legislature, or that it is absolute and without control; although its authority should not be expressly restrained by the Constitution, or fundamental law, of the State. . . . A few instances will suffice to explain what I mean. A law that punished a citizen for an innocent action, or, in other words, for an act, which, when done, was in violation of no existing law; a law that destroys, or impairs, the lawful private contracts of citizens; a law that makes a man a Judge in his own cause; or a law that takes property from A. and gives it to B: It is against all reason and justice, for a people to entrust a Legislature with such powers;

and, therefore, it cannot be presumed that they have done it. The genius, the nature, and the spirit, of our State Governments, amount to a prohibition of such acts of legislation; and the general principles of law and reason forbid them. The Legislature may enjoin, permit, forbid, and punish; they may declare new crimes; and establish rules of conduct for all its citizens in future cases; they may command what is right, and prohibit what is wrong; but they cannot change innocence into guilt; or punish innocence as a crime; or violate the right of an antecedent lawful private contract; or the right of private property. To maintain that our Federal, or State, Legislature possesses such powers, if they had not been expressly restrained; would, in my opinion, be a political heresy, altogether inadmissible in our free republican governments."

18. "It is true, that some speculative jurists have held, that a legislative act against natural justice must, in itself, be void; but I cannot think that, under such a government, any Court of Justice would possess a power to declare it so. Sir William Blackstone, having put the strong case of an act of Parliament, which should authorize a man to try his own cause, explicitly adds, that even in that case, 'there is no court that has power to defeat the intent of the Legislature, when couched in such evident and express words, as leave no doubt whether it was the intent of the Legislature, or no.'

" . . . If . . . the Legislature of the Union, or the Legislature of any member of the Union, shall pass a law, within the general scope of their constitutional power, the Court cannot pronounce it to be void, merely because it is, in their judgment, contrary to the principles of natural justice. The ideas of natural justice are regulated by no fixed standard: the ablest and the purest men have differed upon the subject; and all that the Court could properly say, in such an event, would be, that the Legislature (possessed of an equal right of opinion) had passed an act which, in the opinion of the judges, was inconsistent with the abstract principles of natural justice."

19. Russell Hittinger, *The First Grace: Rediscovering the Natural Law in a Post-Christian World* (Wilmington, Delaware: ISI Books, 2003), Chapter 4.

20. I owe my favorite illustration of this point to Professor Charles E. Rice. The 1932 *Restatement of Contracts* declares in Section 90, "A promise which the promisor should reasonably expect to induce action or forbearance of a definite and substantial character on the part of the promisee and which does induce such action or forbearance is binding if injustice can be avoided only by enforcement of the promise." Put more simply, if breaking a contract would cause injustice, then the contract is binding. Now the *Restatement of Contracts* does not explain what "injustice" means; it expects readers to know that already. Suppose language like this were contained in statutory law. In such a case courts would be forced to work out *some* of the remote implications of the natural law, even if they were utterly deferential and their sole motive were to figure out what the statute meant by "injustice." One may say that in such a case the legislature has legislated badly; it should not have used undefined terms like "injustice"; it should have defined them. But of course, nominal definition merely replaces a single word with a string of words, and the words in the string need definition too.

21. Legal positivism also suffers from other problems that we have no space to discuss. For example, the version holding that law is the command of the sovereign suf-

fers from circularity, because law is necessary to establish who the sovereign is; and the version holding that law is a social convention suffers from infinite regress, for it deems a law valid if it is conventionally accepted as valid. By substitution of terms, we find that it is valid if it is conventionally accepted as conventionally *accepted as* conventionally *accepted as....*

22. *Planned Parenthood v. Casey*, 505 U.S. 833 (1992).

23. Levinson argues the case for this view in detail in *Constitutional Faith* (Princeton, NJ: Princeton University Press, 1988).

24. Rules sometimes migrate among quadrants, as when formerly unwritten rules are formally enacted by the legislature, or declared in opinions of the courts, and thereby become written rules.

25. Thus during the era of Justice Taney, the Supreme Court claimed interpretive supremacy, but President Lincoln disagreed. In the President's view, each branch of government has equal authority to interpret the Constitution, but only in the context of its own work. The Court was within its authority in ordering the runaway slave Dred Scott to be sent home, but not in decreeing that all slaves be regarded as chattels; although its authority to adjudicate cases gave it power to impose upon Congress and President the outcome they had decided for the case, it gave no power whatsoever to impose upon them the principles according to which they had decided it. In the Catholic Church the situation is different, for the Pope and the College of Bishops agree about who has authority to proclaim doctrines of faith and morals as requiring "the adherence of faith." See the apostolic constitution *Lumen Gentium*, as well as the *Catechism of the Catholic Church*, sections 888–892.

26. For a representative expression of his views, see Orestes A. Brownson, "Mission of America," *Brownson's Quarterly Review*, Vol. 4, Ser. 3, No. 4 (October, 1856), 409–444.

27. Ibid., 428.

28. Ibid., 429.

29. Ibid., 428.

30. "Protestantism, basing itself on a subjective fact, private judgment or private illumination,—very good, and never to be spoken lightly of in its sphere,—has no bond of union, and necessarily, where not restrained by outward civil force, splits into innumerable sects and parties. If the civil order has, as with us, for its fundamental principle, its incompetency in spirituals, and is bound to recognize all these sects and parties as standing on a footing of perfect equality before the law, the people in all their political action are obliged to treat them all as alike sacred, and seeing no objective ground of preference among them, very naturally come to regard one sect as good as another, and then to treat them all with indifference, perhaps with a superb indifference, to fall back on the reason and nature on which their political and social order is founded, and practically to place their politics above their religion." Ibid., 429.

31. Ibid., 430.

32. Martin Luther, *Large Catechism*, 2.3. I am using the translation found at the Christian Classics Ethereal Library at www.ccel.org.

33. *Institutes of the Christian Religion*, 2.2.20. I am using the translation found at the Christian Classics Ethereal Library, ibid.

34. For supporting quotations, see J. Budziszewski, *Natural Law for Lawyers* (Scottsdale, Arizona: Blackstone Fellowship, 2006), Chapter 7.

35. George Gaylord Simpson, *The Meaning of Evolution*, rev. ed. (New Haven: Yale University Press, 1967), 344–45.

36. Horace, *Epistles*, I, x, 24.

37. T. S. Eliot, choruses to "The Rock," 1934.

Chapter 10

1. This view of the tendency of religious rationalism is shared by Orestes Brownson; see Chapter 9.

2. Lactantius, *Divine Institutes,* Book 5, Chapter 20, trans. William Fletcher, in Alexander Roberts and James Donaldson, eds., *Ante-Nicene Fathers,* Volume 7, orig. 1886, online edition copyright (c) 2005 by K. Knight, available at http://www.newadvent. org/fathers/07015.htm . I have modernized and Americanized the spelling in all quotations.

3. Hilary of Poitiers, "To Constantius," quoted in Lord Acton, "Political Thoughts on the Church," at 24. The edition is J. Rufus Fears, ed., *Essays in Religion, Politics, and Morality,* which is volume III of *Selected Writings of Lord Acton* (Indianapolis: Liberty Classics, 1988). I have more briefly discussed some of the following quotations in *True Tolerance* (New Brunswick, NJ: Transaction, 1992, 1999) and "On Having Done With It: The Death of Modernist Tolerance," in Gerson Moreno-Riano, *Tolerance in the 21st Century: Prospects and Challenges* (Lantham, MD: Lexington Books, 2006).

4. Isidore of Pelusium, *Epistles,* 3.363, quoted in Margaret A. Schatkin and Paul W. Harkins trans., *Apologist, Saint John Chrysostom,* Volume 73 of *The Fathers of the Church* (Washington, D.C.: Catholic University of America Press, 1985), 83, note 30.

5. Isidore of Pelusium, *Epistles,* 3.129, quoted in ibid.

6. Tertullian, "To Scapula", Chapter 2, from Rudolph Arbesmann, Emily Joseph Daly, and Edwin A. Quain, trans., *Tertullian: Apologetical Works,* and *Municius Felix: Octavius* (New York: Fathers of the Church, 1950), at 152.

7. Tertullian, "Apology", Chapter 24, trans. S. Thelwall, in Alexander Roberts and James Donaldson, eds., *Ante-Nicene Fathers,* Volume 3, orig. 1885, online edition copyright (c) 2004 by K. Knight, available at http://www.newadvent.org/fathers/0301.htm .

8. Gregory Nazianzen, "Second Theological Oration" (Oration 28), trans. Edward Rochie Hardy and Cyril C. Richardson, in Philip Schaff and Henry Wace, *Nicene and Post-Nicene Fathers,* Second Series, Volume 7, orig. 1894, online edition copyright (c) 2005 by K. Knight, available at http://www.newadvent.org/fathers/310228.htm.

9. John Chrysostom, *Discourse on Blessed Babylas and Against the Greeks,* Sec. 13, trans. Margaret A. Schatkin, in Schatkin and Harkins, eds., 83.

10. Ibid., Sec. 42, at 99.

11. Athanasius, *History of the Arians,* 4.33, trans. John Henry Parker, in Philip Schaff and Henry Wace, *Nicene and Post-Nicene Fathers,* Second Series, Volume 4, orig. 1892, online edition copyright (c) 2005 by K. Knight, available at http://www.newadvent. org/fathers/28154.htm.

12. Athanasius, *History of the Arians*, 8:67, in *ibid.*, available at http://www.newadvent. org/fathers/28158.htm. I have modernized "ye."

13. For further support for the thesis, see Ambrose, Letter No. 21, *To Valentinian;* Gregory the Great, Register of Letters I, No. 47, "To Virgilius and Theodorus"; and *idem.*, Register of Letters, III, No. 53, "To John."

14. Augustine of Hippo, Letter No. 185, *To Boniface*, Sec. 30, J.G. Cunningham, trans., in Philip Schaff, ed., *Nicene and Post-Nicene Fathers*, Series One, Volume 1, orig. 1887, online edition copyright (c) 2004 by K. Knight, available at http://www.newadvent. org/fathers/1102185.htm.

15. See also the following passages from Augustine. From Letter No. 23, "To Maximin," Sec. 7: "I do not propose to compel men to embrace the communion of any party, but desire the truth to be made known to persons who, in their search for it, are free from disquieting apprehensions. On our side there shall be no appeal to men's fear of the civil power on your side, let there be no intimidation by a mob of Circumcelliones." From Letter No. 34, "To Eusebius," Sec. 1: "[M]y desire is, not that any one should against his will be coerced into the Catholic communion, but that to all who are in error the truth may be openly declared, and being by God's help clearly exhibited through my ministry, may so commend itself as to make them embrace and follow it." From Letter No. 35, "To Eusebius," Sec. 4, concerning a woman whose father attempted to compel her to return to the Catholic faith: "I was unwilling that this woman, whose mind was so perverted, should be received by us unless with her own will, and choosing, in the free exercise of judgment, that which is better[.]" All texts from http://www. newadvent.org/fathers.

16. Thomas Aquinas, ST, I–II, Q. 91, Art. 4. The internal reference is to Augustine, *On Freedom of the Will*, 1.5.6.

17. Ibid., Q. 96, Art. 2. Saint Thomas bases his line of reasoning on the explanation in Aristotle's *Metaphysics*, 10.3–4, that different things must be ruled by different measures, along with the observation in Isidore of Seville, *Etymologies*, 5.21, that laws should be "possible both according to nature, and according to the customs of the country." I note in passing that Saint Thomas is expressing a version of the "harm principle," commonly and mistakenly thought to have been discovered by John Stuart Mill, who really only promoted a tendentiously misleading version of it. For discussion of the differences between the Thomist and Millian versions, see J. Budziszewski, *True Tolerance: Liberalism and the Necessity of Judgment* (New Brunswick, NJ: Transaction Publishers, 1992, 1999), 18–24, and "Natural Law and Tolerance." *Revue générale de droit* 29:2 (1999): 233–38.

18. John Rawls, *A Theory of Justice* (Cambridge, MA: Harvard University Press, 1971) and *Political Liberalism* (New York: Columbia University Press, 1993).

19. To disavow faith in the religious sense is not the same as to be without faith in a broader sense. The very belief in reasoning requires a kind of faith, for a rational demonstration of its efficacy would be circular. An atheist is not a person who rejects faith in favor of reason alone, but only a person who supposes that he does, because he fails to recognize the elements of faith operative in his beliefs (in particular his belief in reasoning) for what they are.

20. See J. Budziszewski, *The Nearest Coast of Darkness: A Vindication of the Politics of Virtues* (Ithaca, NY: Cornell University Press, 1988), 54–60.

21. Of course the commitments (and their sources) may also be identified in greater or lesser detail, but this point does not presently concern us.

22. "*First, the statute must have a secular legislative purpose;* second, its principal or primary effect must be one that neither advances nor inhibits religion; finally, the statute must not foster 'an excessive government entanglement with religion.'" *Lemon v. Kurtzman,* 403 U.S. 602 (1971), at 612–13; emphasis added.

23. There have been apparent exceptions to the tendency of our courts to treat secular ideologies as nonreligious, for example *Torcaso v. Watkins,* 367 U.S. 488 (1961), at 495: "We repeat and again reaffirm that neither a State nor the Federal Government can constitutionally force a person 'to profess a belief or disbelief in any religion.' Neither can constitutionally pass laws or impose requirements which aid all religions as against non-believers, and neither can aid those religions based on a belief in the existence of God as against those religions founded on different beliefs." *Ibid.,* note 11: "Among religions in this country which do not teach what would generally be considered a belief in the existence of God are Buddhism, Taoism, Ethical Culture, Secular Humanism and others." For the general pattern, however, see *Alvarado v. City of San Jose,* 94 F.3d 1223 (1996), note 2 (internal citations removed):

> In *Torcaso,* in the context of ruling on a state statute requiring notaries to profess belief in God as a condition of office, the Supreme Court assumed without deciding that certain non-theistic beliefs could be deemed "religious" for First Amendment purposes. . . . Much has been made of this footnote, which has been explained as follows by Judge Canby, concurring in *Grove:* "The apparent breadth of the reference to 'Secular Humanism' . . . is entirely dependant upon viewing the term out of context. In context, it is clear that the Court meant 'no more than a reference to the group seeking an exemption, which, although non-Theist in belief, also met weekly on Sundays and functioned much like a church. . . . Thus *Torcaso* does not stand for the proposition that 'humanism' is a religion, although an organized group of 'Secular Humanists' may be." See also *Peloza* ("neither the Supreme Court, nor this circuit, has ever held that evolutionism or secular humanism are 'religions' for Establishment Clause purposes.")

I thank Professor David K. DeWolf, Gonzaga University Law School, for calling my attention to these passages.

24. See Paul Kurtz, *Humanist Manifestos I and II* (New York: Prometheus Books, 1973), and "Humanist Manifesto 2000: A Call for a New Planetary Humanism," *Free Inquiry* 19:4 (Fall 1999).

25. Its supreme and unconditional commitment—as we find in the first proposition of *Humanist Manifesto II*—is that "no deity will save us; we must save ourselves." What it means to save ourselves, and what we are saving ourselves from, must be inferred, with some difficulty, from the rest of the text. The document explicitly declares, however,

that morality is "situational," a term which it does not define but which seems to mean that morality contains no rules, or at least no inviolable prohibitions; in other words, depending on the circumstances, everything is permitted.

26. Had the document's chief draftsman, Thomas Jefferson, been writing for himself alone, he might well have written differently; indeed, its references to Providence were added by the Continental Congress. In a republic, however, the "authors" of a document are not its draftsmen, but those who give it authority—in this case the delegates assembled.

Afterword

1. Acts 5:29; Philippians 3:30; Hebrews 11:13, 16, RSV.

2. Romans 13:1, 1 Peter 2:13–14, 17, RSV.

3. "Even so husbands should love their wives as their own bodies. He who loves his wife loves himself. For no man ever hates his own flesh, but nourishes and cherishes it, as Christ does the church, because we are members of his body. 'For this reason a man shall leave his father and mother and be joined to his wife, and the two shall become one flesh.' This mystery is a profound one, and I am saying that it refers to Christ and the church[.]" (Ephesians 5:28–32, RSV.) For further discussion, see Chapter 3.

4. For the former tendency, see for example the works of Stanley Hauerwas; for the latter, the works of R. J. Rushdoony.

5. I borrow this term from John Paul II, *Veritatis Splendor,* section 41.

6. Deuteronomy 4:8, RSV.

7. See Russell Hittinger, *The First Grace: Recovering the Natural Law in a Post-Christian World* (Wilmington, DE: ISI Books, 2003), xi.

8. Luke 20:22, RSV.

9. Of course the knowledge of their remote implications may require laborious study and experience.

10. Thomas Aquinas, ST, I–II, Q. 94, Art. 4.

11. Ibid., Q. 156, Art. 3; compare Q. 31, Art. 7, and Q. 78, Art. 2. The scriptural reference is to Proverbs 2:14, in the Vulgate. See Chapter 4.

12. As discussed in Chapter 10, this is his reason for concluding that the laws of the earthly city should forbid "only the more grievous vices, from which it is possible for the majority to abstain; and chiefly those that are to the hurt of others, without the prohibition of which human society could not be maintained." Thomas Aquinas, *Summa Theologica,* I–II, Q. 96, Art. 2 and ad. 2. The scriptural reference is to Proverbs 30:33; in the same place he alludes to Matthew 9:17.

13. Wisdom 13:5–9, RSV: "For from the greatness and beauty of created things comes a corresponding perception of their Creator. Yet these men are little to be blamed, for perhaps they go astray while seeking God and desiring to find him. For as they live among his works they keep searching, and they trust in what they see, because the things that are seen are beautiful. Yet again, not even they are to be excused; for if they had the power to know so much that they could investigate the world, how did they fail to find sooner the Lord of these things?" Romans 1:19–21, RSV: "For

what can be known about God is plain to them, because God has shown it to them. Ever since the creation of the world his invisible nature, namely, his eternal power and deity, has been clearly perceived in the things that have been made. So they are without excuse; for although they knew God they did not honor him as God or give thanks to him, but they became futile in their thinking and their senseless minds were darkened."
14. Acts 17:22–23.

Credits, Acknowledgments, Confessions

If I were to attempt to enumerate everyone who offered insight or encouragement during the time when this book was coming together —a temptation to which I have sometimes succumbed in other books— the length of the resulting list would dilute the expression of gratitude where it is most due. My deepest appreciation is for my wise and patient wife, Sandra. I would be gravely remiss to omit mention of many conversations with my friends, Robert C. Koons, Russell Hittinger, and Fr. Albert Laforet. Special thanks are due to Jennifer Connolly of ISI Books, who has demonstrated not only meticulous thoroughness but also grace, since I am at the high end of the authorial persnickettiness scale. To all those known to me and themselves but whom it is not possible to mention here, I express my deep appreciation. Needless to say, the "credit" for any foolishness or error belongs to me alone.

A version of "Natural Law as Fact, as Theory, and as Sign of Contradiction" was originally delivered at the Department of Philosophy, Catholic University of America, November 2005, as part of a series on "Natural Moral Law and Contemporary Society," and is forthcoming from Catholic University Press in a book of essays based on the series and edited by Holger Zaborowski. A shorter version has appeared in *Catholic Social Science Review* 12 (October 2007): 11–32, with responses by Francis J. Beckwith and Kevin Lee, whom I also wish to thank.

A version of "The Second Tablet Project" appeared in *First Things* (June/July 2002): 23–31. Certain sections, though not the whole, were incorporated in *What We Can't Not Know: A Guide* (Dallas: Spence Publishing, 2003).

A highly condensed version of "Nature Illuminated" appeared under the title "Nature Revealed" in *First Things*, No. 188 (December 2008), 29–33.

Versions of "The Natural, the Connatural, and the Unnatural" were presented at the conference "Written on the Heart: The Tradition of Natural Law," Calvin College, Grand Rapids, Michigan, May 2004, and the conference "Saint Thomas and the Natural Law," Jacques Maritain Center, Notre Dame University, Notre Dame, Indiana, July 2004. I am grateful for helpful questions, comments, and suggestions from Steven Brock, Russell Hittinger, Christopher Kaczor, Daniel McInerny, Ralph McInerny, Michael Sherwin, Lance Simmons, and Randall Smith.

A version of "Accept No Imitations: Naturalism vs. Natural Law" appeared in William A. Dembski, ed., *Uncommon Dissent* (Wilmington, DE: ISI Books, 2004).

A version of "Thou Shalt Not Kill . . . Whom? The Meaning of the Person" was presented at the 2002 "annual meeting" of the American Political Science Association. Excerpts appeared in *What We Can't Not Know: A Guide*. Support for the paper came in part from a grant from the Pew Charitable Trusts.

A version of "Capital Punishment: The Case for Justice" was presented at the conference "A Call for Reckoning: Religion and the Death Penalty," University of Chicago Divinity School, January 2002, and appeared with various changes in *Notre Dame Journal of Law, Ethics & Public Policy* 16:1 (2002): 43–56; John Carlson, Eric Elshtain, and Erik Owens, eds., *A Call for Reckoning: Religion and the Death Penalty* (Grand Rapids, MI: Eerdmans, 2004); and *First Things* (August/September 2004): 39–45. I remember with pleasure the graciousness of Avery Cardinal Dulles at the conference in Chicago.

A version of "Constitution vs. Constitutionalism" was presented at the conference "Authority after Authoritarianism: Christian Contributions to Jurisprudence," Intercultural Forum for Studies in Faith and Culture, John Paul II Cultural Center, Washington, D.C., November 2004, and appeared in Patrick McKinley Brennan, ed., *Civilizing Authority: Society, State, and Church* (Lanham, MD: Lexington Books, 2007).

A version of "Constitutional Metaphysics" was presented at The Tocqueville Forum, Georgetown University, October 2007.

A version of "The Liberal, Illiberal Religion" was presented at the conference "Toleration and Truth: The Impact of Liberal Society on Religion," Emory University, Atlanta, Georgia, March 2006.

Versions of "The Architecture of Christian Citizenship: Two Stories with Basement and Mezzanine" were presented at the Northwest Section meeting of the Society of Christian Philosophers, Newberg, Oregon, April 2005, and at the annual meeting of the Evangelical Philosophical Society, Washington, D.C., November 2006.

Finally, I thank the University of Texas at Austin for six weeks of summer support at an early phase of composition.

It seems proper for the mind to make progress rather than always stopping and starting again; new books ought to represent new branches on the same growing tree. For that reason, the new themes in this book are extensions of themes broached in previous writing. On the other hand, in fairness to readers, a book ought to be self-contained. To make this possible, snippets of old DNA are incorporated, not just alluded to, from several places, including the third appendix to my book *True Tolerance: Liberalism and the Necessity of Judgment* (New Brunswick, NJ: Transaction Publishers, 1992) and my introduction to Mitchell S. Muncy, ed., *The End of Democracy? Volume II* (Dallas: Spence Publishing, 1999).

Index

promulgation and, 11, 13–14
Protestantism and, 155–57
prudence and, 28–29
reason and, 41
revelation and, 2, 42–45, 59
as sign of contradiction, 3–6, 17–22
theories on, 199–201
as theory, 2–3, 10–17
witnesses to, 14–17, 157–59, 200–201
See also divine law; law
natural selection, 10, 31, 81, 83, 95, 196
nature
    abolition of, 25–27
    affirmation and, 44, 49–52
    changing, 25–27, 61
    classical understanding of, 12–13
    common good and, 11–12
    corruption of, 68–69
    Darwinism and, 84
    definition of, 42–43
    design and, 12, 15–16, 79, 88
    divine promise and, 45, 56–57
    duty to, 39
    ethics and, 79
    forgiveness and, 56–57
    God and, 27, 28, 51, 146
    grace and, 59, 76, 191–92
    imago Dei (image of God) and,
    42–43
    metaphysical biology and, 50
    morality and, 25
    narrative and, 45, 52–56
    naturalism vs. natural law and, 79,
    81
    natural law and, 11, 27–28, 63, 199
    natural purposes and, 12–13
    natural selection and, 10
    oughtness and, 13
    precept and, 44, 45–49
    providence and, 56–57
    reason and, 11
    sacraments and, 45, 57–59
    second nature and, 61–63
neighbor
    ethics and, 23
    revelation and, 38–39
neutralism
    judgment and, 180

liberalism and, 174–79, 185
religion and, 138
Supreme Court, U. S. and, 174
toleration and, 162, 172–73, 180–82
New Testament, 113
New York Review of Books, 33
Nicene Creed, 182
Ninth Amendment, 139, 150

O

Oakeshott, Michael, 180, 181
Old Testament, 165, 172–73
Olivier, Sir Laurence, 99, 101
One Plausible Principle, 86
On Liberty (Mill), 174
Ophelia, 98
oughtness
    God, natural knowledge of and,
    28–29
    morality and, 35, 83, 84
    nature and, 13
    prudence and, 28–29
    sexual powers and, 28–29

P

Parliament, 132
Paul, St., 14, 15–16, 57, 76–77, 113, 120,
    156, 188–89, 190, 191, 195
Pax Romana, 37
personalism, 3
personhood
    abortion and, 101–4, 110
    absolute regard and, 107–11
    analogy and, 98–99, 100
    assisted suicide and, 106
    being and, 21
    complementarity of the sexes and,
    51
    Constitution, U. S. and, 97
    constitution of, 2, 3, 4, 8
    derivative meanings of, 99–100
    euthanasia and, 104–6
    faith and, 4
    Fifth Commandment and, 100–101,
    104, 107
    functional definition of, 97, 103–4,

About the Author

J. Budziszewski is a professor of government and philosophy at the University of Texas. He is the author of *What We Can't Not Know: A Guide, The Revenge of Conscience, Evangelicals in the Public Square, Natural Law for Lawyers, Written on the Heart, True Tolerance, The Nearest Coast of Darkness,* and *The Resurrection of Nature,* as well as three books about Christian faith for young people.